Learning to Improve the World

How Injaz Al-Arab helps youth

in the Middle East

develop an entrepreneurial mindset

Fernando M. Reimers

With Maria Elena Ortega and Paul Dyer

ISBN-13: 978-1725581371

ISBN-10: 172558137X

Library of Congress Control Number: 2018909570

CreateSpace Independent Publishing Platform

North Charleston, South Carolina

"As the Fourth Industrial Revolution continues to transform economies, businesses and societies, our education and labour markets must be revamped. Injaz Al-Arab, an organization that promotes entrepreneurship education in 14 countries in the Middle East, is a promising model for bridging the gap between labour market demands and youth skills development. The organization's expansion was greatly influenced by Soraya Salti, a Young Global Leader of the World Economic Forum and a 2006 Schwab Social Entrepreneur award winner who strived to reduce un- and underemployment among youth in the region. *Learning to Improve the World* commemorates Salti's passion by taking stock of the transformative work Injaz has done to prepare Arab youth for the changing nature of work. The findings in this study provide lessons for human capital development not just in the region, but around the world."

Klaus Schwab, Founder and Executive Chairman, World Economic Forum

"Prefaced with emotional truthful writing, this book offers an in-depth study of the great role that the entrepreneurship education programs of Injaz Al-Arab & JA Worldwide play in advancing, empowering, and giving voice and agency to youth. In this book Professor Fernando Reimers, an insightful scholar rooted in entrepreneurial thinking, peels the layers of the obvious to reveal the unseen truth of the Injaz program. The book makes a pivotal contribution in measuring and analyzing the actual impact of entrepreneurship. The publication of this book comes at a crucial time for Injaz as it embarks on an ambitious goal to reach one million students annually by 2022.

Soraya once said, to any obstacle, any roadblock, there is one person that will be the gate keeper that can open the door for you". Thank you for opening the door Soraya! The key you have passed on will keep unlocking endless possibilities to our youth and inspire generations to come."

Akef Aqrabawi, President & CEO Injaz Al-Arab

"*Learning to Improve the World* is an inspiring and thorough account of the committed work of Injaz Al-Arab to empower youth across the Arab World to discover, nurture and fulfill their entrepreneurial potential. Personally, it gives me immense pride to see the legacy of my dearly departed partner, Soraya Salti, captured so eloquently. Soraya's spirit clearly lives on – this book is heartwarming testament to that."

Waleed AlBanawi , Founder & Chairman, JISR Venture Partners

"Practical lessons from Injaz Al Arab's extensive experience with young people in the Middle East- an educating read for any organization working to prepare our youth to create and lead a better future for our region."

Nour Abu-Ragheb, Co-Founder and Partner at Edvise ME/ Member of the Board of Trustees at the Crown Prince Foundation

"*Learning to Improve the Word* is a must read for those interested in understanding the important lessons that can be taught through teaching students how to take action and take risks. It has brought to life a unique lens to entrepreneurial education in the Middle East and the immense impact it has on empowering local youth to take ownership of their future ecosystems. In addition this book has also reminded us on the impact a dedicated and passionate individual can have on improving the world one student at a time. Many thanks to Fernando Reimers for keeping Soraya Salti's memory alive by showcasing her commendable work and the impact Injaz continues to have on the future of the youth in the Middle East. "

Haneen Sakakini, Assistant Manager, Ernst & Young Middle East Advisory Services

"*Learning to Improve the Word* presents a compelling narrative for why entrepreneurship education for children and youth is vital as the Arab World moves towards a knowledge economy. It also provides evidence-based policy recommendations and programmatic approaches that will serve governments and other implementers throughout the region."

Bassem Nasir, Education and International Development Expert

Dedicated to the memory of Soraya Salti

A remarkable educational entrepreneur whose great confidence that the future of the Middle East, and of the world, rested in the empowerment of its youth, inspired and helped many of us to think in new ways.

How Injaz Al-Arab helps youth develop an entrepreneurial mindset

Table of Contents

Preface

I first learned about the Injaz Al-Arab Program as I was teaching a class on education at Harvard to a group of Young Global Leaders of the World Economic Forum in the spring of 2007. I challenged that group with the view that, in an increasingly changing world, it was essential that educational institutions empowered children and youth with a broader range of skills that enabled them to become architects of their own lives. In that session, I shared emerging findings of a study I was then conducting, an evaluation of the impact of a civic education program aimed at developing leadership skills among low-income youth in Mexico. One of the young global leaders in that group responded that similar goals could be achieved through a variety of educational programs, not just civic education. At the end of the class, Soraya Salti came to talk to me looking for a way to continue our conversation. I invited her to my office and we extended our conversation about how to empower youth for another couple of hours. She explained that her organization Injaz Al-Arab, had committed in 2004 to extend a series of programs of entrepreneurship education to all countries in the Middle East, and that she was genuinely interested in figuring out how to empower youth in that region. She believed entrepreneurship education was a way forward, but also thought we needed more rigorous study to dig beneath the surface and truly understand what aspects of the process of learning to create a business were truly effective in helping youth develop entrepreneurial mindsets and skills. It was thus that I began a memorable friendship with Soraya, a remarkable social entrepreneur who was committed to bring Injaz entrepreneurship education programs based on the Junior Achievement model, to all countries in the Middle East.

Over the years following our initial meeting, I continued to learn about Soraya's accomplishments and impact. She had become a Young Global Leader in 2006, after winning the Schwab Social Entrepreneur award, and went on to win the Skoll Award for Social Entrepreneurship in 2009. In 2013, Arabian Business recognized her as one of the 100 most powerful Arab women. She was a visionary, whose imagination about a Middle East abundant in opportunities for its youth was matched by her capacity for hard work and by her ability to bring others along in that journey.

In 2009 Soraya invited me to evaluate the impact of Injaz Al-Arab in six Middle Eastern countries. With the collaboration of her organization, we collected the data between the years of 2010 and 2011. By late 2012 we had completed the analysis of the data and a draft manuscript of this book. Soraya and I had discussed the findings of the study several times in phone conversations together with others from the senior staff of Injaz Al-Arab. She was excited about the findings and urged me to publish the book. She believed the findings were not only useful to her organization, by causing them to take a hard look at their work with a view to improving it, but that they would be valuable to other organizations working in the field of entrepreneurship education, and perhaps valuable also to educators more generally in the Middle East and beyond. As it would take me some time to finalize the manuscript, we agreed she would publish the draft of the reports in the website of Injaz Al-Arab, and would have one of her staff summarize the study and publish the highlights of the findings. Two events, however, would delay the publication of the book.

The first was an insight emerging from this study. After evaluating the impact of the Injaz Al-Arab program using similar instruments to those I had developed to evaluate the civic education program in Mexico, building on a decade of research in civic education, I realized Soraya was right. Both interventions had similar effects in how they shaped students' mindsets and skills. Both programs appeared to influence how students viewed themselves, their self-confidence, trust in others, and how they reported the value of a range of skills for collaboration with others. That led me to think differently about how education empowers students and to broaden my interests from civic education and entrepreneurship education. I became less preoccupied with the nomenclature we used for the education programs that empowered students – whether civic education or entrepreneurship education – and more interested in the underlying DNA of those programs, and especially in the instructional design of the learning experiences that undergird these programs.

This mindshift was the origin of the Global Education Innovation Initiative I developed at Harvard University. Travelling the world in 2012 and 2013 to enlist institutions that would eventually form the research and practice collaborative of the Global Education Innovation Initiative, and launching into our first study of curriculum reforms in earnest, caused me to postpone the publication of the book reporting the findings from the study of Injaz Al-Arab. In December of 2014 I received an unexpected call from Soraya. She was in Boston attending a conference of Junior Achievement. I invited her to join me for dinner with some colleagues from Singapore who were in town discussing our work in the Global Education Innovation Initiative. She arrived at my home just as the flurries of a light winter snow were falling outside. She was curious to learn about what we were discovering through the Global Initiative and urged me again, in her ever optimistic, joyful and impatient way, to publish the book. I promised her then that I would publish the book, and would try to do it the following year. The year would go by, however, with all my time focused on the work of the Global Education Innovation Initiative, and no progress on the publication of the study of Injaz Al-Arab. At the end of that year I attended the conference of the World Innovation Summit in Education in Qatar. The conversations about the need to empower youth in the region reminded me again of my promise to Soraya. During my trip home, I received a text from a former student letting me know that Soraya had passed away.

The news of Soraya's passing caused me to regret not having published the book earlier, but, once again, led me to postpone returning to this manuscript. Over the years since I had met her, Soraya had become a generous collaborator, a frequent guest speaker in my course on educational innovation, and someone I would enjoy catching up with during her visits to Cambridge or when we met at international conferences. I had grown to admire her leadership and the significance of her life's work. I dedicated the first book of the Global Education Innovation Initiative, published a few months later, to her, and I arranged for the first launch of this book to be in the Middle East in her memory. I spoke about how conversations with Soraya had inspired the creation of the Global Education Innovation Initiative and about our first study at a regional meeting of Injaz Al-Arab in Abu Dhabi. Visiting with her widower Waleed AlBanawi, with Akef Akwrabawi, the President and CEO of Injaz Al-Arab, and with her former colleagues, helped me realize that the sadness of her passing would require that I wait even longer until I could find the necessary disposition to completing this work.

Last March, attending the Global Education and Skills Forum in Dubai, I ran into Akef and some of his colleagues and learned about the good work which Injaz Al-Arab continues to do. I concluded that publishing this book about the organization Soraya led so well would be a fitting tribute to her memory. The book essentially reflects the manuscript as written in 2012, with minor updates for employment figures in the first chapter. When we describe the country context, or the programs Injaz Al-Arab offers in each country, those descriptions refer to the situation at the time we wrote the book, which may have since changed in some cases. Also, at the time we conducted the study Injaz Al-Arab –the registered brand of the regional organization whose programs we studied-- and Injaz –an organization in Jordan which Soraya had managed prior to embarking on the regional mission of Injaz Al-Arab—had a cooperative agreement. This book is about Injaz Al-Arab not about Injaz, the Jordanian organization. When the term 'Injaz' is used, the reader should understand that I am not referring to the Jordanian organization whose registered brand is Injaz, except when discussing the program in Jordan, but to the programs supported by Injaz Al-Arab, which works as a federation of Injaz organizations in the countries where it operates.

I appreciate the contributions of María Elena Ortega and of Paul Dyer to the analysis presented in this book, and their patience with me over the six years since we finished this work, and the careful editing of Ana Teresa del Toro whose curiosity encouraged me to finally get it done.

Soraya, thank you for everything you did for youth in the Middle East, and for your friendship!

Fernando M. Reimers

Cambridge, MA, August 2018

Chapter 1. Preparing youth to invent the future in the Middle East

1.1. Entrepreneurship Education and 21st Century Skills

The world is changing rapidly. Globalization and technological innovation have created new opportunities and challenges for individuals, communities and nations. With these changes it has become necessary to revisit to what extent children and youth are being prepared to be effective and productive citizens and workers, and to what extent they are equipped not just to understand the future, but to invent it. In the 21st century the skills and dispositions necessary to live meaningful lives, to participate socially, civically and economically, have expanded from those which were sufficient in the past. Over the last decades, an emerging consensus has formed around the idea that knowledge of facts alone is insufficient to prepare youth for a future that is increasingly volatile and uncertain. Students must be educated not just to understand the world, but to improve it, they need to be equipped to become creators and makers, and not just spectators of the world in which they live. There is an emerging consensus that the skills students will need to invent the future must include cognitive, interpersonal, and intrapersonal skills (Pellegrino and Hilton 2012). The growing awareness that the adequate development of these requires deliberate efforts to cultivate them is also stimulating questions and innovations about the kind of educational experiences which can cultivate those skills.

The Global Education Innovation Initiative at Harvard University is a research and practice collaborative focused on understanding how public education systems are changing to address these new demands of the 21st century. We pursue that goal conducting applied research, constructing opportunities for research to inform education policy making and practice, and developing resources, tools and protocols which can support education practitioners in practices which empower students. In a recent study, researchers from the initiative found that governments around the world are broadening curricular goals and aligning them with this multipronged view of competencies that include cognition, but also self-knowledge and the capacity to collaborate, or what is often also termed cognitive and socio-emotional development (Reimers and Chung 2016). Another recent study comparatively examined programs of teacher professional development that aimed at supporting teachers with capacities to educate students holistically in the cognitive, intrapersonal and interpersonal domains. The study found that most of those programs involved public private partnerships in which organizations external to the school worked with networks of schools supporting teachers in multipronged ways to support innovative pedagogies that fostered the development of the whole child (Reimers and Chung 2018). That study, and a report of an expert convening of the Global Education Innovation Initiative, identified the problem of scale as a critical challenge of the transformation of education to empower students with the necessary competencies in a changing world (Reimers 2017).

These heightened aspirations for the competencies youth will need to develop in order to thrive in the future, and the awareness of the potential of public private partnerships to stimulate educational innovation at scale motivate the publication of the results of this study of a program designed to cultivate an entrepreneurial mindset among high school students in the Middle East. The results of this study advance knowledge about how entrepreneurship education helps youth develop some of these competencies, preparing them to '*Improve the world*'. The study focuses on the impact of an entrepreneurship education program administered to high school students in six countries in the Middle East, a region with relatively high levels of youth unemployment. The program is relatively simple, and therefore scalable, it involves bringing to schools a person with business experience, who works with youth teaching them how to create a company.

We think the results of this study will be of interest not only to those who care about the opportunities available to youth in the Middle East. The search for effective avenues to help students develop an expanded set of skills extends beyond the Middle East to the entire global education

14

ecosystem. While the levels of youth unemployment are higher today in the Middle East than in other regions of the world, many predict that the fourth industrial revolution, resulting from increased and ubiqitous automation and the development of artificial intelligence, will eliminate many of the jobs currently available. Together with neurotechnological and genetic developments these changes will create new opportunities as well as serious challenges, which require a heightened commitment to putting humans at the center, and empowerment as a goal (Schwab 2017). These developments create a new urgency to advance knowledge about how to empower youth to invent the future, in the Middle East and beyond.

Entrepreneurship education, a specific set of educational programs aimed at teaching students and adults the skills to initiate and sustain a business, is an avenue to develop some of these skills and attitudes. Entrepreneurship has been defined as the capacity to create something new, usually an innovation or an organization to support new ways to address an unmet need. While many people think of entrepreneurs as those who create businesses, the concept extends more generally to the creation of organizations to serve the needs of identifiable groups of 'customers' or 'beneficiaries'. Gregory Dees, a scholar who advanced the study of 'social entrepreneurship' traces the origins of the term *entrepreneur* to the field of economics in the 17th and 18th century in France:

> "More specifically, it came to be used to identify the venturesome individuals who stimulated economic progress by finding new and better ways of doing things. The French economist most commonly credited with giving the term this particular meaning is Jean Baptiste Say. Writing around the turn of the 19th century, Say put it this way, 'The entrepreneur shifts economic resources out of an area of lower and into an area of higher productivity and greater yield.' Entrepreneurs create value." (Dees 1998, 1).

While the field of entrepreneurship is not new, and efforts to educate and support entrepreneurs extend over many decades, systematic research-based knowledge about how to educate entrepreneurs is more limited and

15

recent. A World Bank study of entrepreneurship education programs identifies four tipes of programs: two focusing on students, and two focusing on entrepreneurs. The former, entrepreneurship education programs, focus on either secondary or higher education students, while the latter, entrepreneurship training programs, focus either on potential or actual entrepreneurs. These programs focus on the development of mindsets and skills, such as self-confidence, leadership, creativity, risk propensity, motivation, resiliency, self-efficacy, awareness of entrepreneurship and business skills. The study concludes that most entrepreneurship education programs at the secondary level have not been rigorously evaluated and that scientific knowledge about their impact is very thin (Valerio et al. 2014). Another synthesis of evaluation studies examining the impact of entrepreneurship education programs found a relatively small number of them (Beary 2012).

This book presents the results of an evaluation of the Injaz Al-Arab Company Program, an entrepreneurship education program designed to help youth in the Middle East develop entrepreneurial mindsets and skills. In this chapter we first describe the challenges facing youth in the Middle East. We then discuss the field of entrepreneurship education, and we present the Injaz Al-Arab program. The following section describes the methods used in this study. We then present the results obtained in this study, and conclude discussing these findings and their implications for policy and practice. Remaining chapters of the book present the evaluation of the program in each of the countries in the study: Egypt, Jordan, Lebanon, Morocco, Saudi Arabia and the United Arab Emirates.

1.2. Why it is important to empower youth in the Middle East to invent the future

Over the past few decades, the Arab world has gone through a dramatic demographic transition. In turn, the region's youth population has surged. Today, those aged 15 to 24 make up nearly 20 percent of the region's population, while those under the age of 25 make up more than 53 percent. The sheer size of this youth population has put intensive pressures on the

16

region's educational systems and labor markets, as these youth seek out opportunities that enable them to start their careers and establish themselves as independent adults. In fact, over the past decade, the Arab world's labor force has grown by an unprecedented annual rate of nearly 3.3 percent, with more than 3 million new individuals entering the job market every year. In this context, the region's economies have failed to create the economic opportunities to meet the needs and expectations of this generation of youth, while regional educational systems have failed in preparing them for a more competitive labor market.

While the Arab world has made significant progress regarding educational attainment and Arab governments have initiated repeated efforts at the reform of educational systems, the region's reforms have not generated significant changes in the quality of education delivered to the region's youth. Rote memorization and teacher-centered instruction remain the core mode of educational delivery across much of the region. Instruction often focuses on the dissemination (and memorization) of facts, rather than the application of such knowledge to analysis, to the solution of problems or to collaborative problem solving. Little focus is placed on the development of creative thinking or soft skills like leadership, teamwork and written and oral communication. This is reinforced by the nature of assessment in much of the region: comprehensive examinations favor transparently assessable multiple- questions rather than essays and application of knowledge, meaning that schools are further incentivized to teach to the test and thus favor rote learning methods. As a result, youth in the region score poorly in internationally comparable examinations which measure the ability to solve problems such as the Trends in International Mathematics and Sciences Study (TIMSS; Figure 1). More tangibly, youth lack the competitive edge needed to secure gainful employment in a tight labor market.

Figure 1.1: Average Math and Sciences Scores, 8th Graders from Arab Countries for TIMSS 2007

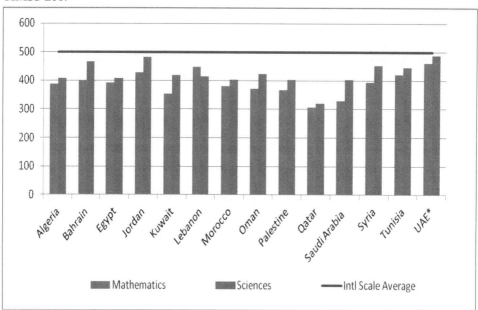

*UAE scores refer only to results from the Emirate of Dubai.
Sources: Mullis, I.V.S., Martin, M.O., & Foy, P. (with Olson, J.F., Preuschoff, C., Erberber, E., Arora, A., & Galia, J.), TIMSS 2007 International Mathematics Report: Findings from IEA's Trends in International Mathematics and Science Study at the Fourth and Eighth Grades (Chestnut Hill, MA: TIMSS & PIRLS International Study Center, Boston College, 2008) and Martin, M.O., Mullis, I.V.S., & Foy, P. (with Olson, J.F., Erberber, E., Preuschoff, C., & Galia, J.), TIMSS 2007 International Science Report: Findings from IEA's Trends in International Mathematics and Science Study at the Fourth and Eighth Grades (Chestnut Hill, MA: TIMSS & PIRLS International Study Center, Boston College, 2008)

In regard to labor market outcomes for youth, the region faces a sustained unemployment crisis. The region faces the highest rate of youth unemployment in the world, 30 percent on average, more than double the world average. Five million workers enter the labor market each year in the Middle East and job creation is in short supply (Stratford 2018). Education does not necessarily provide a bulwark against unemployment; in many countries in the region, the highest rates of unemployment are seen among those with secondary degrees or higher (Middle East Youth Initiative 2009).

Figure 1.2. Youth Unemployment in the Arab World

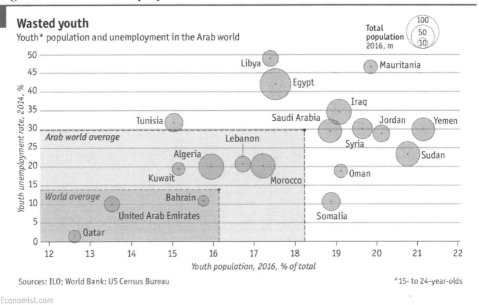

Source: *The Economist*. Youth Unemployment in the Arab World. August 9, 2016. https://www.economist.com/graphic-detail/2016/08/09/youth-unemployment-in-the-arab-world

For those youth able to secure employment, outcomes are not necessarily improved, and many are trading unemployment for underemployment. Across the region, job creation within the public sector – once the engine of job creation for much of the region– has slowed in the context of government cutbacks, and the formal private sector has not filled the void created. In turn, an increasing share of the jobs for youth are found in the informal sector. In fact, Egypt saw the share of jobs for new entrants created in the informal sector rise to nearly 70 percent by 2006 (Middle East Youth Initiative 2009). Such informal jobs provide little in the way of job stability, benefits or access to social safety nets. These jobs rarely offer youth opportunities to build on their human capital with training or experience that helps them to secure formal sector positions over time.

The burdens of poor labor market outcomes in the Arab world are particularly challenging for young women, who average low market participation rates at 21 percent compared with young male participation rates of 52 percent. Those women who are engaged in the labor market are particularly vulnerable to unemployment. On average, the unemployment rate among young women in the region is nearly 38 percent, or twice that of young men. It is important to note that given the conservative nature of many countries in the region, women often face resistance within their families to their working and they have fewer "culturally appropriate" job options open to them than do young men. As such, when they do seek to work, they are often competing with a relatively large number of other women for scarce positions in a limited number of sectors, such as education and government administrative work. In this context, the fact that labor market participation rates are so low while unemployment is so high suggests a high degree of disguised unemployment. Although some women may opt out of the labor market by choice or because of familial expectations, others may be staying out of the labor force because of the perception that there simply are no jobs available to them.

Poor labor market outcomes for Arab youth are rooted in the inability of the educational system to prepare adequately for working life. Indeed, the gap between the skills provided by young job seekers and those sought by the region's employers is often raised by representatives of the private sector when defending their resistance to hiring youth. According to the Arab Human Capital Challenge, only 54 percent of interviewed CEOs across the region feel that the educational system provides graduates with adequate skills, while less than half consider that there are enough graduates with those skills to fill needed positions (Mohammed bin Rashid Al Maktoum Foundation, 2009). In particular, these CEOs voice concerns about the weaknesses of graduates in regard to soft skills such as communication, teamwork and leadership. **Employers are more interested in skills that enable workers to be self-motivated, flexible and innovative in the workplace than in any particular basis of knowledge, and stress that these are the areas in which the educational system is weakest.**

Figure 1.3: CEO Ability to Find Graduates with Adequate Skills (%)

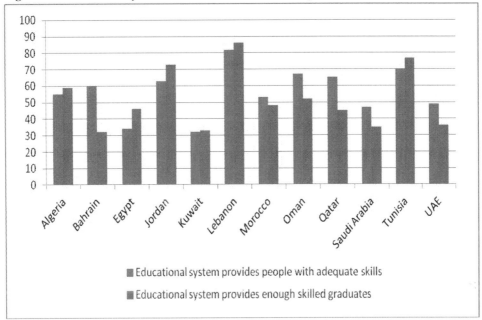

Source: Mohammed bin Rashid Al Maktoum Foundation, *Arab Human Capital Challenge: The Voices of the CEOs* (Dubai: Mohammed bin Rashid Al Maktoum Foundation, 2009). Available online at: http://www.pwc.com/m1/en/publications/arab-human-capital-challenge.jhtml

There are also important structural reasons behind the level and persistence of unemployment and underemployment among youth in the Arab world. Many of the institutions that govern the education and employment markets in the region, unintentionally serve as barriers to youth. Perhaps most important is the legacy of public sector employment in the region. While public sector employment has slowed, the potential for a public-sector job still serves as a strong lure for youth seeking employment, given the non-wage benefits and job security that come with such jobs, if not the relatively high wages provided therein. Educated youth often queue for scarce public sector jobs rather than seeking employment in the private sector or starting their own businesses. Moreover, the lure of public sector employment ensures that, by and large, young people favor educational investments that will ensure access to government employment rather than educational tracks that prepare them for competitive places in the private sector, reinforcing the existent skills gap in the region.

On the other hand, the region's formal private sector has proven hesitant to hire young inexperienced workers largely because of the burdensome labor market regulations that they face. By and large, regulations related to the hiring and firing of workers are fairly restrictive and present high, often unpredictable costs to a potential employer. In terms of hiring, for example, firms are often mandated to pay into the social security scheme, even when taking on an intern. Perhaps more importantly, firms are often required to hire workers using non-conditional, open-term contracts, making it difficult to dismiss workers during downturns in the business cycle or when workers prove to be unproductive. Coupled with the skills gap that they observe with many new entrants, these regulations often keep firms from actively pursuing the risks of taking on new workers.

The frustrations felt by youth about persistently poor labor market outcomes were boldly underlined by the political upheavals of the Arab Spring. In the wake of the youth-led revolutions in Egypt, Libya, Tunisia and Yemen (and in the context of continuing upheaval in Syria), there has been a renewed effort focused on alleviating the economic constraints facing youth in the region. Across the region, organizations –both government and non-governmental– have strengthened programs designed to provide economic opportunities for the region's youth.

Regional policy makers are aware of the need for systematic reforms of the education and labor markets, but such reforms require the investment of significant political capital and take time. The needs of this generation of youth are immediate. As such, there is a significant need for efficient, timely interventions that are able to work within the confines of institutional rigidities to spark opportunities for the region's youth to develop skills, find employment or create their own opportunities through self-employment. In this context, youth entrepreneurship has emerged as an often-cited solution to the employment crisis in the Arab world, and there are a number of emergent interventions related to the promotion of youth entrepreneurship, both initiated by government and initiated by non-governmental organizations or the private sector. Such initiatives run the gamut from angel investment funds to incubation efforts to basic business training programs. One organization that stands out, both because of the scale of its approach as well its efforts to work within the context of existing educational institutions, is Injaz al-Arab.

1.3. Entrepreneurship Education: Injaz Al-Arab and the Company Program

Injaz Al-Arab is an organization established in 2004 by Soraya Salti to promote entrepreneurship education training in the Arab world, as the regional branch of Junior Achievement Worldwide. Between 2001 and 2004 Soraya had managed Injaz, a Jordanian non for profit founded in 1999 to promote entrepreneurship education. While the two organizations are separate entities, Injaz and Injaz Al-Arab partnered for many years through an operating agreement which helped establish Injaz offices in the region. The results presented in this study took place during that period. In the remainder of this text, when we use the term Injaz, it should be understood that we are referring to the Injaz program conducted by the respective organization in each country, and not to the separate Injaz organization in Jordan, except in the chapter when we discuss the program in that country.

Working as the regional branch for Junior Achievement Worldwide, Injaz Al-Arab has served more than three million students in 14 countries across the region, including Algeria, Bahrain, Egypt, Kuwait, Lebanon, Morocco, Oman, Pakistan, Palestine, Qatar, Saudi Arabia, Tunisia, the United Arab Emirates and Yemen in the various Injaz programs described in Table 1.1.

Table 1.1: Injaz Al-Arab Programs [most of these, but not all, are offered in all countries in the region]

Program name	Duration	Age group	Purpose
Banks in Action	8 sessions	Secondary/ university	Promotes understanding of banking fundamentals and operations of competitive banks.
Be Entrepreneurial	Variable	Secondary	Encourages youth to start their own businesses before leaving school.
Business Ethics	7-12 sessions	Secondary	Fosters student's ethical decision-making as they prepare to enter the workforce
Success Skills	7 sessions	Secondary	Works with students to prepare them for job search and interview skills.
Job Shadow	4 sessions	Secondary/ university	Prepares students for careers with 3 classroom sessions and an on-site orientation in the workplace.
Economics for Success	6 sessions	Secondary	Introduces students to personal finance and educational and career options.
More than Money	6 sessions	Grades 3-5	Teaches students about earning, saving and spending money responsibly.
Entrepreneurship Master Class	1 day	Grades 10-12	Provides an introduction to entrepreneurship and self-employment
Community Citizenship	Variable	Secondary/ university	Provides opportunities for the class to participate in a community service project
Innovation Camp	1 day	Secondary/ university	Provides opportunities for participants to discuss a particular business challenge and develop potential solutions.
Company Program	4-6 months	Secondary/ university	Provides opportunities for participants to develop a business plan, launch a business, market and sell their product and then liquidate the business for first-hand experience in entrepreneurship.

By working with local volunteers from the business community and with significant funding support from corporate donors, Injaz Al-Arab seeks to provide a broad base of entrepreneurship training opportunities to Arab youth, with opportunities aimed both at developing the basic business skills and financial literacy they need to start and run their own businesses and the softer job-ready skills that are in increasing demand by the private sector. Working in close coordination with ministries of education and local school administrators, Injaz Al-Arab programs are delivered by private sector volunteers through the school system, either as extra-curricular activities or as part of the curriculum. Programs are designed to provide an experiential learning environment, where youth learn by doing rather than through lectures.

The Company Program is the banner program among Injaz Al-Arab's offerings. During the Company Program, student groups (consisting of about 25 students) work together, with the support of a volunteer from the private sector, to develop a business idea and subsequently a business plan. Following completion of the business plan, students work with the local business community to design and produce their identified product or service and develop a marketing plan before selling their product within the community. Finally, at the close of the program, students undertake the closure of the business, liquidating their student company's assets. Over the course of 4-6 months, students experience the life cycle of a business, gaining hands-on experience in each stage. In all, 162 student companies from 12 countries participated in the Company Program during the 2010-2011 academic year.

At the end of the program, participants from each student company are invited to attend a national competition. In preparation for the competition, students prepare and submit written reports on their companies they have created for consideration by a panel of judges consisting of representatives from the national business community, Injaz Al-Arab board members, teachers and colleagues. During the competition, students are interviewed by the panel of judges and demonstrate their products at company display stands. Judges assess student companies based on criteria that address marketing plans, management reports, and budgeting and environmental considerations.

Winners of the national competitions are invited by Injaz Al-Arab to participate in a regional competition. In 2011, this competition was held in Amman, Jordan. The Palestinian student company ESCO was selected as the "Best Company of the Year," while awards went to the Kuwaiti company Evaluate Me for "Best TV Advertisement", Moroccan company Youth Yell "Most Innovative Product", and Saudi Arabian company "Catalyst" for the team that demonstrated the most improvement in terms of acquisition of business knowledge and know-how. The "FedEx Access Award" for the business plan with the best potential to create jobs, grow small business, expand global development and improve the environment was given to the UAE-based GLights company.

Overall, the experience of participating in the Company Program is designed to expose students to the fundamental elements of business and to spark a greater interest in entrepreneurship. Over the course of the program, however, students are put into situations that demand leadership, teamwork, negotiation and communication, both with each other and the community at large. As such, the experiential approach is designed to improve each participant's ability to work with a team, learning in the process how to effectively communicate their own interests while negotiating toward a common goal. In presenting their business ideas during the competitions and to the community at large, they gain experience in public speaking and communication. In this way, students have an experience that they do not regularly have in the course of their formal education, particularly at secondary level.

1.4. Methods

Since its establishment in 2004 Injaz Al-Arab has not undergone any structured quantitative or qualitative assessment of its programs or of the impact that participation in its programs has on the students involved. For the 2010-2011 school year, Injaz Al-Arab sought to carry out an impact evaluation of its Company Program to measure the impact that participation in this program had on students. Toward this end, the authors, working in collaboration with Injaz Al-Arab management, undertook an effort to evaluate the Company Program as implemented in six Arab countries, including Egypt, Jordan, Lebanon, Morocco, Saudi Arabia and the United Arab Emirates. This book reflects the results of the study.

In order to assess the impact of entrepreneurship education, the Injaz Al-Arab team selected an evaluation focused on the Company Program because of all of Injaz Al Arab's programs it is the most substantive in terms of the duration and scope of participant engagement. Injaz Al-Arab's leadership selected six of the 12 countries in which it operates to participate in the study because they were the countries in which the program had been in place a sufficiently long time to expect that the national teams were implementing it with fidelity. These countries also provided a fairly representative sample of the types of economies within the region, including both poorer and wealthier countries. The following countries were included in this evaluation: Egypt, Jordan, Lebanon, Morocco, Saudi Arabia, and United Arab Emirates.

The original design of this study contemplated a quasi-experimental design, with a treatment and a control group in each of the countries, with an administration of the survey before the Company Program was implemented and an additional administration immediately after the completion of the Company Program. We expected to be able to match the pre and post questionnaires for each student. While the assignment of students to participation in the program would not be random, we had expected that the pre-post comparison and the existence of a quasi-comparison group would have allowed us to reach conclusions about plausible program effects.

In practice, a number of logistical impediments caused modifications to the original design in most countries, and the data in each country were collected in ways that differed from these intended plans. In all countries we collected data for students participating in the Company Program before and after participation, although it was only possible to match pre and post observations for some individual participants in Lebanon, Jordan and the UAE, in the remaining countries we matched schools but not individual students. In regard to a quasi-comparison group, there was an identified comparison group in five countries (all but the UAE, where we were not able to secure a control group). In four of these countries (Morocco, Lebanon, Jordan and Egypt), we surveyed this group before the Company Program took place and after program completion. Only in the case of Jordan and Lebanon was it possible to match the pre and post surveys for some individuals from the comparison group.

The study was conducted in a small number of cities and schools in each of the six countries participating. The data were collected at the upper secondary level in all countries except Egypt. In Egypt, we initially surveyed secondary school students, but in the wake of the Egyptian revolution, extra-curricular activities in secondary schools were suspended. As such, we were not able to run a post survey with secondary students. Instead, the team surveyed university students starting the program and ran a follow-up survey with them at program completion, as well as some students who did not participate in the program. The following table 1.2. summarizes the characteristics of the samples used in the study.

The evaluation focused on the impact of the entrepreneurship education program on entrepreneurial mindset and skills of participating students. In order to measure student knowledge, skills, attitudes and behavioral intentions about entrepreneurship, as well as information about their views regarding their education and exposure to entrepreneurship, we designed a questionnaire that reflected multiple dimensions of the intended and potential impact of Injaz Al-Arab's Company Program. We developed this survey using a conceptual framework that included knowledge and cognitive skills, interpersonal skills and attitudes, and intrapersonal skills and attitudes. Essentially, the survey measures eight constructs which we consider to be pillars of an entrepreneurial mindset and skills:

- o Aspirations, views of self and of others
- o Perceived self-efficacy
- o Educational aspirations
- o Career motivations
- o Interest in starting a business
- o Financial management knowledge
- o Attitudes towards entrepreneurship and business
- o Knowledge about entrepreneurship

Table 1.2. Characteristics of the sample of students and schools in each of the countries participating in the study

	Morocco	Lebanon	Jordan	Saudi	UAE	Egypt
Education Level		Upper Secondary				University
Cities	2	5	1	1	1	3
Schools	14	9	4	4	2	10
Individuals	486	411	76	311	79	91
Individuals in the Comparison Group						
Baseline	219	189	41	123	No	45
Follow-up	No	Yes (61)	Yes (50)	No	No	Yes (45)
Matched	No	Yes (34)	Yes (35)	No	No	No
Individuals in the Company Program						
Baseline	267	222	35	188	79	46
Follow-up	Yes (75)	Yes (43)	Yes (22)	Yes (46)	Yes (61)	Yes (21)
Matched	No	Yes (36)	Yes (15)	No	Yes (58)	No

In designing the questionnaire, we conducted several interviews with the CEO of Injaz Al-Arab and a program manager to ascertain the logic theory of the program. We then discussed several drafts of the questionnaire with them and with senior program staff in each of the countries in which the program operates to ascertain the relevancy of the dimensions we were exploring and the adequacy of the wording of the questions. We made adaptations to this questionnaire based on these conversations. The English version of this questionnaire is presented in Appendix A. The questionnaire was then translated into Arabic and translated back to English for verification of the fidelity of the translation. Data were collected between the months of December 2010 and January 2011 by local teams. Using a modified follow-up survey (Appendix B), data were again collected between July and November 2011.

In spite of the methodological challenges to the design of the study resulting from the Arab spring and other factors which limited our ability to match students' pre and post data and to have a comparison group as described above, which constrain our ability to establish causal inferences about the impact of the Injaz Al-Arab Company Program, the replication of the study in six different countries provides an evidence base that makes visible the most consistent findings across countries. The main strength of this study is the ability to identify which findings are most robust, because they are consistent across countries. This chapter summarizes those findings that are most consistent across countries, and particularly those where the observed differences are greater than five percentage points. Subsequent chapters provide specific findings for each of the countries studied.

1.5. Findings

1.5.1. Who Participates in the Company Program?

In most countries, participation is fairly balanced by gender, with young women representing over 60 percent of the participants in the program in Morocco, Lebanon and Saudi Arabia, and over 45 percent in Jordan, the UAE and Egypt. Students are, on average, between 16 and 17 years old, with the exception of Egypt where, as appropriate to university students, the average age is 21. Most of the participants' fathers hold a secondary or post-secondary diploma, while their mothers have, on average, a secondary degree (except in Egypt, where the fathers' educational attainment, on average, consists of a university education and the mothers' average is between a post-secondary and university degree).

Students have parents who work in a variety of occupations. Students in Saudi Arabia have the highest percentage of fathers working in the public sector (74%) followed by the United Arab Emirates (50%). Lebanon has the lowest percentage of fathers employed in the public sector at 16 percent. The percentage of fathers working in the private sector, likewise, is lowest in Saudi Arabia and UAE and higher in Morocco (26%) and Lebanon (26%). About half of the mothers are unemployed or homemakers. The percentage of mothers working in the public sector is higher in Saudi Arabia (27%) and Egypt (23%) and lower in Lebanon, Jordan and UAE at around 10 percent. The percentage of mothers working in the private sector is higher in Egypt (70%), about 10 percent in Morocco, Lebanon and Jordan, and 0 percent in Saudi Arabia and the UAE. These demographics are comparable to those for the population as a whole, at least for middle class youth living in urban areas.

The overall demographic characteristics of the students in the comparison group are similar to those described for the group of students who participate in the Company Program. Appendix C presents the specific descriptive information of the sample.

1.5.2. How Program Participants and Non-Participants Spend Their Time

Most students who participate in the program report that they spend a lot of time studying, entertaining themselves, chatting with friends, or watching TV or listening to the radio. About half of them report that they spend much time with their parents. About a third spend time exploring career options, researching business opportunities or following the news. For the most part, the patterns of time use are similar for students in the Company Program and in the comparison group, with the exception of Jordan where a greater percentage of students in the program spend time researching business opportunities, with their parents, chatting with their friends and entertaining themselves. In general, except in Jordan, a greater percentage of the students who participate in the Company Program spend time studying than their peers in the comparison group. These findings are summarized in Table 1.3.

Table 1.3. How much time do you spend doing the following activities in a typical week? (Question: On a scale of 1-5, how much time to you spend on the following activities. Table includes percentage who answer that they spent *much time* or a *lot of time*)

	Morocco	Lebanon	Jordan	Saudi	UAE	Egypt
Comparison Group						
Careers	34%	21%	48%	32%	n.a.	34%
Research	41%	25%	39%	35%	n.a.	34%
News	44%	26%	53%	27%	n.a.	57%
Talk parents	63%	50%	59%	53%	n.a.	45%
Studying	65%	64%	78%	47%	n.a.	78%
Entertainment	59%	64%	63%	62%	n.a.	47%
Chating friends	62%	69%	49%	65%	n.a.	55%
TV and Radio	65%	81%	68%	68%	n.a.	55%
Participants in Company Program						
Careers	21%	22%	40%	34%	27%	31%
Research	37%	28%	59%	39%	30%	42%
News	47%	31%	58%	33%	27%	53%
Talk parents	58%	62%	71%	51%	53%	42%
Studying	80%	69%	68%	63%	74%	62%
Entertainment	65%	66%	79%	51%	60%	53%
Chatting friends	61%	74%	79%	59%	63%	62%
TV and Radio	61%	79%	71%	63%	67%	49%

Careers   Investigating career possibilities
Research   Research potential ideas for a new business
News   Following the news
Talk parents   Talking to your parents about career possibilities
Studying   Studying or working on school-related activities
Entertainment   Keeping up-to-date on entertainment, fashion or sports
Chatting friendsChatting with friends
TV and Radio   Watching TV or listening to music

1.5.3.   Exposure to Entrepreneurship before the Company Program

Overall, a large percentage of students report that they know people who are entrepreneurs. Around 80 percent indicate that they have siblings who are entrepreneurs, and between 30 percent to 74 percent report that they have parents and neighbors who are entrepreneurs. This is very similar for students who participate in the Company Program and for those in the comparison group.

Table 1.4. Knowledge of Entrepreneurs (Question: Who among the following people to you know who have started their own business?)

	Morocco	Lebanon	Jordan	Saudi	UAE	Egypt
Comparison Group						
Parent	65%	36%	34%	40%	n.a.	40%
Sibling	76%	77%	74%	80%	n.a.	72%
Family	20%	21%	37%	24%	n.a.	32%
Neighbor	56%	41%	31%	58%	n.a.	38%
Friend	68%	59%	61%	62%	n.a.	51%
Teacher	74%	72%	65%	75%	n.a.	60%
Someone else	35%	32%	23%	30%	n.a.	33%
Participants in Company Program						
Parent	59%	32%	32%	48%	74%	43%
Sibling	83%	81%	66%	80%	88%	78%
Family	33%	15%	18%	28%	27%	30%
Neighbor	52%	39%	43%	53%	79%	54%
Friend	70%	57%	69%	61%	67%	29%
Teacher	79%	60%	38%	78%	91%	68%
Someone else	43%	30%	17%	34%	52%	26%

About half of the students indicate that they could access funding for an entrepreneurial venture from their nuclear family or from a bank, and around a quarter of them say they would from a government grant or from their extended family. Few would obtain those funds from a friend. There are no systematic differences in how students would access financing for those who participate in the Company Program and those in the comparison group.

Table 1.5. Sources of funding. (Q: If you were to start a business, to what extent would you be able to depend on the following financing sources to support your new business? On scale 1-5. Table reports percentage who answered 4 or 5)

	Morocco	Lebanon	Jordan	Saudi	UAE	Egypt
Comparison Group						
Nuclear family	63%	49%	61%	56%	n.a.	52%
Extended family	24%	22%	29%	25%	n.a.	15%
Friends	12%	12%	24%	14%	n.a.	13%
Bank	35%	45%	47%	41%	n.a.	28%
Grant	21%	23%	53%	56%	n.a.	21%
Participants in Company Program						
Nuclear family	47%	48%	58%	49%	40%	56%
Extended family	24%	22%	34%	22%	14%	26%
Friends	13%	10%	31%	19%	9%	20%
Bank	55%	55%	39%	44%	42%	42%
Grant	27%	27%	28%	49%	51%	24%

1.5.4. How Do Participants Differ before and after Participation in the Program?

In this section we examine the differences in the percentage of students who describe their own skills, knowledge and attitudes before and after participation in the Company Program. We especially note differences which are greater than 5 percentage points. In three countries (Morocco, Lebanon and the UAE) we also performed tests of the statistical significance of those differences. However, in the case of Morocco we could not match individuals over time so differences might be result of differences in the composition of the baseline and follow-up samples.

1.5.4.1. Aspirations, Views of Self and Worldviews

Overall, most of the youth surveyed in the program have high aspirations. They believe that they will achieve their goals, they try to learn from their failures, they see challenges as opportunities, they participate in out of school activities for development, and they believe that education is important to get a job in the future. They believe in negotiation as a means to achieve their goals. They set goals for themselves and try to find creative solutions to problems.

In response to most of the questions describing aspirations and views of self, a greater percentage of students report positive aspirations after the Company Program than before. Many of these differences are also greater than 5 percent. They are most consistent in Morocco and Saudi Arabia, and also present for most questions in Jordan and Egypt. For the three countries where we performed a statistical test of the significance of these differences, they are all significant in Morocco, while in the UAE there are significant differences for seeing challenges as opportunities and pursuing enrichment activities outside school.

Given that most of the students have high aspirations and positive views of self even before participating in the Company Program, the extent to which the program could influence those is limited.

Table 1.6. Aspirations and worldviews towards future and self of students before and after participating in the Company Program. (Question: On a scale of 1-5, to what extent do you agree or disagree with the following statements about yourself. Table includes percentage who answer 4 or 5)

	Morocco		Lebanon Matched sample		Jordan Matched sample	
	Before	After	Before	After	Before	After
Achieve goals	74%	95%	89%	92%	93%	100%
Learn from failure	80%	97%	86%	83%	100%	100%
Challenges opport.	66%	88%	75%	83%	87%	67%
Outside school	55%	82%	50%	61%	67%	64%
Educ matters	79%	85%	86%	77%	93%	100%
Negotiate	64%	92%	89%	77%	93%	93%
Leadership	62%	88%	78%	69%	73%	100%
Set goals	76%	96%	81%	81%	87%	93%

	Saudi		UAE Matched sample		Egypt	
	Before	After	Before	After	Before	After
Achieve goals	82%	93%	78%	83%	74%	95%
Learn from failure	87%	93%	86%	91%	85%	100%
Challenges opport.	62%	75%	66%	86%	83%	86%
Outside school	54%	88%	33%	63%	60%	91%
Educ matters	82%	84%	93%	90%	65%	50%
Negotiate	71%	93%	81%	74%	80%	82%
Leadership	73%	82%	74%	78%	73%	73%
Set goals	81%	88%	76%	81%	72%	95%

Achieve goals   I trust that in the future, I will achieve my goals.
Learn from failureIf I fail at something, I try to figure out why so that I can
                   succeed the next time.
Challenges opport.I see challenges as opportunities.
Outside school   Participate in activities outside of school to prepare for future.
Educ matters   I go to school because education is important for getting a
                   job later.
Negotiate   I believe that achieving my goals requires negotiating with others.
Leadership   I can see myself in a leadership position in the future.
Set goals   I set goals for myself in order to attain the things I want.

1.5.4.2. Perceived Self-Efficacy

Students were asked to report their own efficacy on a range of questions. Most students believe that they can work with a team to accomplish a result, can adapt to new situations, can solve problems, can present a topic to a group of classmates or adults, can resolve differences within a group to reach a solution that works for most, can solve community problems, can persuade a group of people about an idea, can negotiate personal conflicts in a peaceful way, and could be competitive in securing a good job. A large percentage of students also believe that they could start and run their own business one day, and that they understand the role of business owners in the economy. Many believe they can lead the members of a group to meet a deadline to produce a result and research the potential market of a company. A large percentage believes there is a clear connection between what they learn in school and the real world.

After participating in the Company Program, a greater percentage of students rated their efficacy more highly than before. These differences exceeded five percentage points in most of these questions in Morocco, Jordan, Saudi Arabia, UAE and Egypt. While there were gains in Lebanon and Jordan in several of the questions, these did not exceed five percentage points.

The tests of the statistical significance of these differences in the three countries in which we were able to match surveys of students before and after participating in the Company Program shows that most of them are highly significant in Morocco and six of them are significant in the UAE

Table 1.7. Perception of Self-Efficacy of students before and after participating in the Company Program. (Question: On a scale of 1-5, to what extent do you feel that you are able to... Table includes percentage for those who answered 4 or 5)

| | Morocco | | Lebanon | | Jordan | |
| | | | Matched sample | | Matched sample | |
	Before	*After*	*Before*	*After*	*Before*	*After*
Teamwork	78%	93%	89%	72%	87%	93%
Adapt	74%	90%	81%	69%	80%	87%
Problemsolve	60%	82%	89%	86%	93%	93%
Presentpeers	64%	85%	69%	81%	87%	71%
Presentadult	64%	70%	66%	78%	93%	67%
Resolvediff	66%	93%	74%	71%	80%	85%
Commproblem	47%	73%	57%	57%	73%	69%
Persuade	60%	88%	83%	71%	93%	77%

| | Saudi | | UAE | | Egypt | |
| | | | Matched sample | | | |
	Before	*After*	*Before*	*After*	*Before*	*After*
Teamwork	79%	96%	76%	81%	80%	91%
Adapt	72%	80%	64%	79%	74%	86%
Problemsolve	72%	89%	67%	76%	74%	91%
Presentpeers	61%	86%	49%	67%	63%	71%
Presentadult	63%	82%	47%	55%	77%	64%
Resolvediff	66%	91%	64%	71%	69%	91%
Commproblem	58%	76%	64%	66%	69%	77%
Persuade	61%	82%	64%	71%	67%	62%

Notes:

Teamwork	Work with a team to accomplish a result
Adapt	Adapt to new situations
Problemsolve	Solve problems
Presentpeers	Present a topic to a group of classmates
Presentadult	Present a topic to a group of adults
Resolvediff	Resolve differences within a group to reach a solution satisfactory to most
Commproblem	Solve community problems
Persuade	Persuade a group of people about an idea

Panel B.

	Morocco		Lebanon Matched sample		Jordan Matched sample	
	Before	*After*	*Before*	*After*	*Before*	*After*
Negconflict	71%	88%	81%	67%	93%	79%
Competejob	83%	93%	86%	91%	100%	93%
Startbusiness	71%	90%	75%	72%	87%	100%
Rolebusiness	62%	64%	58%	53%	100%	33%
Leadteam	64%	86%	83%	60%	67%	86%
Research	67%	71%	77%	53%	79%	73%
Learnrealworld	54%	63%	37%	44%	60%	62%

	Saudi		UAE Matched sample		Egypt	
	Before	*After*	*Before*	*After*	*Before*	*After*
Negconflict	65%	80%	72%	68%	78%	86%
Competejob	83%	93%	85%	93%	87%	95%
Startbusiness	69%	83%	54%	69%	76%	81%
Rolebusiness	49%	50%	41%	41%	68%	64%
Leadteam	66%	91%	59%	71%	80%	67%
Research	59%	63%	52%	48%	62%	65%
Learnrealworld	48%	48%	54%	59%	33%	41%

Notes:

Negconflict	Negotiate personal conflicts in a peaceful way
Competejob	Be competitive in securing a good job
Startbusiness	Start and run your own business someday
Rolebusiness	Understand the role of business owners in our economy
Leadteam	Lead the members of a group to meet a deadline in producing a result
Research	Research the potential market for a company
Learnrealworld	To what extent is there a clear connection between what you are learning in school and the real world?

1.5.4.3. Motivations for Choosing a Job

Students were asked several questions regarding their motivations for choosing a job and their confidence in gaining employment. The range of motivations varies. In general, most students would like to have a job with high status, to earn a lot of money, to have a job with clear career prospects, to have a job that uses their skills and abilities, to have job security, to have a role in decision making, to work independently without supervision, and to have a job that is family friendly. A smaller percentage, but still almost half of the students, would like a job with a lot of vacation time and a job with an easy pace. A large percentage of students are confident that they could successfully complete a job interview and be hired to work in the private sector.

While a higher percentage of students expressed particular motivations for seeking a job after participating in the Company Program, there is not a consistent pattern across countries. There are two questions, however, in which a greater percentage of students express higher confidence after participating in the Company Program across all countries: their confidence in successfully completing a job interview and in their ability to be hired in the private sector. These differences are greater than 5 percent for students in Morocco, Saudi Arabia and Egypt. There are also modest gains in the percentage of students who say they would like to work in a job that gives them a job in decision making and independence from supervision. In Morocco, a greater percentage of students responded positively to all the questions in this section after participating in the Company Program than before.

Table 1.8. Motivations for Choosing a Job of students before and after participating in the company program. (Question: On a scale of 1 to 5, to what extent are the following reasons important to you in choosing a particular job? Percentage who answer important and very important.)

Panel A.

	Morocco		Lebanon Matched sample		Jordan Matched sample	
	Before	*After*	*Before*	*After*	*Before*	*After*
Status	71%	84%	71%	83%	93%	64%
Money	73%	73%	83%	81%	73%	71%
Career	82%	82%	94%	89%	87%	86%
Uses skills	88%	97%	94%	89%	100%	79%
Job security	90%	82%	80%	75%	100%	93%
Role deciding	71%	84%	75%	81%	93%	85%
	Saudi		UAE Matched sample		Egypt	
	Before	*After*	*Before*	*After*	*Before*	*After*
Status	69%	72%	88%	79%	78%	45%
Money	80%	74%	87%	88%	52%	41%
Career	88%	89%	88%	93%	83%	57%
Uses skills	94%	91%	92%	93%	93%	100%
Job security	93%	86%	88%	86%	76%	68%
Role deciding	87%	89%	81%	84%	80%	82%

Notes:

Status	High status of job
Money	Ability to earn a lot of money
Career	Good promotion prospects, clear career path
Uses skills	Uses my skills and abilities
Job security	Job security
Role deciding	Gives me a role in decision making

Panel B.

	Morocco		Lebanon Matched sample		Jordan Matched sample	
	Before	*After*	*Before*	*After*	*Before*	*After*
Ample vacation	47%	54%	42%	39%	67%	43%
Easy pace	37%	38%	44%	47%	62%	62%
Autonomy	58%	61%	50%	77%	73%	69%
Family friendly	57%	79%	51%	56%	87%	50%
Confinter	65%	90%	69%	83%	93%	80%
Confhired	55%	83%	81%	94%	73%	87%

	Saudi		UAE Matched sample		Egypt	
	Before	*After*	*Before*	*After*	*Before*	*After*
Ample vacation	46%	54%	45%	54%	41%	33%
Easy pace	62%	57%	66%	72%	37%	23%
Autonomy	55%	70%	55%	65%	53%	55%
Family friendly	80%	67%	76%	66%	60%	48%
Confinter	73%	89%	73%	93%	74%	82%
Confhired	59%	80%	66%	71%	71%	76%

Notes:

Ample vacation	Has a lot of vacation time
Easy pace	Easy pace of work
Autonomy	Ability to work independently without supervision
Family friendly	Job that is family friendly
Confidence interview	How much confidence do you have that you could successfully complete a job interview?
Confidence hired	How much confidence do you have that you could be hired to work in the private sector?

1.5.4.4. Interest in Starting a Business and Motivations for Business Creation

Students were asked about their interest in starting a business. Most students are interested in starting a business. About half of them think that starting a business is easy and a small percentage has an idea of what kind of business they would like to start. A greater percentage of them were interested in starting a business after participating in the Company Program in Morocco, Saudi Arabia and the UAE. These differences were greater than five percentage points in the first two of these countries and were statistically significant only in the case of Morocco.

Only students in Morocco and Egypt were more prone to think that starting a business was easy after participating in the Company Program, and these differences exceeded five percentage points only in Egypt.

A greater percentage of students indicated that they had an idea for a possible business after participating in the Company Program in Lebanon, Saudi, the UAE and Egypt, but the difference exceeded five percentage points only in Saudi Arabia.

Table 1.9. Interest in opening a business among students before and after participating in the company program. (Question: On a scale of 1 to 5, How interested are you in opening a business Table includes percentage who answer interested or very interested)

	Morocco		Lebanon Matched sample		Jordan Matched sample	
	Before	*After*	*Before*	*After*	*Before*	*After*
Easy start	46%	46%	44%	0%	67%	33%
Startinterest	67%	81%	69%	64%	87%	73%
Businessidea			11%	14%	40%	14%
	Saudi		UAE Matched sample		Egypt	
	Before	*After*	*Before*	*After*	*Before*	*After*
Easy start	50%	36%	37%	28%	30%	41%
Startinterest	72%	89%	47%	52%	87%	68%
Businessidea	25%	43%	19%	22%	13%	14%

Notes:

Easy start	In general, how easy is it to start a business in your country today?
Interest	How interested are you in someday starting your own business?
Idea	Do you have an idea for a business you would like to start?

Students were asked about the role various motivations would play in their eventual decision to open a business. Many students would prefer to work for themselves rather than for someone else, would like to use their skills effectively, would like to create and develop new ideas, would like to resolve important social problems, believe that they can earn more money running their own business, would like to create jobs and foster economic growth, and would like to become famous entrepreneurs. A smaller percentage is interested in creating a business because their friends want them to.

A greater percentage of students, after participating in the Company Program, were motivated to start a business in order to work for themselves in Saudi Arabia. In Morocco and Egypt, a greater share of students were motivated to start a business in order to create and develop new ideas, while in Morocco, Saudi Arabia and Egypt, more wanted to do so in order to use their skills effectively. Motivations related to resolving important social problems, earning more money, creating jobs, becoming famous and responding to their friends' preferences were reported in larger numbers in Morocco, Saudi Arabia and the UAE. These differences were statistically significant only in Morocco.

Table 1.10. Importance of various factors in eventual decision to open a business among students before and after participating in the Company Program. (Question: If you were to start your own business in the future, indicate on a scale of 1-5 how important each of the following is in your decision to start a business. Percentage who answer important or very important)

	Morocco		Lebanon Matched sample		Jordan Matched sample	
	Before	*After*	*Before*	*After*	*Before*	*After*
Work for self	63%	68%	72%	64%	80%	79%
Use skills	84%	97%	92%	83%	93%	86%
Create new ideas	80%	96%	94%	92%	85%	85%
Solve problems	59%	85%	64%	72%	86%	71%
Earn more	64%	73%	72%	81%	86%	86%
Create jobs	68%	90%	72%	72%	93%	79%
Fame	58%	69%	50%	58%	93%	93%
Friends	38%	63%	20%	31%	69%	57%

	Saudi		UAE Matched sample		Egypt	
	Before	*After*	*Before*	*After*	*Before*	*After*
Work for self	61%	78%	56%	63%	72%	43%
Use skills	89%	85%	86%	93%	81%	90%
Create new ideas	83%	85%	81%	86%	79%	90%
Solve problems	74%	84%	64%	70%	65%	76%
Earn more	77%	85%	59%	75%	58%	62%
Create jobs	68%	76%	47%	73%	62%	62%
Fame	58%	65%	61%	70%	60%	52%
Friends	44%	56%	32%	55%	39%	67%

Notes:

Work for self	Prefer to work for yourself rather than someone else
Use skills	To use your skills effectively
Create new ideas	To be able to create and develop new ideas
Solve problems	To resolve important social problems
Earn more	You can earn more money running your own business
Create jobs	To create jobs and foster economic growth
Fame	To become a famous entrepreneur
Friends	Your friends want to start a business

1.5.4.5. Financial Management

Students were asked to report their financial management habits. Most of them plan their spending, budget and save regularly. A greater percentage of them plan how to spend their money, use a budget and save regularly after participating in the program than before in Morocco and UAE, and a greater percentage plan how to spend it in Egypt. These differences are statistically significant in Morocco.

Table 1.11. Financial management habits among students before and after participating in the Company Program. (0=no, 1=yes)

	Morocco		Lebanon Matched sample		Jordan Matched sample	
	Before	*After*	*Before*	*After*	*Before*	*After*
Plan finances	70%	92%	75%	83%	93%	93%
Moneybudget	55%	73%	72%	81%	93%	93%
Moneysave	56%	77%	67%	69%	79%	80%

	Saudi		UAE Matched sample		Egypt	
	Before	*After*	*Before*	*After*	*Before*	*After*
Plan finances	86%		85%	91%	67%	86%
Moneybudget	70%		73%	79%	59%	58%
Moneysave	63%		63%	76%	46%	43%

Notes:

Plan finances	When you have money, do you plan ahead for how to spend it?
Budget	Do you use a budget to manage your spending?
Save	Do you regularly save money?

1.5.4.6. Attitudes towards Entrepreneurship and Business

A number of questions probed student views towards entrepreneurs and entrepreneurship and towards other people more generally. In general, before participating in the Company Program, over half of the students believe that people can get ahead by working hard and about half think that entrepreneurs only think about their own gain. Most think that women can play an important role in the success of a business. A small percentage believe that most people can be trusted, while a large percentage think that there is potential in their country for entrepreneurs to succeed. Many think that entrepreneurs create jobs for others, and more than half of the students think that entrepreneurs contribute to the economic development of the country. A sizable percentage thinks that men are better qualified than women to be business leaders and that, when jobs are scarce, men should have more rights to them.

There are more students, after participating in the Company Program, who think that people can get ahead by working hard in Morocco, Saudi Arabia, the UAE and Egypt. More students believe that women can play an important role in the success of a business in Morocco, Saudi Arabia and Egypt after participating in the Company Program. After participating in the program, more students believe that there is potential for an entrepreneur to be successful in Morocco, Saudi Arabia and the UAE. More students believe, after participating in the program, that entrepreneurs create jobs for others in Morocco, Saudi Arabia and the UAE, while a greater percentage of students believe that entrepreneurs contribute to the economic development of the country after participating in Morocco, Jordan, Saudi Arabia and the UAE.

Table 1.12. Attitudes towards Entrepreneurship. (Question: On a scale of 1-5, to what extent do you agree or disagree with the following statements, percent who agree or strongly agree with the statement)

Panel A

	Morocco		Lebanon Matched sample		Jordan Matched sample	
	Before	*After*	*Before*	*After*	*Before*	*After*
Hard work	56%	86%	35%	42%	67%	60%
Trust	18%	19%	0%	6%	13%	27%
Entrepreneurs selfish	53%	49%	58%	39%	73%	33%
Entrepreneurs succeed	54%	68%	29%	36%	79%	73%
Entr. create jobs	37%	66%	16%	50%	53%	47%
Entrepreneurs contribute	52%	70%	44%	64%	60%	67%

	Saudi		UAE Matched sample		Egypt	
	Before	*After*	*Before*	*After*	*Before*	*After*
Hard work	56%	65%	73%	86%	67%	82%
Trust	28%	24%	18%	32%	29%	19%
Entrepreneurs selfish	60%	36%	40%	35%	38%	50%
Entrepreneurs succeed	57%	63%	72%	86%	62%	50%
Entr. create jobs	34%	52%	39%	70%	58%	55%
Entrepreneurs contribute	39%	48%	56%	74%	64%	59%

Notes:

Hard work	People in your country can get ahead by working hard.
Trust	Most people can be trusted.
Entrepreneurs selfish	Entrepreneurs only think about their own gain.
Entrepreneurs succeed	There is potential in your country for an entrepreneur to become successful.
Entr. create jobs	Entrepreneurs create jobs for others.
Entrepreneurs contribute	Entrepreneurs contribute to the economic development of the country.

Panel B

	Morocco		Lebanon Matched sample		Jordan Matched sample	
	Before	*After*	*Before*	*After*	*Before*	*After*
Women lead	87%	95%	86%	83%	87%	87%
Men lead better	24%	18%	9%	11%	40%	27%
Men more rights	23%	18%	12%	11%	40%	27%

	Saudi		UAE Matched sample		Egypt	
	Before	*After*	*Before*	*After*	*Before*	*After*
Women lead	67%	74%	86%	88%	62%	82%
Men lead better	56%	33%	35%	46%	52%	50%
Men more rights	56%	52%	42%	54%	42%	45%

Notes:

Women lead   Women can play an important role in the success of a business.
Men lead better   Men are better qualified than women to be business leaders
Men more rights   When jobs are scarce, men should have more rights to a job than women.

1.5.4.7. Knowledge about Entrepreneurship

A few questions in the survey assessed student knowledge of basic concepts of entrepreneurship and business. The overall levels of knowledge are low before participating in the program. While there are clear and sizeable differences with the group who had participated in the Company Program in the demonstrating greater knowledge in the cases of Morocco, Jordan, Saudi, UAE and Egypt, participating students are far from achieving mastery of these basic knowledge concepts. These differences are statistically significant in Morocco and Lebanon, and in UAE only for two of the five definitions (liquidation and company). Percentages of students who answered correctly are reported in Table 1.13.

Table 1.13. Knowledge about entrepreneurship (Multiple choice questions)

	Morocco		Lebanon Matched sample		Jordan Matched sample	
	Before	*After*	*Before*	*After*	*Before*	*After*
Sell shares	10%	36%	6%	61%	7%	33%
Vision	9%	29%	31%	56%	33%	73%
Marketing	53%	92%	61%	86%	87%	53%
Liquidation	14%	45%	11%	50%	7%	33%
Company	18%	60%	31%	61%	47%	67%

	Saudi		UAE Matched sample		Egypt	
	Before	*After*	*Before*	*After*	*Before*	*After*
Sell shares	35%	46%	25%	14%	20%	45%
Vision	45%	70%	68%	79%	65%	91%
Marketing	70%	72%	78%	79%	61%	86%
Liquidation	12%	25%	8%	31%	59%	45%
Company	40%	51%	28%	47%	46%	59%

Notes:

Sell shares	Selling shares of stock to get start-up money for a new company is called:
Vision	A _____ represents a company's dream of where it wants to go and what it wants to be.
Marketing	The work you completed in this scenario above is an example of which of the following:
Liquidation	When a company liquidates, it does which of the following:
Company	By definition, a company must have which of the following

1.6. How Do Students in the Company Program Describe the Effects of the Program?

Students who completed the Company Program were asked to rate themselves in a series of questions about possible effects of the program. Most participants who were surveyed after the program were very favorable about the changes they observe in themselves. After participating in the Company Program, over 74 percent of the students feel more empowered to take a leadership role in the workforce in the future; this figure is higher in Morocco, Saudi Arabia and the UAE. Over 80 percent of the students say they understand the importance of managing their finances. The majority say that they have further developed their educational goals. Between 67 percent and 89 percent of participants say they have developed their career goals. Over 70 percent say that they now feel more confident about their ability to successfully compete in the workforce in the future. Over 63 percent say they now know more about entrepreneurship, and over 60 percent say they are now more interested in starting their own business. These ratings about the student experience are least favorable in Lebanon and UAE and most favorable in Morocco and Saudi Arabia.

Table 1.14. Retrospective experience (Compare yourself now to where you were at the beginning of the school year. On a scale of 1-5, to what extent do you agree with the following statements about yourself. Percentage who agree much or very much.)

	Morocco	Lebanon	Jordan	Saudi	UAE	Egypt
Leadership	89%	74%	81%	91%	86%	n.a.
Finances	86%	79%	80%	89%	84%	n.a.
Education goals	96%	62%	68%	93%	79%	n.a.
Career goals	89%	67%	86%	84%	74%	n.a.
Competitive	89%	81%	71%	96%	79%	n.a.
Know entrepreneurship	77%	63%	90%	84%	67%	n.a.
Start business	88%	60%	81%	91%	57%	n.a.

Notes:

Leadership	I feel more empowered to take a leadership role in the workforce in the future.
Finances	I realize more that knowing how to effectively manage my finances is important.
Education goals	I have developed (or further developed) my educational goals.
Career goals	I have developed (or further developed) my career goals.
Competitive	I am more confident in my ability to successfully compete in the workforce in the future.
Know entrepreneurship	I know more about entrepreneurship.
Start business	I am more interested in starting my own business.

When participating students were asked specifically about the Injaz Company Program, most attribute very positive ratings to it. Most found it valuable or very valuable, attribute to the program an enhanced understanding of other people's views and say that the program helped them develop the ability to work with others as a team (Table 1.15). Most also say that it helped them develop citizenship skills, that the program helped them develop the capacity to innovate, that the program taught them critical thinking skills, and that the program taught them useful business skills.

Most students say that the program helped them develop initiative and self-motivation, their abilities as a leader, and knowledge of how to manage a budget, to solve problems, to become a better decision maker, to communicate with others, to negotiate differences with people, to sell ideas or products, to speak in public more easily, and to think more creatively about problems. The most positive ratings relate to the overall value of the program, its help in students learning to work in a team, and its role in fostering motivation. Overall, the ratings are least positive in the UAE.

Table 1.15. Contribution of the Company Program. (In your opinion, on a scale of 1-5, to what extent did your participation in the Injaz Company Program help you with the following. Percent who agree much or very much)

Panel A

	Morocco	Lebanon	Jordan	Saudi	UAE	Egypt
Valuable	93%	92%	86%	95%	70%	n.a.
Empathy	89%	70%	71%	n.a.	67%	n.a.
Team work	93%	90%	95%	91%	74%	n.a.
Citizenship	85%	68%	95%	n.a.	69%	n.a.
Innovation	92%	82%	85%	93%	71%	n.a.
Critical thinking	89%	80%	89%	84%	61%	n.a.
Postbusskill	94%	80%	79%	n.a.	73%	n.a.
Postselfmotiv	96%	93%	100%	87%	72%	n.a.
Postleader	79%	74%	86%	84%	66%	n.a.
Postbudget	80%	87%	80%	95%	66%	n.a.

Notes:
Valuable   In general, how valuable did you find participating in the Injaz company program
Empathy   It helped me develop understanding of other people's views.
Team work   It helped me develop the ability to work with others as a team.
Citizenship   It helped me develop citizenship skills.
Innovation   It helped me develop the capacity to innovate.
Critical thinking It taught me critical thinking skills.
Business   It taught me useful business skills.
Initiative   It helped me development initiative and self-motivation.
Leadership   It helped me develop my abilities as a leader.
Budgeting   It taught me how to manage a budget.

Panel B

	Morocco	Lebanon	Jordan	Saudi	UAE	Egypt
Problem solve	93%	83%	90%	80%	68%	n.a.
Decide	96%	88%	90%	n.a.	74%	n.a.
Postcomm	90%	70%	90%	91%	73%	n.a.
Postnegot	86%	83%	75%	93%	65%	n.a.
Sell	86%	80%	90%	89%	70%	n.a.
Speak	80%	78%	90%	84%	67%	n.a.
Creativity	92%	75%	75%	91%	61%	n.a.

Notes:

Problem solve	It helped me learn to solve problems.
Decide	It helped me to become a better decision maker.
Communicate	It helped me learn to communicate with others.
Negotiate	It helped me learn to negotiate differences with people.
Sell	It helped me learn to sell ideas or products.
Speak	It helped me learn to speak in public more easily.
Creativity	It inspired me to think more creatively about problems.

Students were also asked to evaluate some of the components of the program (Table 1.16). These components are evaluated positively by the majority of the students. Most students say the lectures aroused their interest in the topics and that volunteers presented the content clearly, held lectures in an interactive way, and were helpful and responsive to questions. Most of them found the Student Guides useful or very useful. Most of them would recommend the program to another student or family. The least positive ratings were in the UAE and Lebanon, and the most positive in Morocco and Jordan.

Table 1.16. Evaluation of the Components of the Program. (On a scale of 1-5, to what extent do you agree with the following comments about the Injaz Al-Arab Company Program. Percent who find them valuable or very valuable.)

	Morocco	Lebanon	Jordan	Saudi	UAE	Egypt
Lecture	93%	56%	94%	73%	64%	n.a.
Volunclear	90%	67%	95%	67%	80%	n.a.
Volunrespond	94%	67%	94%	80%	73%	n.a.
Studguide	94%	49%	95%	67%	56%	n.a.
Volunlecture	89%	67%	89%	76%	75%	n.a.
Recommend	97%	100%	100%	n.a.	69%	n.a.

Notes:

Lecture   Company Program lectures aroused my interest for the topics being discussed.

Volunclear   The volunteer presented the program's content in a clear way.

Volunrespond   The volunteer was helpful and responsive to our questions.

Studyguide   The Student Guide was useful.

Volunlecture   The volunteer held lectures in an interactive way.

Recommend   Would you recommend participating in the Injaz Al-Arab Company Program to friends or family members? (1=YES, 0=NO)

1.6. A qualitative synthesis of program effects

Within the follow-up survey, students had the opportunity to answer an open-ended question regarding their experience with the Company Program: "Use the following space to provide any comments – positive or negative – about your experience in the Injaz Al-Arab Company Program." The question received a significant response both in the numbers of youth that took time to provide comments and the detail provided therein. The following section provides an overview analysis of the comments provided by participating students from Jordan, Lebanon, Morocco, Saudi Arabia and the UAE (the question was not included in the Egyptian post survey).

To guide this quantitative analysis, we reviewed the responses provided by survey participants in this section and coded them on the basis of major themes identified within responses, themes that align largely with those presented in the quantitative analysis presented above. While the results cannot be analyzed statistically in the same way that quantitative results can, they are particularly interesting as they come from students without specific prompts. Moreover, students provided feedback that will allow Injaz Al-Arab to take steps to improve the effectiveness of program operations.

In all, 330 students took advantage of the open-ended question to provide feedback on their experience with the Injaz Al-Arab Company Program. Of these responses, the vast majority provided positive views of the program and the learning experience that it provided to them. In all, nearly 68 percent of these responses were only positive, while nearly 25 percent provided critiques in the context of otherwise positive reviews. Less than 6 percent of respondents used the open-ended question to provide criticisms or critiques alone. The majority of negative respondents were found in the UAE, where 35 percent of respondents used the open-ended question to provide only critiques and criticisms; it should be noted that most of the students in this group belonged to one student company that had had problems with a volunteer who had to drop out of the program and that their critiques were related to the volunteer's performance.

Positive Comments about the Program

While most of comments from students were positive, they were also general – with students often describing that they enjoyed or benefitted from the program rather than specifying what the benefits had been. For those who did specify, interpersonal communications and teamwork seem to be the benefits most appreciated by participants. The experience of working with teams and improved teamwork ability stand out as a benefit of Injaz Al-Arab's Company Program, with nearly 25 percent of student responses focus, at least in part, on teamwork or working within groups in describing what the benefitted from during the program. In addition, 14 percent of respondents noted that the Company Program improved their ability to interact and communicate with others, while nearly 8 percent noted an improved respect for others and their opinions.

A few emphasized that the program helped them develop negotiating skills to deal with conflict.

Other self-efficacy factors were also important to participants. Nearly 14 percent stated that the Company Program experience had improved their self-confidence and sense of self-reliance, with many of these noting that the experience had allowed them to overcome shyness and fear. More than 8 percent stressed that participation had taught them how to deal with and overcome problems, while more than 12 percent felt that they had developed a greater sense of responsibility and appreciation for hard work through the Company Program. A further 5 percent stated that they had an improved capacity for creativity and innovation after the program. In addition to the often-repeated areas described above, several students emphasized that after the program, they were more able to persuade others about their ideas, to express themselves more effectively in public settings, to manage time better, to adapt to changing environments, to think more critically about issues, and to lead.

Nearly 28% used the open-ended question to highlight that the program taught them how to establish and manage a business, although only 2% noted that the Company Program had inspired them to start their own businesses. Several respondents focused on very particular aspects of business that participation had drawn them to: buying and selling stocks, developing contracts, marketing, etc. In this regard, several students emphasized the benefit of engaging with members of the business community (volunteers, judges, service providers) and clients.

More than 11 percent student responses acknowledge that Injaz Al-Arab provided them with improved job-relevant skills. Some noted specifically that they improved their abilities in writing and presentations. Others noted an appreciation for how Injaz Al-Arab allowed them to apply their skills, skills that they often were not aware that they had until participating in the Injaz Al-Arab Company Program. Several youth citing the program's role in helping them define and achieve their goals focused specifically on educational goals and career goals.

More broadly, a number of students noted general improvements in their sense of personal wellbeing that resulted from participation. Several noted that the program made them optimistic. Others noted that they had gained a better understanding of themselves or had been able to develop their character or personality. The Company Program also allowed an environment in which several students said that they had met new people and gained new friends.

Criticisms and Critiques

The most often cited criticism of the Company Program by respondents to the open-ended question related to the timing of the program's implementation. Nearly 9 percent of respondents complained the program conflicted with their academic studies. Given a tight delivery schedule, many students did not feel that they had enough time to develop their student company while dealing with other school-related demands. This was particularly the case for those who had to prepare for comprehensive examinations at the end of final year in secondary school. Several students suggested that the Company Program be offered over a longer time period to allow them to manage their academic needs or that it be offered before their final year in school. Some in the UAE suggested that it become a summer program.

A related concern was that the Company Program's implementation itself was not held over long enough period, so that the program did not provide enough time for participants to develop and implement their ideas for student companies. This was voiced by 6 percent of participants. Some of these students suggested that the responsibility for this constraint lay with the school administration, which they felt was not flexible enough in giving them time to work on their student companies.

Other issues of potential concern were voiced with much less frequency. About 4 percent of students voiced concerns about the lack of preparedness or cooperation among their peers engaged in the Company Program. Several students voiced concerns about the tensions that arose at times within their groups, as individuals conflicted with each other over decisions related to the development of their student companies. At the same time, many of these students noted that this initial tension was eventually overcome, providing a lesson in problem solving and conflict resolution. Others felt that many of their peers were simply not engaged, did not attend sessions, did not carry out their share of the responsibilities or were unorganized. Some viewed this issue holistically, stating that the lack of cooperation among their peers had given them valuable experience in managing people and their expectations of them. Importantly, these comments should be read in the context of the fact that most of the students voicing these concerns were part of classes placed in the program rather than being run as extra-curricular activities in which students participate by choice.

Several students complained about the quality of instruction and engagement provided by the volunteers appointed to their student groups (4%). These students expressed concern that the volunteers working with their student companies were frequently late or did not show up as expected; that the volunteer did not communicate effectively with students; or that the program could benefit from more instructors in general. It is important to keep in mind the small number of these cases; however, at the same time, Injaz Al-Arab's dependence on volunteers to provide instruction means that the program is vulnerable to the schedules and demands of these busy professionals. Some problems are thus to be expected, but can have significant reputational costs for the organization.

A surprising number of students (nearly 6%) complained about the way in which the national competition was carried out. Particular complaints were that the rules and assessment criteria were vague, that judges' questions were unclear or disconnected from the experience of the Company Program, or that they had not been aware of the criteria when developing their company business plan. Others felt that the competition (one day in duration) was too short for the student companies to adequately present their cases. One student protested that awards at the national competition had been given only to those students who represented the student company at the national competition (company managers) rather than all students involved in that company.

Many of these critiques touch on areas that Injaz Al-Arab should investigate more thoroughly to alleviate issues that can be readily resolved in the future. Others are simply reflective of the experiential nature of the program: challenges and uncertainty will arise in the course of any endeavor, and many of the issues faced by youth during the program provided opportunities to gain experience in addressing such challenges in terms of problem solving, conflict resolution, negotiating and adapting.

Finally, several students provided critiques that can be viewed as a positive response to program participation. For example, several students lamented the fact that, having created companies with products that they were proud of, they had to liquidate and close the company as part of the program. They wanted to continue building what they had worked so hard to create. Similarly, a number of students wished that they would be allowed to participate in the Company Program in the future, or a follow-up program, but understood that students can only participate in the program once.

Sample Responses by Students

The following are selected responses from student answers to the open-ended question described above. While not drawn randomly, they are chosen to reflect a representative sample of the responses provided. They are intended to provide additional perspective on the student experience during the Company Program. (Responses have been edited for grammar and clarity, but care has been taken to ensure that no change to meaning takes place in doing so.)

"Injaz's Company Program helped us in all of life's aspects. It made us think about future more seriously and made us insist on achieving what we dream about." – Jordanian participant

"It helped us in building our personalities and self-confidence, and taught us how to express our ideas clearly." – Jordanian participant

"How the program helps with improving ideas is positive, but it needs someone who has free time for meetings." – Jordanian participant

"It was an unforgettable experience. It helped me to fulfill my dream of establishing a company. It gave me self-confidence. We learned that the secret to success is to believe in what you do and team work." – Moroccan participant

"In fact, it was an amazing experience. I learned how to take responsibility for my actions, interact with my team, self-confidence, trusting the team, be optimistic, recognition of my mistakes, and thinking about the others before myself." – Moroccan participant

"The program helped me to improve my communication skills, managing disputes, and respecting the opinions of others. It helped me to be courageous and to be able to confront any one. I think the program should give others the opportunity to participate and expand the program to the whole country." – Moroccan participant

"The negative part was that some participants didn't pay any attention to the project, even the people who should have. Otherwise I learned a lot from this program. I have started initiating conversations, I am not that shy anymore, and I learned the principles of management and accounting." – Moroccan participant

"It's a dream come true; it's an adventure that I've always wanted to live. The program taught us a lot of things like working in teams, responsibility, listening to others, solving conflicts in a peaceful way, accepting the others opinion, and that making a company is not a difficult thing , it just needs managing and planning." – Moroccan participant

"Negatives: some difficulties at the beginning, miscommunication between the team members. But by listening to each other and communicating in the right way, we managed to overcome all the obstacles we faced and we managed to reach our goals and a profit we didn't expect. All the team members behaved with lots of responsibility, and acted like part of a big family." – Moroccan participant

"This experience gave me a lot because I gained team spirit and group work. I also learned to be patient, responsible, helpful and understanding. This experience has served a lot socially, helping me to get rid of my shyness and letting me make a fair business by working in groups." – Moroccan participant

"It helped me become a stronger person who is not afraid to express her opinion in public. I can express myself in a more creative way." – Lebanese participant

"It is such a great experience. It changed me a lot. It built a part of my character and allowed me to see the other part of life: work and reality. It is hard and it takes a lot of time, but it is worth it! I'm so proud of this program. It's amazing. And I wish my company the best of luck. Thank you, Injaz. I am hoping to live up to all your expectations." – Lebanese participant

"I learned a lot from this experience! It helped me make some changes about my future career." – Lebanese participant

"We had a great experience, but I think the Company Program is somehow not close to reality." – Lebanese participant

"It has been an unbelievable experience; however, if the final report and competition could have been rescheduled until after exams, it would have been much easier." – Lebanese participant

"The program was a great help as I ran a project and a full staff. Now I can also do that from the beginning of any project." – Saudi Arabian participant

"My participation was a transformational part of my life. The disadvantages lie in reconciling school and the company." – Saudi Arabian participant

"Injaz is a success, and I encourage those who do not have any experience in trade to participate because it tells us a lot in our lives." - UAE participant

"Pros: I learned how to run a company and choose an attractive product. Cons: We did not have enough time because of the pressure of examinations and the need to review many lessons every day." - UAE participant

1.6. Conclusions and Implications

The findings of this evaluation of an entrepreneurship education program in six countries in the Middle East are remarkably consistent: Youth participating in the Injaz Al-Arab Company Program have, in general, very high levels of access to entrepreneurs in their lives, medium levels of knowledge of basic entrepreneurial concepts, and high and positive aspirations, views of self and others, self-efficacy and interest in business creation, and favorable attitudes towards entrepreneurship and business.

While this study does not allow us to establish to what extent these youth are representative of other youth in their countries, indirect evidence suggests that this is a self-selected group of the population. The level of education of their parents is higher than the level of education of the average student. In this sense we should keep in mind that this study was not designed to assess the effects of the Injaz Al-Arab program in an average student, but to examine the impact of the program on the students who participate in it, who are for the most part middle class urban youth. We do not know whether the findings of this study would apply to a very different group of students. This is the first limitation of this study, the limitation of the sample of students on which the impact of the study was evaluated. However, it would seem reasonable to expect that an engaging educational experience might have even more positive impact in a group of students who came from less privileged backgrounds, or who had less exposure to entrepreneurs than the students in this evaluation do. Given that the students who participate in the Company Program have fairly positive attitudes towards entrepreneurship and themselves before participating in the program, there is a limit to the extent that these positive views can increase. So regarding the first limitation of the study it is plausible that Injaz Al-Arab would have an impact at least similar to the impact documented in this evaluation with other students.

The evidence in this study, however, is very consistent across the various domains examined and across countries in showing that these views and knowledge increase. This regularity of these changes in the views and knowledge of students before and after participation in the program leads us to conclude that in all likelihood participating in the Injaz Al-Arab Company Program has positive effects for the students. This is what the students themselves say: they rate the program positively and the changes in their responses to the survey administered before and after suggest this.

There are two obvious limitations of this study to establish this impact conclusively. The first is that the design of the study is such that we cannot eliminate competing hypotheses for the changes observed. This report is based only on changes before and after participation in the study –although individual reports for each country include an analysis that examines changes in students in a comparison group, when available. There are clear changes across most dimensions examined in this study. Many of these reach a level of statistical significance when appropriate tests are used in the three countries where we were able to match surveys before and after for the same student. Given that the sample sizes are small, the lack of statistical significance does not mean necessarily that the observed differences should be discounted as small sample sizes make it difficult to determine effects, even when those effects exist.

The most serious limitation to interpreting the findings is that the observed changes may not be the result of participating in the Injaz Al-Arab program, but because of other factors not measured in this study, or of the particular characteristics of students who participate in the program interacting with participation in the program. Given the methodological limitations of these studies resulting from challenges to implementing the research, we are unable to discount that possible objection. Ultimately, the fact that similar findings are consistently found across countries and across all dimensions is a strong indication that, in spite of the methodological limitations, participating in the program has positive effects on the students.

Another limitation to this study concerns the fact that the data collected are based on self-reports of the students. In this sense, the data are 'subjective.' They reflect reality as perceived by the students, not by an independent observer. It is possible that students rate themselves on many of the dimensions evaluated in this study more favorably than an independent observer would rate them. There is no analysis of the actual competencies of the students –other than a few questions to assess their knowledge of basic business concepts. But the subjective reality through which we assess the impact of the program is the way in which students make meaning of the world and, as such, is a legitimate object of study in its own right. If students believe that in the future they will achieve their goals, for example, this attitude is important, independently of what a third person might believe about the ability of the students to achieve their goals, or independently of whether they in fact are able to achieve their goals.

With these caveats in mind, the overall findings of this report are that students who participate in the Injaz Al-Arab Company Program spend most of their time studying, and with friends and family. A smaller, but still significant, number devote time to think about their career or to research future business opportunities. After participation in the program, their aspirations and sense of self-efficacy improve, as do their skills, knowledge and attitudes towards entrepreneurship and their financial management skills. Their interest in starting a business increases in some, but not all countries. Students have very positive attributions to the Injaz Al-Arab program in terms of its aid in developing their leadership skills, confidence and soft skills. They evaluate the program and all of its components in very positive ways.

These consistently positive results across so many different domains are striking, given that the program is a relatively modest and short-term intervention. It is remarkable that students can gain so much from a few months in which they are provided the opportunity to create a business, motivated to participate in a competition and supported by a mentor who spends a few hours with them each week over a short period.

Given the indications that school systems are not currently helping students develop some of these skills, and given that these skills are highly valued by employers and likely to be necessary for students to develop agency and become contributing members of their societies, this suggest that programs such as the Injaz Al-Arab Company Program are a valuable educational opportunity for students in the region. A policy challenge is whether and how these programs can be scaled up to serve a larger, and perhaps more diverse, group of students. Because these programs depend on the mentorship of individuals with actual business experience, there may be limits to how many volunteers are available to scale up the program to serve a much greater number of students. There are also likely to be organizational challenges to training and supporting mentors, as well as students, as they participate in the various tiered competitions if the program is to serve a much larger number of students.

Perhaps the search for options to extend the apparent benefits of this program to a larger number of students could follow several avenues. One is the exploration of alternatives to extend programs of this kind to more students, in more settings. Another is the analysis of what aspects of the experience of participating in this program contribute to the results documented in this study. Are some of these outcomes the result of providing students the opportunity to decide what project to work on as they set out to create a business? Are they the result of engaging students with authentic problems? Are they the result of providing students a project based experience that allows them to integrate what they have learned and are learning in different disciplines? Are they the result of engaging students with people who have professional expertise in the real world? These might be approaches that could be integrated into the curriculum and pedagogy of the schools these students attend, thus allowing much greater impact at scale.

All the evidence examined in this report, while limited, suggests that the road ahead to identify ways to help youth in the Arab world become architects of their own lives and contributing members of their communities, will gain much from expanding options for the kind of learning by doing that Injaz Al-Arab makes possible to students who participate in the Company Program.

1.7. References

Vanessa Beary, The Effectiveness of Entrepreneurship Education Programs for Youths and Young Adults: A Best-Evidence Synthesis. (Cambridge, MA: Harvard Graduate School of Education. Unpublished Qualifying Paper, 2012)

Gregory Dees "The meaning of social entrepreneurship". (Kauffman Foundation and Stanford University, 1998) https://community-wealth.org/content/meaning-social-entrepreneurship

International Labour Organisation, *Global Employment Trends 2012: Preventing a deeper jobs crisis* (Geneva: International Labour Organisation, 2012)

International Labour Organisation, *Global Employment Trends 2010* (Geneva: International Labour Organisation, 2010)

Middle East Youth Initiative, "Missed by the Boom, Hurt by the Bust: Making Markets Work for Young People in the Middle East"

(Washington, DC and Dubai: Wolfensohn Center for Development and Dubai School of Government, 2009)

Mohammed bin Rashid Al Maktoum Foundation, *Arab Human Capital Challenge: The Voices of the CEOs* (Dubai: Mohammed bin Rashid Al Maktoum Foundation, 2009). Available online at: http://www.pwc.com/m1/en/publications/arab-human-capital-challenge.jhtml

Michael O. Martin, Ina V.S. Mullis and Pierre Foy in collaboration with John F. Olson, Corinna Preuschoff, Ebru Erberber & Joseph Galia, TIMSS 2007 International Mathematics Report: Findings from IEA's Trends in International Mathematics and Science Study at the Fourth and Eighth Grades (Chestnut Hill, MA: TIMSS & PIRLS International Study Center, Boston College, 2008)

Michael O. Martin, Ina V.S. Mullis, Pierre Foy in collaboration with John F. Olson, Ebru Erberber, Corinna Preuschoff, Joseph Galia, TIMSS 2007 International Science Report: Findings from IEA's Trends in International Mathematics and Science Study at the Fourth and Eighth Grades (Chestnut Hill, MA: TIMSS & PIRLS International Study Center, Boston College, 2008)

James Pellegrino and Margaret Hilton (Eds.) Education for Life and Work: Developing Transferable Knowledge and Skills in the 21st Century. (Washington, DC: National Academies Press, 2012)

Fernando Reimers and Connie Chung (Eds.) Teaching and Learning for the Twenty First Century. (Cambridge, MA: Harvard Education Publishing, 2016)

Fernando Reimers and Connie Chung (Eds.) Preparing Teachers to Educate Whole Students. An International Comparative Study. (Cambridge, MA: Harvard Education Publishing, 2018)

Klaus Schwab The Fourth Industrial Revolution. (New York: Crown Business, 2017)

Stratford Youth Unemployment: The Middle East ticking bomb. Stratford. February 28, 2018.   https://worldview.stratfor.com/article/youth-unemployment-middle-east-teen-jobless

Alexandria Valerio, Brent Parton and Alicia Robb Entrepreneurship Education and Training Programs around the world. (Washington, DC: The World Bank, 2014)

How Injaz Al-Arab helps youth develop an entrepreneurial mindset

Appendix A: English Version of Baseline Questionnaire

Youth Education, Employment and Entrepreneurship Survey

We are conducting a survey of 11th grade students in COUNTRY with the aim of understanding student perspectives on education, employment and entrepreneurship (starting a new business or other venture). In this survey, we will ask you a number of questions to get to know your views and aspirations about the future, as well as questions about your experience with school and your knowledge about certain financial and business issues. The information you provide is important for helping us better understand the needs and desires of young people in your country, and the results of the study will help to improve the quality of programs offered to youth in the future.

The information you provide will be held in the strictest confidentiality. Your answers will be analyzed and presented only in the form of 'averages' to characterize what groups of students answered. No one student will be identified individually. Your teachers, parents or peers will not know how you answer this questionnaire. Please answer honestly and freely. Participation in this survey is voluntary, and you can choose not to answer any particular question if you feel that it is too personal.

What time is it now? _____

On a scale of 1-5, to what extent do you agree or disagree with the following statements about yourself:

    1. If I fail at something, I try to figure out why so that I can succeed the next time.

    2. I trust that in the future, I will achieve my goals.

    3. I see challenges as opportunities.

    4. I do things outside of school to prepare for my future.

    5. Studying is very important to me.

    6. I go to school because education is important for getting a job later.

7. The things that I am learning now will help me in the future.

8. I believe that achieving my goals requires negotiating with others.

9. I can see myself in a leadership position in the future.

10. I set goals for myself in order to attain the things I want.

On a scale of 1-5, to what extent do you feel that you are able to:

11. Work with a team to accomplish a result

12. Adapt to new situations

13. Solve problems

14. Present a topic in front of a group of classmates

15. Present a topic you know well to a group of adults

16. Resolve differences within a group to reach a solution satisfactory to most

17. Understand your purpose in life

18. Solve community problems

19. Persuade a group of people about an idea

20. Negotiate personal conflicts in a peaceful way

21. Be competitive in securing a good job

22. Start and run your own business someday

23. Understand the role of business owners in our economy.

24. Lead the members of a group to meet a deadline in producing a result

25. Research the potential market for a company.

26. To what extent is there a clear connection between what you are learning in school and the real world? (1-5 scale: To a large extent ----- no connection)

27. What is the highest level of education that would like to complete?
- Will not finish secondary school
- Will finish Secondary school
- Post-secondary training program or diploma
- University (Bachelor)
- Post-graduate degree (Masters or PhD)
- Other _____ (please specify)

28. What do you plan to do once you leave secondary school?
- Work or look for a job
- Continue with my formal education (post-secondary diploma or university)
- Participate in additional training programs
- Establish my own business
- Stay at home
- Other _____ (please specify)

29. If you are planning to go to university or a post-secondary diploma program, what subject do you intend to study?

Arts

Social sciences

Physical sciences

Computer science

Mathematics

Commerce

Engineering

Military studies

Religious Studies

Language Studies

Social Sciences

Law

Architecture

Medicine

Business administration

Education/teaching

Nursing

Vocational/technical skills _____ (please specify)

Other _____(please specify)

Don't know

30. If you are planning to go to university, how confident are you that you will meet the requirements of entry into the program of your choice? (1-5 scale: very confident to not confident at all)

31. In the future, what kind of job would you like to have?
- To work for the government
- To work for the army or the police
- To work for a large private organization
- To work for a small private organization
- To work for a family business
- To own my own business

- To create my own non-profit organization
- To work for a non-profit organization
- To NOT work
- Other _____ (please specify)
- Don't know

To what extent are the following reasons important to you in choosing a particular job? (For each answer, a 1-5 scale: Very important to not important at all)

32. High status of job

33. Ability to earn a lot of money

34. Good promotion prospects, clear career path

35. Uses my skills and abilities

36. Job security

37. Gives me a role in decision making

38. Has a lot of vacation time

39. Easy pace of work

40. Ability to work independently without supervision

41. Job that is family friendly (able to combine work with domestic/childcare responsibilities)

42. Opportunity to travel

OPTION: Do not plan to work

43. How much confidence do you have that you could successfully complete a job interview? (1-5 scale: very confident to not confident at all)

44. How much confidence do you have that you could be hired to work in the private sector? ((1-5 scale: very confident to not confident at all)

45. Do you think that there is <u>more</u> job security owning your own business or working for a private company?

- Owning your own business
- Working for a private company
- Don't know

46. Which of these work experiences have you had? (Check all that apply.)
- Internship/apprenticeship without pay in a private company
- Internship/apprenticeship without pay in a public company
- Work with pay in a private company
- Work with pay in a public company
- Work in a family business
- Volunteer work for a charity or similar service organization
- Self-employment
- Other work experience _____ (please specify)
  I have never worked.

Who among the following people you know have started their own business?
- (choice of yes or no for each person)
- 47. Parent
- 48. Sibling
- 49. Another family member (not a parent or sibling) yes no
- 50. A neighbor
- 51. A friend
- 52. A teacher
- 53. Someone else you know

54. In general, how easy do you believe it is to start a business in COUNTRY today? (1-5 scale: very easy to very difficult)

55. How interested are you in someday starting your own business?
1-5 scale (not all all interested to very interested)
56. Do you have an idea for a business you would like to start?
- Yes
- No
- Don't know

If you were to start your own business in the future, indicate on a scale of 1-5 how important each of the following is in your decision to start a business: (1-5 scale for each answer: very important to not important at all)

57. You prefer to work for yourself rather than someone else

    58. To use your skills effectively

    59. To be able to create and implement new ideas

    60. To resolve important social problems

    61. You can earn more money by running your own business

    62. To create jobs and foster economic growth

    63. To become a famous entrepreneur

    64. Your friends want to start a business

    65. Other _____ (specify)

    66. When you have money, do you plan ahead for how to spend it?Yes/No

67. Do you use a budget to manage your spending?
Yes/No

68. Do you regularly save money?
Yes/No

On a scale of 1 to 5, how much time do you spend doing the following activities in a typical week:

    69. Investigating career possibilities

    70. Researching potential ideas for a new business

    71. Following the news

    72. Talking to your parents about career possibilities

    73. Studying for comprehensive examinations

    74. Keeping up-to-date on entertainment, fashion or sports news

    75. Chatting with friends (personally, by phone or online)

    76. Watching television or listening to music

    77. Doing homework or school-related research

On a scale from 1 to 5 to what extent do you agree or disagree with the following statements:

    78. People in COUNTRY can get ahead by working hard.

    79. Entrepreneurs only think about their own gain.

    80. Entrepreneurs create jobs for others.

    81. Entrepreneurs contribute to the economic development of the country.

82. There is potential in COUNTRY for an entrepreneur to become successful.

83. Women can play an important role in the success of a business.

84. When jobs are scarce, men should have more rights to a job than women.

85. Men are better qualified than women to be business leaders.

86. Most people can be trusted.

The following questions ask you factual information about business and entrepreneurship. Please answer to the best of your ability.

87. An entrepreneur is someone who:
- Owns land and rents it to others
- Is wealthy
- Invests in the stock market
- Creates a business
- Works for a businessman
- Lends money to others
- I don't know
-

88. Selling shares of stock to get start-up money for a new company is called:
- Liquidation
- Bankruptcy
- Capitalization
- Dividends

89. A _____ represents a company's dream of where it wants to go and what it wants to be.
- Mission statement
- Business plan
- Stock portfolio
- Vision statement

Read the statement below and answer question 90:

You are the head of the Marketing Department at a start-up company that produces and distributes mobile phone to electronic stores across the country. To ensure success, you identify your target market as electronic stores that already carry mobile phones, develop an advertising plan that includes distributing free samples in target electronic stores, and project the number of mobile phones that you think your company will sell.

90. The work you completed in this scenario above is an example of which of the following:

- Market strategy
- Liquidation
- Capitalization
- Cost-benefit analysis

91. When a company liquidates, it does which of the following?

- Streamlines its processes to be more fluid
- Counts the number of finished products
- Converts company assets to cash
- Obtains additional funding to purchase new assets

92. By definition, a company must have which of the following:

- Stockholders
- Many branch offices
- Large capital assets
- Government subsidies

Read the statement below and then answer questions 93 and 94.

The Bright Ideas Company has decided to sell specialty high-tech light bulbs that use a new infrared technology. The company is comprised of 10 employees who work 30 hours a week and are paid $12 an hour. The marketing department requires $200 a month for supplies and rent for office space is $500 a month. For the month of June, the company sold 150 light bulbs and paid its employees a 10 percent sales commission and is responsible for a sales tax rate of 5 percent. Can we change the situation, as they won't relate to it like they did the previous question?

93. Using the information above, what are the Bright Ideas company's total FIXED COSTS for the month of June?
- $3,600
- $4,300
- $4300 + 5% sales tax rate

  $4300 + 10% sales commission and 5% sales tax rate

94. In addition to the information provided in the description above, what information would we need to calculate the number of units that must be sold to cover the company's costs?
- The number of salespeople employed by Bright Ideas
- The net price of the light bulbs
- The country where Bright Ideas is located
- Information about the retail company buying Bright Ideas' light bulbs

Read the statement below and then answer question 95.

The Bright Ideas Company has decided to close shop after 30 years in business despite record sales of its newest product - an infrared light bulb. The company's financial records reveal that there is a net profit of $75,000 after bonuses are paid. Capital stock totals $10,000 and there are 250 shares of stock sold in the company. (I think this question is too technical for the students and they will either ignore it or just fill out anything)

95. What is the formula used to calculate the book value of the Bright Ideas Company stock upon liquidation?
- (Net profit after bonuses + capital stock)/shares of stock
- (Capital stock +shares of stock)/net profit after bonuses
- Net profit/number of years in business
- Number of employees/(number of years in business/shares of stock)

96. Are you currently participating in the INJAZ Company Program?
- Yes
- No

97. If yes, how were you chosen to participate in the INJAZ Company Program?
- My teacher assigned me to the program.
- My parents told me to participate.
- I chose to participate.
- I don't know

98. In the past, have you ever participated in any of the following INJAZ programs? If yes, what year did you participate?
- Banks in Action
- Be Entrepreneurial
- Business Ethics
- Success Skills
- Company Program
- Job Shadow
- Economics for Success
- More than Money
- Entrepreneurship Master Class
- Community Citizenship
- Innovation Camp

99. Have you ever taken an entrepreneurship or business training program other than INJAZ? If yes, what program did you participate in?

100. What is your gender?

102. How old are you? _____ years

103. What is the highest level of education completed by your father and mother?
- No formal education
- Primary
- Basic (intermediate)
- Secondary
- Post-secondary diploma
- University
- Post-graduate degree
- Don't know

104. What best describes the work that your father and mother do?

                                Father   Mother

Professional or technical work

Administrative or managerial work

Clerical and related work

Salesperson

Agriculture

Factory production worker

Manual labor or construction

Government worker

Member of the police or armed forces

Home-based worker or subcontractor

Other service worker

Unpaid family worker

Housework

Student

Unemployed (looking for work)

Outside the labor force or retired

Parent deceased

105. How many books are there in your home?
- 0 to 10
- 10 to 25
- 26 to 100
- 101 to 200
- More than 200

106. How satisfied are you with your family's standard of living (all the things you can do or buy)?

1-5 scale (Very satisfied to very dissatisfied)

107. If you were to start a business, to what extent would you be able to depend on the following financing sources to support your new business? (1-5 scale for each answer: from very much to none)
- Nuclear family
- Extended family
- Friends

- Bank loans
- Governmental grants
- Other _____ (please specify)

Time at which you ended the survey: _____

We are interested in improving this questionnaire. Can you please write down any comments on questions you found unclear or confusing, or any suggestions about how to improve this questionnaire:

On balance, the questions in this questionnaire were

1. Very clear
2. Sufficiently clear
3. OK
4. Somewhat unclear
5. Very unclear

○ Did you feel that it was possible for you to provide honest answers to the questions in this questionnaire? If not, what would have helped you provide honest answers?

○ Did you feel that it was possible for you to concentrate and think about each question in the questionnaire before answering?

○ On balance, do you feel that the length of this questionnaire is

1. Way too long
2. Too long
3. About right
4. Short
5. Too short

- What is your name?
- What is your date of birth?

Appendix B: English Version of Follow-up Questionnaire

Youth Education, Employment and Entrepreneurship Survey

We are conducting a follow-up survey based on a survey which you completed earlier in the year, with the aim of understanding student perspectives on education, employment and entrepreneurship (starting a new business or other venture). As with the previous survey, we will ask you a number of questions to get to know your views and aspirations about the future, as well as questions about your experience with school and your knowledge about certain financial and business issues. The information you provide is important for helping us better understand the needs and desires of young people in your country in regard to education and employment, and the results of the study will help to improve the quality of programs offered to youth in the future.

As when you took the previous survey, the information you provide will be held in the strictest confidentiality. Your teachers, parents or peers will not know how you answer this questionnaire. Please answer honestly and freely.

	1	2	3	4	5
1. I trust that in the future, I will achieve my goals.					
2. If I fail at something, I try to figure out why so that I can succeed the next time.					
3. I see challenges as opportunities.					
4. I do things outside of school to prepare for my future.					
5. Studying is very important to me.					
6. I go to school because education is important for getting a job later.					
7. The things that I am learning now will help me in the future.					

8. I believe that achieving my goals requires negotiating with others.					
9. I can see myself in a leadership position in the future.					
10. I set goals for myself in order to attain the things I want.					

On a scale of 1-5, to what extent do you agree or disagree with the following statements about yourself:

On a scale of 1-5, to what extent do you feel that you are able to:

	Not at all				To a large extent
	1	2	3	4	5
11. Work with a team to accomplish a result					
12. Adapt to new situations					
13. Solve problems					
14. Present a topic in front of a group of classmates					
15. Present a topic you know well to a group of adults					
16. Resolve differences within a group to reach a solution satisfactory to most					
17. Understand your purpose in life					
18. Solve community problems					
19. Persuade a group of people about an idea					
20. Negotiate personal conflicts in a peaceful way					

21. Be competitive in securing a good job					
22. Start and run your own business someday					
23. Understand the role of business owners in our economy					
24. Lead the members of a group to meet a deadline in producing a result					
25. Research the potential market for a company					

26. To what extent is there a clear connection between what you have learned in school and the real world?

No connection				To a large extent
1	2	3	4	5

27. What is the highest level of education that you would plan to complete?
____ Will not finish secondary school
____ Will finish secondary school
____ Post-secondary training program or diploma
____ University (Bachelor)
____ Post-graduate degree (Masters or PhD)
____ Other _____ (please specify)

28. What do you plan to do first, once you leave secondary school? (Choose only one option).
____ Work or look for a job

___ Continue with my formal education (post-secondary diploma or university)

___ Participate in additional training programs

___ Establish my own business

___ Stay at home

___ Other _____ (please specify)

---

29. If you are planning to go to university or a post-secondary diploma program, what subject do you intend to study? (Choose only one option.)

___ Arts

___ Social sciences

___ Physical sciences

___ Computer science

___ Mathematics

___ Commerce

___ Engineering

___ Military studies

___ Religious Studies

___ Language Studies

___ Social Sciences

___ Law

___ Architecture

___ Medicine

___ Business administration

___ Education/teaching

___ Nursing

___ Vocational/technical skills

_____ (please specify)

___ Other _____(please specify)

___ Don't know

30. In the future, what kind of job would you like to have? (select one)

___ To work for the government

___ To work for the army or the police

___ To work for a large private organization

___ To work for a small private organization

___ To work for a family business

___ To own my own business

___ To create my own non-profit organization

___ To work for a non-profit organization

___ To NOT work

___ Other _____ (please specify)

___ Don't know

On a scale of 1 to 5, to what extent are the following reasons important to you in choosing a particular job?

	1	2	3	4	5
31. High status of job					
32. Ability to earn a lot of money					
33. Good promotion prospects, clear career path					
34. Uses my skills and abilities					
35. Job security (low risk of being dismissed)					
36. Gives me a role in decision making					
37. Has a lot of vacation time					
38. Easy pace of work					
39. Ability to work independently without supervision					
40. Job that is family friendly (able to combine work with domestic/childcare responsibilities)					

□ I do not plan to work

41. How much confidence do you have that you could successfully complete a job interview?

No confidence   Very
                                                 confident

1	2	3	4	5

42. How much confidence do you have that you could be hired to work in the private sector?

No confidence   Very
                                                 confident

1	2	3	4	5

43. Do you think that there is <u>more</u> job security owning your own business or working for a private company?

___ Owning your own business
___ Working for a private company
___ Don't know

44. To date, which of these work experiences have you had? (Check all that apply.)

___ Internship/apprenticeship without pay in a private company
___ Internship/apprenticeship without pay in a public company
___ Work with pay in a private company
___ Work with pay in a public company
___ Work in a family business
___ Volunteer work for a charity or similar service organization
___ Self-employment
___ Other work experience _____ (please specify)
___ I have never worked.

45. In general, how easy do you believe it is to start a business in your country today?

Very difficult   Very easy

1	2	3	4	5

46. How interested are you in someday starting your own business?

Not interested   Very interested

1	2	3	4	5

47. Do you have an idea for a business you would like to start?

___ Yes

___ No

___ Don't know

If you were to start your own business in the future, indicate on a scale of 1-5 how important each of the following is in your decision to start a business:

	1	2	3	4	5
48. You prefer to work for yourself rather than someone else					
49. To use your skills effectively					
50. To be able to create and implement new ideas					
51. To resolve important social problems					
52. You can earn more money running your own business					
53. To create jobs and foster economic growth					
54. To become a famous entrepreneur					
55. Your friends want to start a business					
56. Other					

_____ (specify)					

57. When you have money, do you plan ahead for how to spend it?

___ Yes

___ No

58. Do you use a budget to manage your spending?

___ Yes

___ No

59. Do you regularly save money?

___ Yes

___ No

On a scale of 1 to 5, how much time do you spend doing the following activities in a typical week:

	No time				A lot of time
	1	2	3	4	5
60. Investigating career possibilities					
61. Researching potential ideas for a new business					
62. Following the news					
63. Talking to your parents about career possibilities					
64. Studying or working on school-related projects					
65. Keeping up-to-date on entertainment, fashion or sports					

66. Chatting with friends (personally, by phone or online)					
67. Watching television or listening to music					

On a scale from 1 to 5, to what extent do you agree or disagree with the following statements:

	1	2	3	4	5
68. People in your country can get ahead by working hard.					
69. Entrepreneurs only think about their own gain.					
70. Women can play an important role in the success of a business.					
71. Most people can be trusted.					
72. There is potential in your country for an entrepreneur to become successful.					
73. Men are better qualified than women to be business leaders.					
74. Entrepreneurs create jobs for others.					
75. When jobs are scarce, men should have more rights to a job than women.					
76. Entrepreneurs contribute to the economic development of the country.					

77. How satisfied are you with your family's standard of living (all the things you can do or buy)?

Not satisfied   Very satisfied

1	2	3	4	5

THE FOLLOWING QUESTIONS (90-95) ASK YOU ABOUT FACTUAL INFORMATION RELATED TO BUSINESS AND ENTREPRENEURSHIP. PLEASE ANSWER TO THE BEST OF YOUR ABILITY. PICK ONLY ONE ANSWER FOR EACH QUESTION.

78. An entrepreneur is someone who: (pick one)

___ Owns land and rents it to others

___ Is wealthy

___ Invests in the stock market

___ Creates a business

___ Works for a businessman

___ Lends money to others

___ I don't know

79. Selling shares of stock to get start-up money for a new company is called (pick one):

___ Liquidation

___ Bankruptcy

___ Capitalization

___ Dividends

___ I don't know

80. A _____ represents a company's dream of where it wants to go and what it wants to be.

___ Mission statement

___ Business plan

___ Stock portfolio

___ Vision statement

___ I don't know

Read the statement below and answer question 81:

You are the head of the Marketing Department at a start-up company that produces and distributes mobile phone to electronic stores across the country. To ensure success, you identify your target market as electronic stores that already carry mobile phones, develop an advertising plan that includes distributing free samples in target electronic stores, and project the number of mobile phones that you think your company will sell.

81. The work you completed in this scenario above is an example of which of the following:

___ Market strategy

___ Liquidation

___ Capitalization

___ Cost-benefit analysis

___ I don't know

82. When a company liquidates, it does which of the following?

___ Streamlines its processes to be more fluid

___ Counts the number of finished products

___ Converts company assets to cash

___ Obtains additional funding to purchase new assets

___ I don't know

83. By definition, a company must have which of the following:

___ Stockholders

___ Many branch offices

___ Large capital assets

___ Government subsidies

___ I don't know

Did you participate in Injaz's company program this year?

Yes

No

Overall, how valuable did you find participating in the company program?

Not valuable at all

Not very valuable

Don't know

Somewhat valuable

Very valuable

How effective was the mentor who supported your group?

1. Not effective at all
2. Not very effective
3. Don't know
4. Somewhat effective
5. Very effective

In your view, in general, to what extent has participating in the Company Program helped you with the following: (scale 1 to 5, 1 not at all, 5 very much)

- Promote my academic engagement with my studies
- It helped me develop empathy with other people
- It helped me develop problem solving skills
- It helped me learn about health issues

- It helped me develop public speaking skills
- It helped me develop negotiation skills
- It helped me become a changemaker
- It helped me develop the ability to work with others
- It helped me develop citizenship skills
- It helped me develop the capacity to innovate
- It helped me develop critical thinking skills
- It helped me learn about history
- It helped me develop entrepreneurial skills
- It helped me learn about business
- It helped me develop initiative
- It helped me learn to achieve results in my work
- It helped me develop discipline
- It helped me develop emotionally
- It helped me develop leadership skills
- It helped me learn how to manage a budget
- It helped me learn to solve problems
- It helped me to make decisions
- It helped me learn to communicate with others
- It helped me learn to negotiate differences
- It helped me learn to sell ideas or products
- It helped me learn to speak in public

Compare yourself now to where you were at the beginning of the school year. On a scale of 1-5, to what degree do you agree with the following statements:

84. I feel more empowered to take a leadership role in the workforce in the future.

85. I recognize that knowing how to effectively manage my finances is important.

86. I have developed or further developed my educational goals.

87. I have developed or further developed my career goals.

88. I am more confident in my ability to successfully compete in the workforce in the future.

89. I know more about entrepreneurship.

90. I am more interested in owning my own business.

84. Did you participate in the INJAZ Company Program this year?

___ Yes (GO TO QUESTION 85)

___ No (GO TO QUESTION 115)

IF ANSWER YES TO 84…

Participating in the INJAZ Al-Arab Company Program…Scale of 1-5

85. Helped prepare me for the world of work

86. Connected what I learned in the classroom to real life

87. Made me realize the importance of staying in school

88. Helped me to be more competitive in a business environment

89. Helped me to more effectively manage my money

90. Prepared me to start my own business

91. Helped me identify my future career path

92. Changed the way that I think about the economy.

93. Improved my ability to understand the economy.

Participating in the INJAZ Al-Arab Company Program strengthened the following skills for me: (Scale of 1-5)

94. Ability to work with a team

95. Solving problems

96. Making decisions

97. To think about problems critically

98. Managing a budget

99. Interpersonal communications

100. Thinking creatively

101. Negotiating with others

102. Managing time

103. Speaking in public

104. Conducting research

105. Acting as an effective salesperson.

On a scale of 1-5, to what extent do you agree with the following comments:

106. Company Program classroom lectures aroused my interest for the topics being discussed.

107. The content was presented in a clear way.

108. The content was difficult

109. The instructor was helpful and responsive to our questions.

110. The instructional materials were useful.

111. The instructor held lectures in an interactive way.

112. To what extent has your experience in the Company Program introduced you to knowledge that you have not learned elsewhere in your schooling? 1-5

113. Use the following space to provide any comments about your experience in the INJAZ Company Program. What did you get out of the program?

114. Use the following space to provide any criticisms that you have about your experience in the INJAZ Company Program:

IF "NO" TO ANSWER 84

115. Have you heard about the INJAZ Company Program?
Yes
No

115A. How did you hear about the INJAZ Company Program?

115B. From what you have heard, would you have liked an opportunity to take the INJAZ Company Program?

ALL RESPONDENTS

116. Have you participated in any other business or entrepreneurship training programs besides INJAZ Al Arab?
Yes
No

116A. IF YES: Provide the name of the program(s) in which you participated.

117. In general, to what extent do you think that taking part in entrepreneurship or business training programs increases people's chances of getting a job or getting a better job in your country?
1-5

Appendix C: Descriptive Statistics of the Samples

	Morocco	Lebanon	Jordan	Saudi	UAE	Egypt
Education Level		Upper Secondary				University
Cities	2	5	1	1	1	3
Schools	14	9	4	4	2	10
Individuals	486	411	76	311	79	91
Individuals in the Comparison Group						
Baseline	219	189	41	123	No	45
Follow-up	No	Yes (61)	Yes (50)	No	No	Yes (45)
Matched	No	Yes (34)	Yes (35)	No	No	No
Individuals in the Company Program						
Baseline	267	222	35	188	79	46
Follow-up	Yes (75)	Yes (43)	Yes (22)	Yes (46)	Yes (61)	Yes (21)
Matched	No	Yes (36)	Yes (15)	No	Yes (58)	No

How Injaz Al-Arab helps youth develop an entrepreneurial mindset

Treatment Group

	Morocco	Lebanon	Jordan	Saudi	UAE	Egypt
Participants in Company Program						
Individuals	267	222	35	188	79	46
Females	63%	63%	45%	61%	48%	55%
Age (average)	16.5	16.3	16.9	17.3	16	20.8
Father's Education (average)	Sec/ Post-sec	Post-sec	Sec	Post-sec/ Univ	Sec/ Post-sec	Univ
Mother's Education (average)	Sec	Post-sec	Interm/ Sec	Sec	Sec	Post-sec/ Univ
Father's work						
Public sector	31%	16%	26%	74%	50%	28%
Private sector	27%	26%	13%	0%	3%	19%
Mother's work						
Public sector	17%	11%	10%	27%	10%	23%
Private sector	9%	13%	10%	0%	0%	70%
Housework / unemployed	61%	53%	57%	40%	57%	42%
Follow-up	Yes (75)	Yes (43)	Yes (22)	Yes (46)	Yes (61)	Yes (21)
Matched	No	Yes (36)	Yes (15)	No	Yes (58)	No

Comparison Group

	Morocco	Lebanon	Jordan	Saudi	UAE	Egypt
Comparison Group						
Individuals	219	189	41	123	n.a.	45
Females	60%	63%	73%	33%	n.a.	38%
Age (average)	16.5	16.5	16.7	17.2	n.a.	20.5
Father's Education (average)	Post-sec	Post-sec	Secondary	Post-sec/ Univ	n.a.	Post-sec/ Univ
Mother's Education (average)	Sec	Post-sec	Interm/ Sec	Sec	n.a.	Post-sec
Father's work						
Public sector	34%	15%	23%	50%	n.a.	20%
Private sector	28%	27%	17%	0%	n.a.	30%
Mother's work						
Public sector	25%	7%	3%	19%	n.a.	14%
Private sector	11%	14%	7%	0%	n.a.	12%
Housework / unemployed	49%	48%	71%	38%	n.a.	40%
Follow-up	No	Yes (61)	Yes (50)	No	No	Yes (45)
Matched	No	Yes (34)	Yes (35)	No	No	No

How Injaz Al-Arab helps youth develop an entrepreneurial mindset

Chapter 2. An exploratory study of the Injaz Company Program in Egypt.

1.1. Introduction

Egypt has, over the past two decades, undergone a dramatic demographic shift, wherein youth have made up a large and growing share of the population. Even though the country's youth population peaked in 2005, those between the ages of 15 and 24 still make up nearly 20 percent of the population, while those ages 15 to 29 make up nearly 30 percent. Almost 61 percent of Egypt's population is under 30 years of age. This large cohort of youth concurrently seeking opportunities in the fields of education and employment has put tremendous strains on the country's ability to meet their economic needs, strains that will continue for the foreseeable future.

Egypt has long been struggling with high rates of youth unemployment. In 2007, youth unemployment (ages 15-24) was estimated at nearly 25 percent. At the time, youth made up nearly 63 percent of the total unemployed, with an unemployment rate 5.8 times that of Egyptian adults. Moreover, the challenge of unemployment is particularly acute for young Egyptian women. While overall participation rates are low for young women, with less than 20 percent of women ages 15 to 24 in the labor force, they are gradually increasing. Yet, as more young women enter the work force, they face an unemployment rate of nearly 48 percent. Furthermore, the fact that this rate is so high suggests that some of those women outside of the labor force may be staying out due to discouragement rather than lack of desire to work.

At the same time, labor market outcomes for those youth who are able to find work are also increasingly discouraging. Not too long ago, a secondary or university education in Egypt was a guarantee of public sector employment. In recent years, public sector positions have dried up given serious budgetary constraints, while the formal private sector has only demonstrated modest gains in regard to employment. According to Assaad and Barsoum, the formal sector accounted for only 28 percent of jobs for new entrants in 2005.[1] On the other hand, the vast majority of new entrants found work in informal positions, which do little to help young people establish their careers and to build their human capital.

The onset of the Egyptian revolution represented a bold manifestation of the frustrations inherent in this situation for young people, and Egypt's youth have naturally come out of the 2011 revolution with high expectations of improving economic circumstances. Yet, in the political instability that has marked the transition, Egypt has not seen any dynamic economic improvements. In fact, with trade, tourism and foreign investment down, the Egyptian economy has seen economic growth slow significantly. During 2011, GDP growth was 0.4 percent compared with an average annual rate of 4.1 percent over the past 20 years. As the government struggled to meet the demands of the country's costly subsidy system, foreign currency reserves fell from $36 billion before the revolution to about $10 billion by March 2012. They eventually rose to $15 billion, but only because of an influx of Saudi Arabian financial aid. The currency is still under severe pressure, and a steep drop in the exchange rate could bring painful inflation and more social unrest. In the meantime, little has been accomplished in regard to creating employment opportunities for the country's youth and, while official unemployment rates are not available, there is a risk that the youth unemployment rate has risen considerably since the revolution.

As Egypt moves forward, finding solutions to the youth employment crisis is a priority for the government, the private sector and non-

---

[1] See Assaad, Ragui and Ghada Barsoum, "Rising Expectations and Diminishing Returns for Egypt's Young," in Navtej Dhillon and Tarik Yousef, eds., Generation in Waiting: The Unfulfilled Promise of Young People in the Middle East (Washington, DC: Brookings Institution Press, 2009)

governmental actors seeking to stabilize Egypt's economic situation. In the long term, this will require a coordinated approach that includes regulatory reforms that incentivize private sector hiring and significant changes to the education sector that ensure that youth are building job-relevant skills. As in most other Arab countries, Egypt's school system is largely failing to provide youth with the knowledge and skill development that would enable them to be competitive in a knowledge economy or in an innovation based economy.

Evidence of this lack of preparedness is found in the 2007 Trends in International Mathematics and Sciences Study (TIMSS), an international examination testing student abilities to apply learned concepts, 8th graders in Egypt earned average scores of 406 in sciences and 393 in mathematics.[2] These respective average scores place Egypt far below the international scale average of 500. More directly, Egyptian employers regularly decry the lack of job preparedness among Egyptian graduates. When Egyptian CEOs were asked in 2008 whether the school system provided people with adequate skills and sufficient qualities to be economically productive, only 34 percent reported affirmatively that they were able to find those with the skills they needed and 46 percent affirmed that they were able to find those with other qualities for which they were looking.[3] In particular, the report notes a demand for communications skills, teamwork, self-motivation, initiative, creative and innovative thinking, flexibility and leadership. These soft skills are not

---

[2] Mullis, I.V.S., Martin, M.O., & Foy, P. (with Olson, J.F., Preuschoff, C., Erberber, E., Arora, A., & Galia, J.), *TIMSS 2007 International Mathematics Report: Findings from IEA's Trends in International Mathematics and Science Study at the Fourth and Eighth Grades* (Chestnut Hill, MA: TIMSS & PIRLS International Study Center, Boston College, 2008); Martin, M.O., Mullis, I.V.S., & Foy, P. (with Olson, J.F., Erberber, E., Preuschoff, C., & Galia, J.), *TIMSS 2007 International Science Report: Findings from IEA's Trends in International Mathematics and Science Study at the Fourth and Eighth Grades* (Chestnut Hill, MA: TIMSS & PIRLS International Study Center, Boston College, 2008)

[3] Mohammed bin Rashid Foundation, *Arab Human Capital Challenge: The Voice of CEOs* (Dubai: Mohammed bin Rashid Foundation, 2009).

developed adequately by an educational system that continues to favor rote memorization and theoretical knowledge.

Long-term reforms in these areas do not alleviate the immediate and significant needs of Egyptian youth. In this context, it becomes necessary to find innovative programs and policies which, in the short term, can provide opportunities for the country's youth to improve their job skills, to search for jobs and, if they are so inclined, to start their own small businesses. In this regard, there are a growing number of training and skills development programs open to young Egyptians.

Among the most noted is Injaz Egypt, which seeks to provide a growing number of Egyptian students with a broad base of entrepreneurship training opportunities. Delivered within the school system with the cooperation of the Ministry of Education and local school administrators, Injaz Egypt runs a number of programs focusing on various core business skills, financial literacy, job-readiness skills and citizenship that are increasingly in demand from the private sector. For each of these programs, Injaz provides instructional materials, secures and trains volunteers to implement the programs, and works with local school administrators to arrange for program delivery within schools. Particular programs range from day-long interventions like Innovation Camp to programs carried out over the course of the academic year, like the Company Program (see table 2.1).

The Company Program is arguably the most important program among Injaz's offerings in Egypt. With the support of a local volunteer, groups of students work together to develop an idea for a business and subsequently a business plan. Following completion of the business plan, students work with the local business community to design and produce their identified product or service and develop a marketing plan before selling their product within the community. At the close of the program, students undertake the closure of the business, liquidating their student company assets. Over the course of 4-6 months, students experience the life cycle of a business, gaining hands-on experience in each area of this life cycle.

Table 2.1: Injaz Programs Offered in Egypt

Program name	Duration	Age group	Purpose
Banks in Action	8 sessions	Secondary/ university	Promotes understanding of banking fundamentals and operations of competitive banks.
Be Entrepreneurial	Variable	Secondary	Provides interactive classroom activities aimed to encourage youth to start their own businesses before leaving school.
Business Ethics	7-12 sessions	Secondary	Fosters student's ethical decision-making as they prepare to enter the workforce
Success Skills	7 sessions	Secondary	Works with students to prepare them for job search and interview skills.
Job Shadow	4 sessions	Secondary/ university	Prepares students for careers with 3 classroom sessions and an on-site orientation in the workplace.
Economics for Success	6 sessions	Secondary	Introduces students to personal finance and educational and career options.
More than Money	6 sessions	Grades 3-5	Teaches students about earning, saving and spending money responsibly.
Entrepreneurship Master Class	1 day	Grades 10-12	Introduces students to entrepreneurship and self-employment
Community Citizenship	Variable	Secondary/ university	Provides opportunities to participate in a community service project
Innovation Camp	1 day	Secondary/ university	Provides opportunities to discuss a particular business challenge and develop potential solutions.
Company Program	4-6 months	Secondary/ university	Provides opportunities for students to develop a business plan, launch a business, market and sell their product and then liquidate the business for first-hand experience in entrepreneurship.

1.2. Evaluating Injaz's Impact on Participants

In the context of Egypt's youth employment crisis – and that experienced more broadly throughout the Arab world – there are a growing number of programs and interventions aimed at resolving aspects of the economic challenges that youth face. Entrepreneurship training – both for the sake of encouraging more youth to engage in self-employment and to provide youth with opportunities to develop job-readiness skills – is an area of emerging focus, both by governments and non-governmental organizations involved in the field. Injaz in particular has developed a reputation in the Arab public sphere as an innovative organization that provides students with early exposure to business training and exposure to entrepreneurship. Through the exposure provided by its national and regional competitions, Injaz's Company Program in particular has earned recognition as a way to inspire more Arab youth to become entrepreneurs and small business owners.

The design and methods of the study are described in chapter one. As explained the implementation of the design varied by country. Particularly important to the evaluation of the Egyptian program, the Arab Spring resulted in the elimination of secondary schools that had been initially surveyed in Egypt, because the lost instructional time resulting from the revolution led the Ministry of Education to suspend all extra-curricular programs for the remainder of the academic year.

In Egypt, we originally surveyed 113 students from four private secondary schools that were set to participate in the 2010-2011 Company Program. As a baseline, we delivered our questionnaire to students in each of the classes from which students were eligible to enroll in the Company Program. However, as noted above, after the start of the Egyptian revolution, secondary schools suspended extra-curricular programs in order to make up instructional time lost during the revolution. At that point Injaz Company Program sessions ceased for the 2010-2011 academic year, and we were not able to follow up with participants as they were not able to complete the course.

At a fairly late date, we were able to run baseline surveys among university students participating in the program. As part of this process, we were able to survey 46 university student participants in the Company Program. To provide some comparison to these university students, we were also able to survey 45 university students from the same universities (and programs of study). After completion of the Company Program, however, we were only able to survey 22 participants, and we were unable to match the surveys obtained before and after participation in the Company Program. In this report, we analyze the responses of the secondary and university students in the control and participant group prior to participating in the Company Program, and compare them with the responses of the students who participated in the Company Program at the conclusion of the program.

1.3. Who Participates in the Company Program?

Slightly more women than men participate in the program, although the difference is small. For the group of secondary school students, 43 percent of the students are women. For the group of university students who did not participate in the program, only 36 percent are women. For those who participated in the program, 55 percent are women at pre-test. The group of students included in the post-test, however, is only 48 percent female.

As would be expected, the secondary school students are younger, on average, than the university students. Among the secondary school students, 50 percent were 16 years old, whereas 38 percent where 17 years old. The university students range in age from 17 to 24 years old. The control group has a greater percentage of students under 20 (34%) compared to those who participate in the program, either before (16%) or after (19%) program participation. Most students are under the age of 22.

The level of parental education is similar across the four groups. For secondary school students all fathers and mothers have at least post-secondary education. Among university students those who participate in the program have, on average, fathers with higher levels of education. Those who finish the program have fathers with even higher levels of education. Whereas 14 percent of those in the university control group had fathers with secondary education or less, only 2 percent of the university students who participated in the program had fathers with that level of education. Among university students who finished the program all had fathers with at least a university education and 36 percent had fathers with a graduate degree. Before participating in the program, 91 percent of the students had fathers with at least a university education, and 14 percent had fathers with a graduate degree. Among those in the control group, 77 percent had fathers with at least a university education, and 25 percent had a graduate degree.

In terms of maternal education, in the group of secondary school students 99 percent have at least post-secondary education, 73 percent have completed university and 21 percent have post-graduate degrees. Among university students, the level of education of mothers of those in the control group are lower, with 21 percent of them with less than post-secondary education, 52 percent with university degrees and 14 percent with post-graduate degrees. For those who participated in the Company Program, only 5 percent had less than post-secondary education.

Fathers of the students have a range of occupations. Among secondary school students, 12 percent work as government employees, police or armed forces or in a public sector enterprise. This percentage is much greater among the university students. For those in the comparison group, 20 percent work in these occupations, as do 28 percent of those who participate in the Company Program at pre-test and 38 percent of them at post-test.

Among secondary school students, 37 percent have fathers working in a large private sector company, and 6 percent in a small private sector company, 17 percent work in a family business and 12 percent are self employed. For university students in the control group, 25 percent work

110

in a large private sector company, 5 percent in a small private sector company, 9 percent in a family business and 14 percent are self-employed. For those who participate in the Company Program, 14 percent work in a large private sector company, 5 percent in a small private sector company, and 37 percent are self-employed. For those university students who finish the program, 10 percent work in a large private sector company, 5 percent in a small private sector company, 10 percent in a family business and 24 percent are self-employed.

The occupational profile of mothers is different. Among high school students only 5 percent work for the government, policy or public sector company, whereas 13 percent work in a large private sector company and 6 percent in a small private sector company, 9 percent work in a family business, 7 percent are self-employed, 35 percent are homemakers and 3 percent are unemployed. For university students in the comparison group, 14 percent work for the government, police or a public sector company, 12 percent work in a large private sector company and 2 percent work in a small private sector company, 2 percent work in a family business, 12 percent are self-employed, 33 percent are engaged in housework and 7 percent are unemployed. Those university students who participate in the Company Program have mothers with different occupations, at pre-test 23 percent worked for the government, police or a public sector company, 7 percent in a large private sector company, and 42 percent in housework. For those who complete the Company Program, the percentage in government, policy and public sector increases to 48 percent, large private companies 10 percent, small private companies 5 percent and housework 29 percent.

The students come from homes that vary with regards to how much literacy is valued, although the pattern of responses is similar across the four groups of students. When secondary school students were asked how many books were in their homes 5 percent said less than 10 books, 9 percent reported having 11-25 books, 35 percent reported having 26-100 books, 17 percent had 101-200 books, and 35 percent had more than 200.

For university students in the comparison group, 4 percent had less than 10 books, 18 percent had between 11-25 books, 33 percent had 26-100 books, 18 percent had 101-200 books, and 27 percent had over 200 books. The percentages are similar for those who participate in the Company Program.

We asked the students how satisfied they were with their standard of living, and the majority of them in all groups was either very satisfied or satisfied, although the percentage of dissatisfied students is lower among university students than among secondary school students. The percentage of students satisfied or very satisfied was 96 percent at the secondary level, 87 percent for university students who did not participate in the Company Program, 91 percent for those who participated in the program at pre-test, and 77 percent for those who participated in the Company Program at post-test.

1.4. How Do Participants Spend Their Time, and How Do They Differ from Other Students?

Students were asked, in the pre-questionnaire, how much time they spent in several activities. There are no systematic differences in the way the four groups of students spend their free time although secondary school students spend less time investigating career possibilities or researching business ideas. Secondary school students also report spending more time watching TV and radio, chatting with friends, enjoying various forms of entertainment, talking to their parents and studying than do university students. These figures are summarized in table 2.2.

Table 2.2. How much time do students in Egypt spend on the following activities in a typical week? Responses before participating in the company program (Question: On a scale of 1-5, how much time to you spend on the following activities. Table includes percentage who answer that they spent *much time* or a *lot of time*)

	Control Secondary	Control University	Participant University Before	Participant University After
Careers	25%	34%	31%	14%
Research	22%	34%	42%	45%
News	25%	57%	53%	41%
Talk parents	55%	45%	42%	50%
Studying	70%	78%	62%	59%
Entertainment	67%	47%	53%	55%
Chatting friends	75%	55%	62%	77%
TV and Radio	73%	55%	49%	55%

Careers	Investigating career possibilities
Research	Research potential ideas for a new business
News	Following the news
Talk parents	Talking to your parents about career possibilities
Studying	Studying or working on school-related activities
Entertainment	Keeping up-to-date on entertainment, fashion or sports
Chatting friends	Chatting with friends
TV and Radio	Watching TV or listening to music

1.5. How Do Participants Differ Before and After the Program?

Because this section of the analysis does not match questionnaires before to those after the program by student, it is important to note that the differences identified could be the result of program effects, the result of differences between the students who completed the survey after program completion from those who abandoned the program or did not fill out the follow-up survey (selection effects), or the result of an interaction between program effects and selection effects (i.e., the program may have effects on the kind of students who remain in the program).

1.5.1. Aspirations, Views of Self and Worldviews

Overall, students have high aspirations and expansive worldviews in the four groups. There are no differences among the students in secondary school and university for the control group or participant group at pre-test, with the exception that participating university students before and after the program are more likely to participate in activities outside the school to prepare for their future than the secondary school students and the university students in the comparison group. In spite of these overall similarities, the participating students are more likely to trust that they will achieve their goals in the future, to see challenges as opportunities, to see studying as important to them, and to set goals for themselves. A surprising finding is the fact that students who participate in the program are less likely to see education as important for getting a job in the future, and this is more the case for students who complete the program. There are no differences in how students in the four different groups think about the future value of what they are learning at present, their view of negotiation as an approach to achieve their goals, their view of themselves as leaders in the future, or their propensity to set goals for themselves.

Each of these aspirations and worldviews was measured with a five-point scale in which students were asked to rate themselves from completely disagree (1) with completely agree (5). In table 2.3, we have calculated the percentages for each item represented by the students who selected agree or completely agree (points 4 and 5 in the scale).

Table 2.3. Aspirations and worldviews towards future and self of students in Egypt before and after participating in the Company Program. (Question: On a scale of 1-5, to what extent do you agree or disagree with the following statements about yourself. Table includes percentage who answer 4 or 5)

	Control Secondary	Control University	Participant University	
			Before	After
Achieve goals	80%	73%	74%	95%
Learn fr. Failure	83%	75%	85%	100%
Challenges/opport.	61%	66%	83%	86%
Outside school	57%	52%	60%	91%
Studying matters	61%	59%	65%	82%
Educ matters	84%	75%	65%	50%
Learnfuture	72%	75%	80%	86%
Negotiate	74%	77%	80%	82%
Leadership	69%	75%	73%	73%
Set goals	75%	89%	72%	95%

Achieve goals I trust that in the future, I will achieve my goals.
Learn from failure   If I fail at something, I try to figure out why so that I can succeed the next time.
Challenges opport.   I see challenges as opportunities.
Outside school   Participate in activities outside of school to prepare for my future.
Studying matters   Studying is important to me
Educ matters   I go to school because education is important for getting a job later.
Learnfuture   What I learn now will help me in the future.
Negotiate with   I believe that achieving my goals requires negotiating others.
Leadership   I can see myself in a leadership position in the future.
Set goals   I set goals for myself in order to attain the things I want.

1.5.2. Perceived Self-Efficacy

Students were asked to what extent they felt capable of performing a series of tasks. Table 2.4 summarizes the percentage of those students who felt capable of doing them to a great extent – values 4 and 5 in the 5-point scale. While most students tend to report high levels of self-efficacy on those dimensions, there no differences among the reported levels of self-efficacy of secondary school students and university students in the comparison group and in the participant group at pre-test. There are, however, higher levels of self-efficacy for the participant students at post-test in ability to work in a team to accomplish a result, ability to adapt to new situations, ability to solve problems, ability to resolve differences within a group to reach a satisfactory solution, having a sense of life purpose, being able to solve community problems, being able to negotiate conflicts in a peaceful way and being competitive in securing a job.

There are no differences among the four groups in ability to present a topic to a group of classmates or adults, ability to persuade a group of an idea, ability to start and run a business someday, understanding of the role of business owners in the economy, ability to lead the members of a group to meet a deadline, ability to research the potential market for a company (more participating students report self-efficacy in this domain, but there are no differences between pre and post-tests) and seeing a clear connection between what they learn in school and the real world.

Table 2.4. Perception of Self-Efficacy of students in Egypt before and after participating in the Company Program. (Question: On a scale of 1-5, to what extent do you feel that you are able to. Table includes percentage who answer 4 or 5)

	Control Secondary	Control University	Participant University	
			Before	After
Teamwork	78%	77%	80%	91%
Adapt	70%	70%	74%	86%
Problemsolve	82%	84%	74%	91%
Presentpeers	63%	72%	63%	71%
Presentadult	61%	79%	77%	64%
Resolvediff	61%	73%	69%	91%
Purpose	66%	68%	63%	77%
Commproblem	47%	71%	69%	77%
Persuade	73%	67%	67%	62%
Negconflict	62%	79%	78%	86%
Competejob	77%	74%	87%	95%
Startbusiness	67%	81%	76%	81%
Rolebusiness	62%	55%	68%	64%
Leadteam	62%	52%	80%	67%
Research	50%	59%	62%	65%
Learnrealworld	51%	51%	33%	41%

Teamwork   Work with a team to accomplish a result
Adapt   Adapt to new situations
Problemsolve Solve problems
Presentpeers Present a topic to a group of classmates
Presentadult Present a topic to a group of adults
Resolvediff   Resolve differences within a group to reach a solution
                      satisfactory to most
Purpose   Understand your purpose in life
Commproblem Solve community problems
Persuade   Persuade a group of people about an idea
Negconflict   Negotiate personal conflicts in a peaceful way
Competejob   Be competitive in securing a good job
Startbusiness Start and run your own business someday
Rolebusiness Understand the role of business owners in our economy
Leadteam   Lead the members of a group to meet a deadline in producing a

	result
Research	Research the potential market for a company
Learnrealworld	To what extent is there a clear connection between what you Are learning in school and the real world?

1.5.3.   Educational Aspirations

There are no differences in the educational aspirations of the four groups of students. About 40% aspire to finish university and 60 percent to pursue graduate studies.   As would be expected, few secondary school students aim to look for a job immediately upon graduation (5 percent), whereas a greater percentage of the university students do (29 percent for those in the comparison group, 35 percent for those in the participant group at pre-test and 23 percent at post-test.). The percentage planning to continue studying is 76 percent for secondary school students, 36 percent for university students in the comparison group, 17 percent for participant students at pre-test and 18 percent at post test. A small percentage plans to continue additional training programs: 4 percent for secondary school students, 9 percent for university students in the comparison group, 7 percent at pre-test and 14 percent at post-test for those participating. The percentage of students who plans to establish their own business is 7 percent for secondary school students, 16 percent for university students in the comparison group, 33 percent for participant students at pre-test and 41 percent for participant students at post-test.

1.5.4.   Motivations for Choosing a Job

We asked students to what extent a range of reasons were important to them in choosing a particular job. There were very few differences between the students in the four groups before participation in the program. The university students participating in the program, however, differ in five areas from their peers.   First, they are less likely to be motivated by the status of a job, ability to earn a log of money, a clear career path and an easy pace of work, and they are more likely to be interested in a job that gives them a role in decision making. A job that is

118

family friendly was mentioned as being important by 75 percent of participants. Most students in all groups are confident they were that they could successfully complete a job interview and that they could be hired to work in the private sector.

Table 2.5. Motivations for Choosing a Job of students in Egypt before and after participating in the company program. (Question: On a scale of 1 to 5, to what extent are the following reasons important to you in choosing a particular job? Percentage who answer 4 and 5)

	Control Secondary	Control University	Participant University	
			Before	*After*
Status	74%	76%	78%	45%
Money	84%	62%	52%	41%
Career	86%	80%	83%	57%
Uses skills	91%	93%	93%	100%
Job security	81%	80%	76%	68%
Role deciding	80%	84%	80%	82%
Ample vacation	48%	40%	41%	33%
Easy pace	53%	53%	37%	23%
Autonomy	71%	55%	53%	55%
Family friendly	62%	76%	60%	48%
Confidence interview	74%	75%	74%	82%
Confidence hired	73%	69%	71%	76%

Status   High status of job
Money   Ability to earn a lot of money
Career   Good promotion prospects, clear career path
Uses skills   Uses my skills and abilities
Job security   Job security
Role deciding Gives me a role in decision making
Ample vacation Has a lot of vacation time
Easy pace   Easy pace of work
Autonomy   Ability to work independently without supervision
Family friendly   Job that is family friendly
Confidence interview How much confidence do you have that you could
                      successfully complete a job interview?
Confidence hired   How much confidence do you have that you could be
                      hired to work in the private sector?

1.5.5. Interest in Starting a Business and Motivations for Business Creation

Students were asked for their views on the ease of starting a business and their interest in starting one (Table 2.6). When asked how easy they thought it was to start a business in Egypt today, about 30 percent of the university students said it was easy or very easy. This figure is smaller for secondary school students.

In response to the question of whether they had an idea for a business to start, few students responded affirmatively. The percentage of students who do is smaller for those who participate in the Company Program, and remains consistent before and after participation.

Table 2.6. Interest in opening a business among students in Egypt before and after participating in the company program. (Question: On a scale of 1 to 5. Table includes percentage who answer 4 or 5)

	Control Secondary	Control University	Participant University	
			Before	*After*
Easy start	17%	30%	30%	41%
Interest	73%	82%	87%	68%
Idea	19%	20%	13%	14%

Easy start	In general, how easy is it to start a business in your country today?
Interest	How interested are you in someday starting your own business?
Joininterest	How interested are you in someday joining somebody else's business?
Idea	Do you have an idea for a business you would like to start

A number of questions in the survey explored the motivations students had to start a business. These are summarized in table 2.7.

Table 2.7. Importance of various factors in eventual decision to open a business among students in Egypt before and after participating in the Company Program. (Question: If you were to start your own business in the future, indicate on a scale of 1-5 how important each of the following is in your decision to start a business. Percentage who answer 4 or 5)

	Control Secondary	Control University	Participant University	
			Before	*After*
Work for self	72%	60%	72%	43%
Use skills	92%	80%	81%	90%
Create new ideas	89%	84%	79%	90%
Solve problems	65%	64%	65%	76%
Earn more	75%	82%	58%	62%
Create jobs	52%	53%	62%	62%
Fame	55%	51%	60%	52%
Friends	25%	48%	39%	67%

Work for self	Prefer to work for yourself rather than someone else
Use skills	To use your skills effectively
Create new ideas	To be able to create and develop new ideas
Solve problems	To resolve important social problems
Earn more	You can earn more money running your own business
Create jobs	To create jobs and foster economic growth
Fame	To become a famous entrepreneur
Friends	Your friends want to start a business

There are few of these factors where there are differences between the group who participated and those who did not participate in the Company Program. These differences include a lower percentage of students who would prefer to work for themselves among those who finish the program than in the other three groups, and a higher percentage of university students who complete the program who indicate that they want to open a business because their friends want to do it too. For all other motives to open a business there are no systematic differences between the three groups.

1.5.6. Financial Management

Students were asked about their financial management habits in terms of whether they planned how to spend money, used a budget and saved regularly. Table 2.8 summarizes these results. There are clear differences between these four groups in terms of whether they plan their spending, use a budget or save regularly.

Table 2.8. Financial management habits among students in Egypt before and after participating in the Company Program (0=no, 1=yes)

	Control Secondary	Control University	Participant University	
			Before	After
Plan finances	80%	80%	67%	86%
Budget	63%	76%	59%	58%
Save	65%	40%	46%	43%

Plan finances When you have money, do you plan ahead for how to spend it?
Budget   Do you use a budget to manage your spending?
Save   Do you regularly save money?

1.5.7. Attitudes towards Entrepreneurship and Business

Students in the four groups held similar views towards entrepreneurship in most domains measured. The only differences are that university students who complete the program are more likely to believe that people in the country can get ahead by working hard (62 percent) and more likely to believe that women can play an important role in the success of a business, which 82 percent of them do. About half of the students, after program participation, believe that entrepreneurs only think about their own gain, believe that there is potential in the country for entrepreneurs to succeed, believe that men are better qualified than women to be business leaders, believe that entrepreneurs create jobs for others, believe that men have more rights to jobs than women and believe that entrepreneurs contribute to the economic development of the country. Only one in five persons believes that most people can be trusted.

Table 2.9. Attitudes towards Entrepreneurship in Egypt. (Question: On a scale of 1-5, to what extent do you agree or disagree with the following statements)

	Control Secondary	Control University	Participant University Before	Participant University After
Hard work	56%	58%	67%	82%
Entrepreneurs selfish	61%	51%	38%	50%
Women lead	78%	77%	62%	82%
Trust	9%	25%	29%	19%
Entrepreneurs succeed	42%	55%	62%	50%
Menleadbetter	34%	36%	52%	50%
Entr.createjobs	66%	39%	58%	55%
Menmorerights	43%	43%	42%	45%
Entrepreneurs contribute	58%	51%	64%	59%

Hard work   People in your country can get ahead by working hard.
Entrepreneurs selfish Entrepreneurs only think about their own gain.
Women lead   Women can play an important role in the success of a business.
Trust   Most people can be trusted.
Entrepreneurs succeed   There is potential in your country for an entrepreneur to become successful.
Men lead better Men are better qualified than women to be business leaders.
Entr. create jobs Entrepreneurs create jobs for others.
Men more rights When jobs are scarce, men should have more rights to a job than women.
Entrepreneurs contribute   Entrepreneurs contribute to the economic development of the country.

In addition, students were asked whether they knew someone who was an entrepreneur. Most students know entrepreneurs who are relatives, family members or friends. Most students have access to entrepreneurs among siblings and teachers, less so among parents. There are no systematic differences in access to entrepreneurs among the four groups.

Table 2.10. Knowledge of Entrepreneurs in Egypt. (Q: Who among the following people do you know who have started their own business?)

| | Control Secondary | Control University | Participant University | |
			Before	After
Parent	36%	40%	43%	56%
Sibling	91%	72%	78%	83%
Family	21%	32%	30%	19%
Neighbor	60%	38%	54%	37%
Friend	57%	51%	29%	26%
Teacher	81%	60%	68%	81%
Someone else	31%	33%	26%	28%

Furthermore, the group of students who participated in the program and those who did not are very similar in terms of where they imagine they could access funds to create a business. Over half of them expect that they could find support within their nuclear family. About a third believed that they could secure support from a bank, and about a fifth from their extended family, friends, or government grant.

Table 2.11. Sources of funding in Egypt. (Q: If you were to start a business, to what extent would you be able to depend on the following financing sources to support your new business? On scale 1-5. Table reports percentage who answered 4 or 5)

| | Control Secondary | Control University | Participant University | |
			Before	After
Nuclear family	71%	52%	56%	41%
Extended family	35%	15%	26%	9%
Friends	21%	13%	20%	18%
Bank	35%	28%	42%	18%
Grant	16%	21%	24%	0%

Nuclear family   Nuclear family
Extended family   Extended family
Friends   Friend
Bank   Bank loans
Grantrant   Government grants

1.5.8. Knowledge about Entrepreneurship

A few questions in the survey assessed student knowledge of basic concepts of entrepreneurship and business. A greater proportion of the university students who participate in the program know the definition of capitalization, vision, and marketing. There are no differences in knowledge of the definition of entrepreneurship, liquidation or company. These results are reported in Table 2.12.

Table 2.12. Knowledge about entrepreneurship in Egypt. (Percentage of correct answers in multiple choice questions)

	Control Secondary	Control University	Participant University Before	After
Entrepredefine	88%	51%	67%	59%
Sell shares	41%	27%	20%	45%
Vision	44%	36%	65%	91%
Marketing	77%	67%	61%	86%
Liquidation	53%	40%	59%	45%
Company	56%	36%	46%	59%

Entrepredefine	An entrepreneur is someone who
Sell shares	Selling shares of stock to get start-up money for a new company is called:
Vision	A _____ represents a company's dream of where it wants to go and what it wants to be.
Marketing	The work you completed in this scenario above is an example of which of which of the following:
Liquidation	When a company liquidates, it does which of the following:
Company	By definition, a company must have which of the following

1.6. Discussion and Program Implications

Our inability to secure follow-up surveys for secondary students (due to the fact that they did not complete the program) and comparison university students poses a stark challenge for the interpretation of results. As noted above, because the differences seen in responses of

Company Program participants before and after the program are not comparable to a counterfactual, it is impossible to confirm that such differences are the result of program participation. Indeed, they could be the result of a number of factors, including student maturation or external changes that affected all students (not just participants). In this regard, it is especially important to note that between pre- and post-survey, these individuals have all experienced a cultural shock in the context of the Egyptian revolution, which could have impacted student perceptions on a host of issues related to perspectives on the future and their own ability to shape their lives.

Moreover, because we were not able to match individual responses in the post-survey to responses in the pre-survey for university students, it is not possible to eliminate other biases. As such, evidence of positive program impact could be related to the types of individuals who stayed with the program and completed the survey, rather than reflecting program impact per se.

Still, with these caveats strongly emphasized, the aggregate differences in answers provided by participants before and after program participation do suggest a positive impact of the Company Program. Strikingly, participants do not demonstrate an increase in desire to start their own businesses, although they generally see it as an easier prospect after participation than before participation and they demonstrate an increased understanding of basic business concepts. However, in regard to aspirations, self-efficacy and development of soft skills, participant responses suggest fairly bold, positive shifts.

Following participation in the Company Program, respondents – at the aggregate level – are more prone to state that they feel that they are able to achieve their goals, that they learn from failures and apply this learning to future success, and that they set goals for the future. In terms of self-efficacy, participants demonstrate large increases in how they perceive their own abilities regarding working with teams, adapting to new situations, resolving differences with peers, negotiating conflict and solving problems, both at a personal and community level. Perhaps more tangibly, in regard to their economic futures, participants feel more able to compete in the job market and are more prone to plan ahead with regard to their finances.

There are no differences among students who participate in the program and those who do not in terms of their educational aspirations or immediate plans. There are also no systematic differences among groups of students in terms of their motivations to choose a job, the reasons why they would chose to open a business or in their motivation to start a business. There are also no visible differences in the financial management habits or attitudes towards entrepreneurship, and there are modest differences in terms of knowledge about entrepreneurship, with students participating in the program demonstrating greater knowledge after participation of the concepts of shares, vision, marketing and company.

Overall, these results do suggest that Injaz has been successful in effecting positive outcomes among students in at least some of the areas deemed central to improving their long-term status in Egypt's labor market. While results do not show a particularly positive result in relation to the promotion of entrepreneurship and self-employment, these results should be viewed in a long-term context, given that these students are still in school and are likely to see employment and job experience as a necessary step before considering self-employment. It is somewhat surprising that among university students, closer to entering the labor market, the apparent effects of participating in the program are not greater than at the secondary level in the other countries included in this study. On the other hand, the program does seem to provide students with experiential learning that enables them to practice the development of soft skills, an area that has been highlighted by the Egyptian private sector as a stark need that is not being met by the conventional approach of educational institutions in Egypt.

That said, the results herein should not be taken to represent the causal evidence of impact that would be provided in the context of a more rigorous impact evaluation. Towards this end, the team suggests that Injaz should engage in an experimental evaluation that is able both to determine the exact causal relationship between participation in the program and outcomes in regard to entrepreneurial activity, job-relevant skills development, and employment. Moreover, such an evaluation should take place over a longer time span, allowing for an assessment of actual outcomes within the labor market after youth leave school.

Chapter 3. An exploratory study of the Injaz Company Program in Jordan.

3.1. Introduction

Like many countries in the Arab world, Jordan is facing a youth employment crisis. In 2010, the unemployment rate for those ages 15-24 in Jordan was 28.1 percent. Moreover, 46 percent of the youth in Jordan were out of school; only 41 percent of those not enrolled in school were working, while 42 percent were not active in the labor market. The situation is particularly dire for young women. Young women are staying in school slightly longer than their male peers, but their labor market participation rates upon completion of school are much lower. The total female labor force participation rate among 15-24-year-old women was estimated in 2010 at 10.5 percent (24 percent for women not in school). While reflective in part of Jordan's conservative culture and family concerns about young women working, it also reflects a high level of discouraged employment. With unemployment rate for young women at 46.8 percent, many young women are opting out of the labor force entirely rather than continuing their search for work.

Jordan's employment crisis comes about in the context of a dramatic demographic shift, wherein youth make up a large share of the population. Currently, those between the ages of 15 and 24 make up nearly 19 percent of the population, while those aged 15 to 29 make up nearly 30 percent. This large cohort of youth concurrently seeking opportunities in the fields of education and employment has put tremendous strains on the country's ability to meet the economic needs of Jordan's youth. At the same time, however, it is important to note that job creation in Jordan overall has been fairly strong. For example, between 2004 and 2006, total employment grew by 6 percent a year, far surpassing the labor force growth rate of 4.3 percent. However, during that period, employment among the Jordanian population grew by only 3 percent a year while employment of non-Jordanians grew by nearly 19 percent.[4]

A significant part to the puzzle of youth employment in Jordan has been identified as a skills gap, a marked differentiation between the skills and expectations that young Jordanians bring to the labor market and the needs of Jordan's emerging private sector. In part, this reflects an emphasis within the private sector on low-skill industries like construction (which has boomed in recent years to meet the needs of Jordan's expanding housing sector), industries that have not attracted Jordanian youth in large numbers because of poor job quality and wages provided therein. However, it also reflects a more general lack of marketable, job-ready skills that those leaving school to enter the labor market have. In particular, Jordanian CEOs decry the lack of soft skills (or life skills) among young applicants, including skills related to communications, teamwork, self-motivation and initiative, creative and innovative thinking, flexibility and leadership.[5]

Jordan has been playing a leading role in the region in regard to efforts to closing its skills gap. The country's educational reform program – Education Reform for the Knowledge Economy (ERfKE) – has made significant strides in reforming curricula away from an emphasis on rote memorization and providing youth with more exposure to internet and communications technology. In turn, Jordan leads the larger Arab world in terms of educational outcomes. In the 2007 Trends in International Mathematics and Sciences Study (TIMSS), an international examination testing student abilities to apply learned concepts, 8th graders in Jordan were second in the region (behind Lebanese youth) in terms of average

---

[4] Kanaan, Taher and May Hanania, "Education, Job Growth and Employment in Jordan" in Navtej Dhillon and Tarik Yousef, eds., Generation in Waiting: The Unfulfilled Promise of Young People in the Middle East (Washington, DC: Brookings Institution Press, 2009).

[5] See Mohammed bin Rashid Foundation, Arab Human Capital Challenge: The Voice of CEOs (Dubai: Mohammed bin Rashid Foundation, 2009).

scores on both the sciences examination and the mathematics examination. With respective average scores of 482 and 427, however, Jordanian students still failed to meet the international scale average of 500.

There are also a growing number of training and skills development programs open to young Jordanians. Among the most notable is Injaz Jordan. Established in 1999, in cooperation with the US-based Junior Achievement Worldwide, Injaz Jordan seeks to provide a growing number of Jordanian students with a broad base of entrepreneurship training opportunities. Delivered within the school system with the cooperation of the Ministry of Education and local school administrators, Injaz Jordan runs a number of programs focusing on various core business skills, financial literacy, job-ready skills and citizenship that are increasingly in demand from the private sector. For each of these programs, Injaz provides instructional materials, secures and trains volunteers to run the programs, and works with local school administrators to arrange for program delivery within schools. Particular programs range from day-long interventions like Innovation Camp to programs carried out over the course of the academic year, like the Company Program (see table 3.1). The *Company Program* is perhaps the most important program among Injaz's offerings in Jordan, serving as a culmination of the series of programs offered to Jordanian youth.

Table 3. 1: Injaz programs offered in Jordan

Program name	Duration	Age group	Purpose
Banks in Action	8 sessions	Secondary/university	Promotes understanding of banking fundamentals and operations of competitive banks.
Be Entrepreneurial	Variable	Secondary	Provides interactive classroom activities aimed to encourage youth to start their own businesses before leaving school.
Business Ethics	7-12 sessions	Secondary	Fosters student's ethical decision-making as they prepare to enter the workforce
Success Skills	7 sessions	Secondary	Works with students to prepare them for job search and interview skills.
Job Shadow	4 sessions	Secondary/university	Prepares students for careers with 3 classroom sessions and an on-site orientation in the workplace.
Economics for Success	6 sessions	Secondary	Introduces students to personal finance and educational and career options.
More than Money	6 sessions	Grades 3-5	Teaches students about earning, saving and spending money responsibly.
Entrepreneurship Master Class	1 day	Grades 10-12	Provides an introduction to entrepreneurship and self-employment
Community Citizenship	Variable	Secondary/university	Provides an opportunity to participate in a community service project
Innovation Camp	1 day	Secondary/university	Provides an opportunity to discuss a particular business challenge and develop potential solutions.
Company Program	4-6 months	Secondary/university	Provides students an opportunity to develop a business plan, launch a business, market and sell their product and then liquidate the business for first-hand experience in entrepreneurship.

3.2. Evaluating Injaz's Impact on Participants

The design and methods of the study are described in chapter one of this book. Four Jordanian schools participated in the Company Program, with the program run as an extra-curricular activity. As a baseline, we delivered our questionnaire to students in each of the classes from which students were eligible to enroll in the Company Program (one from each school). From this group, students were invited to participate in the Company Program's initial instructional classes: some opted out from the beginning, others dropped out after one or two sessions. In the end, there were 46 participants who entered and completed the Company Program from the four identified schools. In all, we were able to secure 141 pre surveys for our baseline (including 41 non-participants, 35 participants and 65 dropouts (students who identified themselves as participants but who dropped out of the program). After completion of the Company Program, we were able to survey each group again, collecting post surveys from 22 participants who completed the entire program and the national competition; however, only 15 of these were able to be matched to specific baseline responses. In addition, we were able to secure 50 surveys from non-participants, 35 of which were matched to baseline non-participant surveys. Finally, we were able to match 46 baseline dropout surveys with follow up surveys. In total, we collected 118 post surveys.

In this analysis we focus on the responses provided by the three groups of students (control, participants and dropouts) at pre-test and post-test, and subsequently analyze the differences observed for the matched students. Because the sample size of each of the matched groups is too small, we do not estimate the statistical significance of the observed differences.

Table 3.2. Number of students surveyed in Jordan for control and participant groups

| | Jordan Sample | | | | | |
| | Control | | Participants | | Dropouts | |
	Before	After	Before	After	Before	After
Full Sample	41	50	35	22	65	46
Male Students	11		19		28	
Matched Sample	35	35	15	15	46	46
Male Students	8	8	5	5	16	16

3.2. Who Participates in the Company Program?

In this section of the report, we characterize the 121 students who completed the questionnaire before participating in the Company Program. This allows us to detail the demographics of Injaz participants in Jordan, while also assessing the similarities and differences observed when comparing the three groups under study.

First, there is an important gender differential between our three groups. Whereas only 27 percent of the students in the control group are female, 54 percent of those who participated in the Company Program are female, as are 43 percent of those who dropped out of the program.

In terms of age, 41 percent of the students in the control group are 16 years old and 51 percent are 17 years old. The ages of students range from 16 to 19. Students in the Company Program group are slightly older, as only 15 percent are 16 whereas 82 percent are 17. Students who dropped out of the Company Program are 16 (30 percent) and 17 (63 percent).

The level of parental education varies and is similar across the three groups. In the control group, 47 percent of students' fathers have up to secondary education, whereas 26 percent have university education and 21 percent have post-graduate studies. In the Company Program group, 60 percent of fathers have up to secondary education, 15 percent have university education and 18 percent have post-graduate studies. Among dropouts, 51 percent of the fathers have up to secondary education, 21 percent have college education and 19 percent have post-graduate studies.

For mothers of students in the control group, 70 percent have up to secondary education, 24 percent have university education and 5 percent have post-graduate studies. Among mothers of students in the Company Program group, 66 percent have up to secondary education, 19 percent have university studies and 13 percent have post-graduate studies. Among dropouts, 43 percent of the mothers have up to secondary education, 30 percent have university studies, and 23 percent have post-graduate studies.

Fathers of the students have a range of occupations. For those in the comparison group, 23 percent of fathers work as government employees, in the police or armed forces, or in a public sector company. For those in the program 26 percent, and among dropouts 43 percent do. In the comparison group, 14 percent of the fathers work in a large private sector company and 5 percent in a small private sector company. A small percentage of them work in a family business (9 percent) and seventeen percent are self-employed. One student defines their work as housework, and another one is unemployed. Less than 11 percent are outside the labor force or retired.

In the Company Program group 26 percent of the fathers work for the government administration or police or armed forces, 10 percent for a large private sector company, 3 percent for a small private sector company, 13 percent for a family business and 23 percent are self-employed. Only 2 (6 percent) are unemployed and none defines their work as housework.

For the group of students who began the Company Program but dropped out, 43 percent of the fathers work for the government administration, police or public sector company, 12 percent work for a large private sector company, 2 percent for a small private sector company, 24 percent are self-employed, 2 percent housework and 4 percent outside the labor force or retired.

The occupational profile of mothers is different. For those in the comparison group only 10 percent of mothers work outside the house, 65 percent work in housework, 6 percent are unemployed and 13 percent are outside the labor force. For those in the Company Program group, 19 percent work outside the house, 10 percent on a family business, 43 percent work in housework, 14 percent are unemployed and 5 percent are outside the labor force. For those who dropped out 23 percent work outside the house, 56 percent work in housework and 7 percent are outside the labor force.

The students come from homes which vary with regards to how much literacy is valued. When students in the comparison group were asked how many books were in their homes 20 percent said less than 10 books, 35 percent reported having 11-25 books, 33 percent reported having 26-100 books, 5 percent had 101-200 books, and 8 percent had more than 200. For those in the Company Program group, 13 percent had less than 10 books, 31 percent had between 11-25 books, 44 percent had 26-100 books, 6 percent had 101-200 books, and 6 percent had over 200 books. For those who dropped out, 3 percent had less than 10 books, 38 percent had between 11-25 books, 33 percent had 26-100 books, 14 percent had 101-200 books and 12 percent had over 200 books.

Finally, we asked the students how satisfied they were with their standard of living, and the majority of them in the comparison group were either very satisfied (38%) or satisfied (33%); only 8 percent were not satisfied or barely satisfied. In the Company Program group, 39 percent were very satisfied and 45 percent satisfied, while no one was not satisfied or barely satisfied. In the group that dropped out, 51 percent were very satisfied and 31 percent satisfied, and only 7 percent not satisfied or barely satisfied.

3.3. How Do Participating Students Spend Their Time, and How Do They Differ from Other Students?

Students were asked, in the pre-questionnaire, how much time they spent in several activities. There are no systematic differences in the way that students who participate in the program and those who do not participate spend their time. Most students report spending much time watching TV and radio, chatting with friends, enjoying various forms of entertainment, talking to their parents and studying. These figures are summarized in table 3.3.

Table 3.3. How much time do students in Jordan spend on the following activities in a typical week? Responses before participating in the company program (Question: On a scale of 1-5, how much time to you spend on the following activities. Table 3.4. includes percentage who answer that they spent *much time* (4) or a *lot of time* (5).)

	Control	Participant	Dropout
Careers	48%	40%	43%
Research	39%	59%	54%
News	53%	58%	44%
Talk parents	59%	71%	63%
Studying	78%	68%	70%
Entertainment	63%	79%	61%
Chatting friends	49%	79%	59%
TV and Radio	68%	71%	67%

Notes:

Careers	Investigating career possibilities
Research	Research potential ideas for a new business
News	Following the news
Talk parents	Talking to your parents about career possibilities
Studying	Studying or working on school-related activities
Entertainment	Keeping up-to-date on entertainment, fashion or sports
Chatt friends	Chatting with friends
TV and Radio	Watching TV or listening to music

3.4. How Do Participants and Non-participants Differ before and after Participation?

In this section, we compare six groups: three groups before the Company Program took place (pre- questionnaire) and three groups after the Company Program took place (post-questionnaire). The groups are the comparison group, the participant group and the dropout group, which consists of students who participated, but did not complete, the Company Program.

Because this section of the analysis does not match questionnaires before to those after the program per students, the differences identified in this section could be the result of program effects, the result of differences between the students who completed the survey after program completion from those who abandoned the program or did not fill out the follow-up survey (selection effects), or the result of an interaction between program effects and selection effects (i.e., the program may have effects on the kind of students who remain in the program). A subsequent section performs the same analysis only for the much smaller sample for which we are able to match students before and after the program.

3.4.1. Aspirations, Views of Self and Worldviews

Overall, students in all three groups have high aspirations and broad worldviews. There are no differences among the groups at the pre-survey. The students who participate in the Company Program show gains in several of dimensions: trust in ability to achieve goals in the future, seeing challenges as opportunities, believing that achieving their goals requires negotiating with others, and seeing themselves in a leadership position in the future. There are no differences between the three groups in whether the students see challenges as opportunities, participate in activities outside the to prepare for their future, believe that studying and education is important to them, and have ambition to find creative solutions to problems.

Each of these aspirations and worldviews was measured with a five-point scale in which students were asked to rate themselves from "completely disagree" (1) to "completely agree" (5). In Table 3.5, we have calculated the percentages for each item represented by the students who selected "agree" or "completely agree" (points 4 and 5 in the scale).

Table 3. 5. Aspirations and worldviews towards future and self of students in Jordan before and after participating in the Company Program. (Question: On a scale of 1-5, to what extent do you agree or disagree with the following statements about yourself. Table includes percentage who answered 4 or 5.)

	Control		Participant		Dropout	
	Before	*After*	*Before*	*After*	*Before*	*After*
Achieve goals	90%	73%	91%	100%	89%	80%
Learn from failure	85%	76%	91%	100%	82%	76%
Challenges opport.	71%	66%	79%	73%	81%	66%
Outside school	55%	51%	57%	58%	66%	36%
Studying matters	88%	.	91%	.	89%	.
Educ matters	93%	83%	94%	95%	89%	70%
Learnfuture	93%	.	82%	.	88%	.
Negotiate	73%	78%	79%	90%	80%	71%
Leadership	88%	69%	80%	95%	91%	65%
Set goals	83%	73%	89%	90%	86%	79%
Creativity	.	69%	.	70%	.	69%

Notes:

Achieve goals	I trust that in the future, I will achieve my goals.
Learn from failure	If I fail at something, I try to figure out why so that I can succeed the next time.
Challenges opport.	I see challenges as opportunities.
Outside school	Participate in activities outside of school to prepare for my future.
Studying matters	Studying is important to me

Educ matters	I go to school because education is important for getting a job later.
Learnfuture	The things that I am learning now will help me in the future.
Negotiate	I believe that achieving my goals requires negotiating with others.
Leadership	I can see myself in a leadership position in the future.
Set goals	I set goals for myself in order to attain the things I want.
Creativity	I try to find creative solutions to problems.

Most students indicate that studying and education are important to them, and the majority trust that in the future they will achieve their goals, believe that achieving those goals requires negotiating with others, see themselves in a leadership position in the future, and set goals for themselves in order to achieve what they want.

With regards to trust in their own capacity to achieve their goals in the future, there are no differences between the control group and the groups who participated in the Company Program at the pre-survey. At the post-survey, however, in the comparison group, the percentage of students who believe in their own ability to achieve their goals declined from 90 percent to 73 percent. It also declines in the group that dropped out of the program from 89 percent to 90 percent, but for the students who completed the Company Program it increased from 91 percent to 100 percent.

With respect to the question of whether they try to figure out why they fail at something so they can be successful the next time, there are no differences between the three groups (in the participant group, there are more students who do this than in the other groups). At the post-survey, this percentage has declined for the control group and for the dropout group, but increased for the participant group from 91 percent to 100 percent.

When asked whether education is important to help them get a job in the future, over 90 percent of the students feel this way at the pre-survey. At the post survey, however, this figure has declined for the students in the control group and for those who dropped out, but it holds high for the students who participated in the Company Program.

Most students understand that achieving their goals requires negotiating with others, slightly more so for those who participate in the program. After the Company Program this figure increased from 79 percent to 90 percent for the students who participated, increased slightly for students in the control group from 73 percent to 78 percent and declined for the students who dropped out from 80 percent to 71 percent.

While most of the students see themselves as leaders in the future at pre-survey, these figures decline for the control group (from 88 percent to 69 percent) and for the dropout group (from 91 percent to 65 percent) while they increase for the students who participated in the Company Program (from 80 percent to 95 percent).

Most students set goals for themselves, but the percentage of students who do so declines for those in the control group, from 83 percent to 73 percent, and for those in the group that dropped out, from 86 percent to 79 percent. It held for the students who participated in the Company Program, from 89 percent at pre-survey to 90 percent at post-survey.

Most students, over 70 percent, report an interest in finding creative solutions to problems, at the end of the program.

To sum up, most students score on the high end of the various dimensions explored in this section. There are a few differences in these various aspects of worldviews and views of themselves between students who did not participate in the program and those who did prior to participation. After participation, however, there are greater observed gains for students who participated in the program in several dimensions reflecting their aspirations and worldviews towards the future.

3.4.2. Perceived Self-Efficacy

Students were asked to what extent they felt capable of performing a series of tasks. Table 3.6. summarizes the percentage of those students who felt capable of doing them to a great extent (values 4 and 5 in the 5-point scale). While most students tend to report high levels of self-efficacy on those dimensions, there are important gains after participation in the Company Program, which are not observed in the students in the control group and in the dropout group. These differences are observed in self-efficacy with regard to working with a team to accomplish a result, ability to resolve differences within a group to achieve a satisfactory result, ability to solve community problems, ability to start and run their own business someday, ability to lead the members of a group to meet a deadline in producing a result.

In addition, in some dimensions, the students in the group that participates in the Company Program maintain their high levels of perceived self-efficacy, whereas the students in the control and dropout groups reduce those levels. This is the case with ability to solve problems, ability to present a topic to a group of peers, ability to negotiate personal conflicts in a peaceful way, be competitive for a job, and ability to research the potential market for a company. There are no gains in the ability to adapt to new situations, to present to adults, to persuade a group of people about an idea, to understand the role of business owners in the economy, or to find a clear connection between what is learned in school and the real world.

The three groups had a similar percentage of students who saw themselves as capable of working with a team to accomplish a result, 80 percent for the participant and dropout group and 71 percent for the control group at pre-survey. Upon completion of the Company Program, the percentage of students who saw themselves as capable to work with a team to accomplish a result had increased to 86 percent, whereas this figure had decreased to 62 percent for the control group and to 72 percent for the dropout group.

A similar pattern is observed with the ability to resolve differences within a group to resolve differences within a group to reach a solution satisfactory to most group members. For this question, the percentage who see themselves as efficacious in the participant group increases from 71 percent to 80 percent, whereas these figures decline from 78 percent to 65 percent in the control group, and increase slightly from 78 percent to 80 percent for the dropout group.

The same pattern is observed with the ability to solve community problems. For the group participating in the Company Program, the percentage who report high ability increases from 66 percent to 75 percent, but this figure declines from 73 percent to 68 percent for the control group, and from 72 percent to 69 percent for the dropout group.

Table 3.6. Perception of Self-Efficacy of students in Jordan before and after participating in the Company Program. (Question: On a scale of 1-5, to what extent do you feel that you are able to. Table includes percentage who answer 4 or 5)

	Control		Participant		Dropout	
	Before	After	Before	After	Before	After
Teamwork	71%	62%	80%	86%	80%	72%
Adapt	83%	60%	83%	76%	87%	71%
Problemsolve	88%	64%	91%	91%	86%	73%
Presentpeers	80%	65%	83%	81%	75%	65%
Presentadult	74%	69%	85%	72%	70%	66%
Resolvediff	78%	65%	71%	80%	78%	80%
Purpose	93%	.	91%	.	92%	.
Commproblem	73%	68%	66%	75%	72%	69%
Persuade	69%	69%	87%	75%	83%	84%
Negconflict	76%	48%	85%	86%	74%	70%
Competejob	87%	74%	91%	90%	85%	74%
Startbusiness	72%	73%	83%	95%	81%	77%
Rolebusiness	66%	38%	76%	45%	69%	28%
Leadteam	75%	59%	68%	86%	83%	72%
Research	76%	47%	76%	73%	88%	48%
Learnrealworld	76%	70%	73%	63%	66%	49%

Notes:

Teamwork	Work with a team to accomplish a result
Adapt	Adapt to new situations
Problemsolve	Solve problems
Presentpeers	Present a topic to a group of classmates
Presentadult	Present a topic to a group of adults
Resolvediff	Resolve differences within a group to reach a solution satisfactory to most
Purpose	Understand your purpose in life
Commproblem	Solve community problems
Persuade	Persuade a group of people about an idea
Negconflict	Negotiate personal conflicts in a peaceful way
Competejob	Be competitive in securing a good job
Startbusiness	Start and run your own business someday
Rolebusiness	Understand the role of business owners in our economy
Leadteam	Lead the members of a group to meet a deadline in producing a result
Research	Research the potential market for a company
Learnrealworld	To what extent is there a clear connection between what you are learning in school and the real world?

A similar trend is observed with ability to start and run one's own business someday. For those students participating, self-efficacy increases from 83 percent to 95 percent after participating in the Company Program, whereas these figures change only slightly from 72 percent to 73 percent in the comparison group, and decline from 81 percent to 77 percent in the dropout group.

When asked about their ability to lead the members of a team to meet a deadline in producing a result, the percentage of students in the Company Program group who rated themselves highly increased from 68 percent to 86 percent, whereas these figures declined for the control group from 75 percent to 59 percent, and in the dropout group from 83 percent to 72 percent.

In the following items, the students in the group that participated in the Company Program maintained their relatively high levels of perceived self-efficacy, whereas those levels declined in the other two groups. In terms of ability to solve problems, the percentage of students who reported high levels of ability among those in the Company Program remained at 91 percent, whereas these figures declined from 80 percent to 64 percent for those in the comparison group, and from 86 percent to 73 percent in the dropout group. A similar trend is observed in terms of ability to present a topic to a group of classmates, which declined slightly from 83 percent to 81 percent for the group participating in the Company Program, compared to much steeper declines for the control group, from 80 percent to 65 percent or for the dropout group, from 75 percent to 65 percent.

A similar pattern is observed with regards to ability to negotiate personal conflicts in a peaceful way, which increases slightly from 85 percent to 86 percent for the group in the Company Program. This figure declines significantly for the students in the control group, from 76 percent to 48 percent, and declines somewhat for those who dropout, from 74 percent to 70 percent.

Similarly, perceived ability to compete for a job declines slightly from 91 percent to 90 percent for those participating in the Company Program. In comparison, there are steeper declines for the control group, from 87 percent to 74 percent, and for the dropout group, from 85 percent to 74 percent.

Paradoxical results include the decline in perceived self-efficacy, for all groups, in ability to present a topic to a group of adults, ability to persuade a group of people about an idea, understanding the role of business owners in the economy and ability to see a clear connection between what is learned in school and the real world.

3.4.3. Educational Aspirations

There are minimal differences in the educational aspirations of the students in the control group who took the post-questionnaire and those who took the pre-questionnaire. For those in the control group, at pre-test, 35 percent aspired to complete university and 46 percent aspired to complete graduate studies. At post-test, the figures were, respectively, 37 percent and 51 percent.

Among those in the Company Program, 31 percent aspired to complete university and 53 percent aspired to complete graduate studies at pre-test, compared to 32 percent and 59 percent after participating in the program.

For those who did not complete the program, 29 percent and 54 percent reported their willingness to complete university and post-graduate studies, respectively. The distribution was similar in the post test, with 27 percent aspiring to complete university and 53 percent to complete post-graduate studies.

A higher percentage of the students reported plans to continue with their studies immediately after leaving secondary study at post-test than at pre-test. For those in the comparison group, these figures were 64 percent at baseline vs. 67 percent at post-test. Figures were 63 percent vs. 68 percent for those who completed the company program and 75 percent vs. 61 percent for those who did not complete the program.

3.4.4. Motivations for Choosing a Job

We asked students to what extent a range of reasons were important to them in choosing a particular job. There were few differences between those students who participated in the Company Program and those in the comparison group and in the dropout group: before the program, high status of a job was important to about 80 percent of the students; ability to earn a lot of money was important to 75 percent of the students (less so to students in the control group at 61 percent); good promotion prospects and a clear career path were important to 90 percent of the students (declines for all groups); the opportunity to use their skills and abilities was a motivation for over 90 percent of the students (declines for all groups); and job security was important to 90 percent of the students (increases slightly for students in the Company Program but not for the other groups); autonomy to have a role in decision making was important to 90 percent of the students; having a lot of vacation time was mentioned by about half of the students; easy pace of work was mentioned by about two-thirds of the students; ability to work independently without supervision was mentioned by about 75 percent of the students; a job that is family friendly was mentioned by 75 percent of the students. About 75 percent mentioned the kind of people they would work with as an important factor (this question was not asked of students before the program).

When asked how confident they were that they could complete successfully a job interview, about 90 percent of the students felt confident. We also asked students how much confidence they had that they would be hired to work in the private sector, this percentage increases only for the students who participated in the Company Program, from 71 percent to 86 percent. For the control group it decreases from 77 percent to 69 percent, and for the dropout group it decreases slightly from 72 percent to 71 percent.

Table 3.7. Motivations for choosing a job before and after participating in the Company Program in Jordan. (Question: On a scale of 1 to 5, to what extent are the following reasons important to you in choosing a particular job? Percentage who answer 4 and 5)

	Control		Participant		Dropout	
	Before	*After*	*Before*	*After*	*Before*	*After*
Status	80%	69%	89%	76%	75%	67%
Money	61%	55%	74%	71%	75%	65%
Career	93%	66%	89%	81%	90%	77%
Uses skills	95%	88%	94%	86%	89%	82%
Job security	97%	76%	91%	95%	90%	78%
Role deciding	90%	78%	89%	90%	97%	82%
Ample vacation	46%	64%	57%	50%	57%	44%
Easy pace	78%	63%	67%	63%	67%	62%
Autonomy	58%	68%	74%	80%	75%	70%
Family friendly	73%	60%	74%	52%	77%	64%
Jobcolleagues	.	78%	.	76%	.	72%
Confidence interview	89%	74%	97%	81%	93%	78%
Confidence hired	77%	69%	71%	86%	72%	71%

Notes:

Status	High status of job
Money	Ability to earn a lot of money
Career	Good promotion prospects, clear career path
Uses skills	Uses my skills and abilities
Job security	Job security
Role deciding	Gives me a role in decision making
Ample vacation	Has a lot of vacation time
Easy pace	Easy pace of work
Autonomy	Ability to work independently without supervision
Family friendly	Job that is family friendly
Confidence interview	How much confidence do you have that you could successfully complete a job interview?
Confidence hired	How much confidence do you have that you could be hired to work in the private sector?

3.4.5. Interest in Starting a Business and Motivations for Business Creation

Students were asked for their views on the ease of starting a business and their interest in starting one. When asked how easy they thought it was to start a business in their country today, about 50 percent said it was easy or very easy before participating in the Company Program. This figure declines for the group that participated in the Company Program and for those who dropout, but increases for those in the control group (Table 3.8.).

In response to the question of how interested they were in starting a business someday in the country, over 80 percent of students surveyed said they were interested or very interested before participating in the Company Program. This figure declines for all groups, but less so for those in the Company Program than for the control group or for those who dropped out.

We asked students how interested they were in someday joining somebody else's business (we did not ask this question in the pre-survey). There are differences between the three groups: 43 percent in the control group, 27 percent in the group that participated in the Company Program and 31 percent for those who dropped out.

We asked students whether they had an idea for a business they would like to start. A small percentage of them do. This figure declines for those students who participated in the Company Program, but not for the other two groups.

Table 3.8. Interest in opening a business before and after participating in the Company Program in Jordan. (Question: On a scale of 1 to 5. Table includes percentage who answer 4 or 5)

	Control		Participant		Dropout	
	Before	*After*	*Before*	*After*	*Before*	*After*
Easy start	56%	60%	54%	41%	47%	42%
Interest	85%	74%	86%	82%	84%	60%
Joininterest	.	43%	.	27%	.	31%
Idea	15%	21%	20%	10%	12%	17%

Notes:

Easy start	In general, how easy is it to start a business in your country today?
Interest	How interested are you in someday starting your own business?
Joininterest	How interested are you in someday joining somebody else's business?
Idea	Do you have an idea for a business you would like to start

A number of questions in the survey explored the motivations students had to start a business. These are summarized in table 3.9.

Table 3.9. Importance of various factors in eventual decision to open a business among students in Jordan before and after participating in the Company Program. (Question: If you were to start your own business in the future, indicate on a scale of 1-5 how important each of the following is in your decision to start a business. Percentage who answer 4 or 5)

	Control		Participant		Dropout	
	Before	*After*	*Before*	*After*	*Before*	*After*
Work for self	76%	64%	74%	81%	78%	56%
Use skills	93%	68%	91%	86%	89%	71%
Create new ideas	93%	66%	91%	90%	83%	75%
Solve problems	83%	73%	65%	75%	76%	71%
Earn more	80%	72%	82%	86%	80%	67%
Create jobs	69%	80%	88%	79%	75%	72%
Fame	80%	65%	94%	91%	75%	58%
Friends	59%	60%	69%	60%	63%	47%

Notes:

Work for self	Prefer to work for yourself rather than someone else
Use skills	To use your skills effectively
Create new ideas	To be able to create and develop new ideas
Solve problems	To resolve important social problems
Earn more	You can earn more money running your own business
Create jobs	To create jobs and foster economic growth
Fame	To become a famous entrepreneur
Friends	Your friends want to start a business

There are few of these factors where there are differences between the group who participated and those who did not participate in the Company Program. These include, as a reason to open a business, a preference to work for themselves, which is about 75 percent at pre-survey for all groups. This increases to 81 percent after the Company Program for the group that participated, whereas it declines for the control group and for those who dropped out. A similar pattern is observed with regards to the motivation to open a business in order to resolve important social problems which for the group participating in the

Company Program increases from 65 percent to 75 percent, whereas for those in the control group it declines from 83 percent to 73 percent, and for those who dropout it declines from 76 percent to 71 percent. Also, we see a similar pattern with regards to the belief that it is possible to earn more money running their own business, which is expressed by 82 percent of the students in the group that participates in the Company Program before the program, increasing to 86 percent after the program. This declines for those in the control group, from 80 percent to 72 percent, and declines also in the group that dropped out, from 80 percent to 67 percent.

For all other motives to open a business there are no systematic differences between the three groups.

3.4.6.   Financial Management

Students were asked about their financial management habits in terms of whether they planned how to spend money, used a budget and saved regularly. Table 3.10 summarizes these results. There are clear gains in the financial management habits of students who participate in the Company Program, which are not mirrored for the students in the control group – where in fact we observe declines between pre- and post-surveys—or in the dropout group.

Table 3.10. Financial management habits among students in Jordan before and after participating in the Company Program. (0=no, 1=yes)

	Control		Participant		Dropout	
	Before	*After*	*Before*	*After*	*Before*	*After*
Plan finances	73%	66%	89%	91%	92%	80%
Budget	76%	67%	80%	95%	74%	78%
Save	73%	66%	71%	77%	86%	77%

Notes:

Plan finances   When you have money, do you plan ahead for how to spend it?
Budget   Do you use a budget to manage your spending?
Save   Do you regularly save money?

3.4.7.   Attitudes towards Entrepreneurs and Business

Students who participated in the Company Program held similar views towards entrepreneurs, business and related social issues at pre-survey to those who did not participate. However, after participation in the program, these views had shifted in different directions, or at different levels.   In essence, participants were more inclined towards seeing entrepreneurs in a positive light. They were also more open to women's participation in business, and demonstrated a stronger feeling of trust in others.

The percentage of students who believe that there is potential in Jordan for entrepreneurs to succeed increased from 64 percent to 77 percent. Also, the percentage of students who believe that there is potential in Jordan for entrepreneurs to succeed increased from 64 percent to 77 percent for the students participating in the Company Program, but it declined in the other two groups, from 74 percent to 57 percent in the control group, and from 67 percent to 44 percent in the group that dropped out.

The percentage of students who agree that entrepreneurs create jobs for others increased from 57 percent to 64 percent for those in the Company

Program. For those in the control group, it increased from 53 percent to 59 percent, while it declined for the students who dropped out of the program from 52 percent to 48 percent. Similarly, the percentage of students who believe that entrepreneurs contribute to the economic development of the country increased for those in the Company Program, from 63 percent to 68 percent, and in the control group, from 65 percent to 70 percent, but it declined for those who dropped out, from 60 percent to 51 percent.

There were similar changes in attitudes among the three groups for several related concepts. For example, the percentage of students who thought that entrepreneurs only think about their own gain declined for those participating in the Company Program from 71 percent to 41 percent. It declined also, albeit less, for those in the control group from 68 percent to 54 percent and in the group that dropped out from 63 percent to 44 percent.

Those participating in the Company Program tended to shift their views towards greater appreciation of the potential contributions made by women. With regards to the notion that women can play an important role in the success of a business, those participating in the Company Program increased their agreement with that idea from 83 percent to 86 percent. This is in contrast to those in the control group, where figures decreased from 85 percent to 77 percent, or to those who dropped out, where figures decreased from 81 percent to 76 percent. Similarly, the percentage of students who agreed with the notion that men are better qualified than women to be business leaders decreased from 46 percent to 36 percent for those participating in the program, whereas it increased from 49 percent to 54 percent for those in the control group, and from 40 percent to 45 percent for those who dropped out. The percentage of students who agreed that when jobs are scarce men should have more rights to them than women decreased for those who participated in the Company Program from 50 percent to 36 percent, whereas it increased from 53 percent to 61 percent for those in the control group, and from 38 percent to 40 percent in the comparison group.

Trust in other people changed in similar directions. For those in the Company Program, the percentage who think that most people can be trusted increased from 20 percent to 35 percent. It increased less for those in the control group, from 46 percent to 50 percent, and it declined in the group that dropped out, from 38 percent to 34 percent.

Paradoxically, all groups saw a decline in the percentage of students who believe that people can get ahead by working hard.

Table 3.11. Attitudes towards entrepreneurship in Jordan. (Question: On a scale of 1-5, to what extent do you agree or disagree with the following statements) (Percentage of students who reply 4 or 5)

	Control		Participant		Dropout	
	Before	*After*	*Before*	*After*	*Before*	*After*
Hard work	54%	49%	71%	59%	61%	51%
Entrepreneurs selfish	68%	54%	71%	41%	63%	44%
Women lead	85%	77%	83%	86%	81%	76%
Trust	46%	50%	20%	35%	38%	34%
Entrepreneurs succeed	74%	57%	64%	77%	67%	44%
Men lead better	49%	54%	46%	36%	40%	45%
Entr. create jobs	53%	59%	57%	64%	52%	48%
Men more rights	53%	61%	50%	36%	38%	40%
Entrepreneurs contribute	65%	70%	63%	68%	60%	51%

Notes:

Hard work	People in your country can get ahead by working hard.
Entrepreneurs selfish	Entrepreneurs only think about their own gain.
Women lead	Women can play an important role in the success of a business.
Trust	Most people can be trusted.

Entrepreneurs succeed	There is potential in your country for an entrepreneur to become successful.
Men lead better	Men are better qualified than women to be business leaders.
Entr. create jobs	Entrepreneurs create jobs for others.
Men more rights	When jobs are scarce, men should have more rights to a job than women.
Entrepreneurs contribute	Entrepreneurs contribute to the economic development of the country.

In addition to these questions about their views on entrepreneurs, business and related social issues, students were asked whether they knew someone who was an entrepreneur. Most students know entrepreneurs who are relatives, family members or friends. There are no differences in this respect between the students who participate in the Company Program and those who do not. About 70 percent of the students have a sibling or a friend who is an entrepreneur. About one in three have a parent or a neighbor who is an entrepreneur.

Table 3.12. Knowledge of entrepreneurs in Jordan. (Q: Who among the following people do you know who have started their own business?)

	Control	Participant	Dropout
Parent	34%	32%	25%
Sibling	74%	66%	77%
Family	37%	18%	37%
Neighbor	31%	43%	40%
Friend	61%	69%	67%
Teacher	65%	38%	57%
Someone else	23%	17%	22%

Furthermore, the group of students who participated in the program and those who did not are very similar in terms of where they imagine they could access funds to create a business. Over half of them expect that they could find support within their nuclear family. About 40 percent from a bank, and about a third from their extended family, friends, or government grant.

Table 3.13. Sources of funding in Jordan. (Q: If you were to start a business, to what extent would you be able to depend on the following financing sources to support your new business? On scale 1-5. Table reports percentage who answered 4 or 5))

	Control	Participant	Dropout
Nuclear family	61%	58%	55%
Extended family	29%	34%	35%
Friends	24%	31%	27%
Bank	47%	39%	43%
Grant	53%	28%	40%

Notes:

Nuclear family	Nuclear family
Extended family	Extended family
Friends	Friend
Bank	Bank loans
Grant	Government grants

3.4.8. Knowledge about Entrepreneurship

A few questions in the survey assessed student knowledge of basic concepts of entrepreneurship and business. While there are clear and sizeable differences, with the group who had participated in the Company Program demonstrating greater knowledge, this group is far from achieving mastery of these basic knowledge concepts. Percentages of students who answered correctly are reported in Table 3.14.

Table 3.14. Knowledge about entrepreneurship in Jordan. (Multiple choice questions)

	Control		Participant		Dropout	
	Before	*After*	*Before*	*After*	*Before*	*After*
Entrepredefine	51%	only in baseline	57%	only in baseline	48%	only in baseline
Sell shares	2%	14%	9%	41%	12%	11%
Vision	34%	30%	26%	73%	29%	37%
Marketing	66%	32%	71%	55%	68%	48%
Liquidation	10%	24%	17%	41%	5%	17%
Company	39%	28%	40%	55%	38%	33%

Notes:

Entrepredefine An entrepreneur is someone who

Sell shares — Selling shares of stock to get start-up money for a new company is called:

Vision — A _____ represents a company's dream of where it wants to go and what it wants to be.

Marketing — The work you completed in this scenario above is an example of which of the following.

Liquidation — When a company liquidates, it does which of the following:

Company — By definition, a company must have which of the following

Before participation in the Company Program, students were asked to provide a definition for "an entrepreneur." Over half of the students in all groups could identify the correct definition.

When asked to identify the term for selling shares of stock to get start-up money for a new company, for the students who participated in the Company Program these figures increased from 9 percent to 41 percent, compared to 2 percent to 14 percent for the control group and 12 percent to 11 percent for the group that dropped out.

When asked to fill in the term for the definition of a vision statement among students who participated in the Company Program, the percentage who identified the term correctly increased from 26 percent to 73 percent, compared to 34 percent to 30 percent in the control group and 29 percent to 37 percent in the group that dropped out.

Paradoxically, when asked to recognize a scenario representing a marketing strategy, the percentage of students who could do so correctly declined in all three groups.

When asked to recognize the definition of liquidation, the percentage of respondents who could do so correctly in the group who participated in the Company Program increased from 17 percent to 41 percent, compared to 10 percent to 24 percent in the control group and 5 percent to 17 percent in the group that dropped out.

Lastly, when asked to identify that a company must have stockholders, only in the Company Program group did the percentage of students responding correctly increased, from 40 percent to 55 percent. In comparison, there was a decline from 39 percent to 28 percent in the control group, and from 38 percent to 33 percent in the group that dropped out.

3.5. Participant, Non-participants and Dropout Differences from Matched Questionnaires

As mentioned above, we were only able to match the pre- and post-questionnaires of 35 students in the comparison group, 15 students who participated in the Company Program and 46 students who dropped out after initially signing up for the program. These students differ in a number of dimensions from the original sample of students, as will become evident in the following section. However, they represent the best group on which to draw conclusions about possible program effects, because there is information for all students before and after the Company Program. This is unlike the previous section, which was based on data for all students who began the study and all those who completed it, meaning that some of the differences might be simply due to a selection effect, as students who took the post- questionnaire differed, even in the pre-test, from those who did not complete the post questionnaire.

3.5.1. How Do Participants Differ from Comparison Students in How They Spend Their Time?

There are no differences in the way that students who participated in the program and those who did not spend their time. The percentage of students who devote time to the activities summarized in the table below is very similar for this matched sample as it is for the entire sample analyzed in the previous section.

Table 3.15. How much time do students in Jordan spend on the following activities in a typical week? Responses before participating in the company program (Question: On a scale of 1-5, how much time to you spend on the following activities. Table includes percentage who answer that they spent *much time* or a *lot of time*)

	Control	Participant	Dropout
Careers	44%	47%	39%
Research	43%	43%	52%
News	51%	57%	50%
Talk parents	60%	71%	68%
Studying	77%	79%	73%
Entertainment	62%	71%	58%
Chatting friends	49%	57%	62%
TV and Radio	69%	64%	69%

Notes:

Careers	Investigating career possibilities
Research	Research potential ideas for a new business
News	Following the news
Talk parents	Talking to your parents about career possibilities
Studying	Studying or working on school-related activities
Entertainment	Keeping up-to-date on entertainment, fashion or sports
Chatting friends	Chatting with friends
TV and Radio	Watching TV or listening to music

3.6.2. How Do Participants and Non-Participants Differ before and after the Program?

In this section, we compare three matched groups before and after the program: the 35 students in the comparison group who did not participate in the Company Program, the 15 students who participated in the Company Program, and the 46 students who dropped out of the Company Program.

3.6.2.1. Aspirations, Views of Self and Worldviews

Overall, students have high aspirations and broad worldviews in both groups. The trends in changes from pre- to post-surveys are in line with those described for the entire sample in the previous section.

Each of these aspirations and worldviews was measured with a five-point scale in which students were asked to rate themselves from completely disagree (1) with completely agree (5). In table 3.16, we have calculated the percentages for each item represented by the students who selected agree or completely agree (Corresponding to a 4 and 5 on the scale).

Table 3. 16. Aspirations and worldviews towards future and self of students in Jordan before and after participating in the Company Program. (Question: On a scale of 1-5, to what extent do you agree or disagree with the following statements about yourself. Table includes percentage who answer 4 or 5)

	Control		Participant		Dropout	
	Before	*After*	*Before*	*After*	*Before*	*After*
Achieve goals	89%	77%	93%	100%	87%	80%
Learn from failure	86%	83%	100%	100%	76%	76%
Challenges opport.	69%	66%	87%	67%	80%	66%
Outside school	50%	44%	67%	64%	60%	36%
Studying matters	85%	.	100%	.	87%	.
Educ matters	91%	81%	93%	100%	87%	70%
Learnfuture	91%	.	73%	.	82%	.
Negotiate	74%	80%	93%	93%	74%	71%
Leadership	86%	71%	73%	100%	91%	65%
Set goals	83%	76%	87%	93%	82%	79%
Creativity	.	73%	.	71%	.	69%

Notes:

Achieve goals	I trust that in the future, I will achieve my goals.
Learn from failure	If I fail at something, I try to figure out why so that I can succeed the next time.
Challenges opport.	I see challenges as opportunities.
Outside school	Participate in activities outside of school to prepare for my future.
Studying matters	Studying is important to me
Educ matters	I go to school because education is important for getting a job later.
Learnfuture	The things that I am learning now will help me in the future.
Negotiate	I believe that achieving my goals requires negotiating with others.
Leadership	I can see myself in a leadership position in the future.
Set goals	I set goals for myself in order to attain the things I want.
Creativity	I try to find creative solutions to problems.

162

3.6.2.2. Perceived Self-Efficacy

Students were asked to what extent they felt capable of performing a series of tasks. Table 3.17 summarizes the percentage of those students who felt capable of doing them to a great extent – values 4 and 5 in the 5-point scale. In most of the dimensions evaluated, there are no differences between the students who participated in the Company Program and those who did not or in the changes observed between the pre- and post-tests for each group.

Table 3.17. Perception of Self-Efficacy of students in Jordan before and after participating in the Company Program. (Question: On a scale of 1-5, to what extent do you feel that you are able to do the following? Table includes percentage who answer 4 or 5)

	Control		Participant		Dropout	
	Before	*After*	*Before*	*After*	*Before*	*After*
Teamwork	71%	69%	87%	93%	76%	72%
Adapt	80%	62%	80%	87%	88%	71%
Problemsolve	91%	66%	93%	93%	84%	73%
Presentpeers	82%	71%	87%	71%	76%	65%
Presentadult	76%	71%	93%	67%	67%	66%
Resolvediff	80%	71%	80%	85%	76%	80%
Purpose	94%	.	100%	.	89%	.
Commproblem	71%	66%	73%	69%	76%	69%
Persuade	73%	74%	93%	77%	83%	84%
Negconflict	71%	56%	93%	79%	71%	70%
Competejob	91%	82%	100%	93%	87%	74%
Startbusiness	73%	71%	87%	100%	80%	77%
Rolebusiness	69%	44%	100%	33%	67%	28%
Leadteam	76%	62%	67%	86%	80%	72%
Research	77%	42%	79%	73%	87%	48%
Learnrealworld	81%	77%	60%	62%	59%	49%

Notes:

Teamwork	Work with a team to accomplish a result
Adapt	Adapt to new situations
Problemsolve	Solve problems
Presentpeers	Present a topic to a group of classmates
Presentadult	Present a topic to a group of adults
Resolvediff	Resolve differences within a group to reach a solution satisfactory to most
Purpose	Understand your purpose in life
Commproblem	Solve community problems
Persuade	Persuade a group of people about an idea
Negconflict	Negotiate personal conflicts in a peaceful way
Competejob	Be competitive in securing a good job
Startbusiness	Start and run your own business someday
Rolebusiness	Understand the role of business owners in our economy
Leadteam	Lead the members of a group to meet a deadline in producing a result
Research	Research the potential market for a company
Learnrealworld	To what extent is there a clear connection between what you are learning in school and the real world?

Overall, the changes between pre-survey and post-survey follow the same trends as those described for the full sample in the earlier section, except for adapting to new situations and finding a connection between what is learned in school and the real world. The refined analysis shows a gain for the students in the Company Program, whereas they showed a decline for the full sample. Paradoxically, efficacy in making presentations to adults or peers now declines for the students in the Company Program, as well as for students in the other two groups. Similarly, the ability to solve common problems, to negotiate conflicts and to appreciate the role of business owners in the economy diminishes for students in the Company Program in the refined analysis.

3.6.2.3. Educational Aspirations

There are increases in the educational aspirations of the students in the control group at post questionnaire relative to those expressed at pre-questionnaire. At pre-test, 40 percent aspired to complete university and

34 percent aspired to complete post-graduate studies. At post-test, the respective figures were 37 percent and 51 percent. For those in the Company Program, these figures were 31 percent who aspire to complete university and 62 percent who aspired to complete post-graduate studies at pre-test, compared to 40 percent and 47 percent after participating in the program. This suggests that for the matched sample, there is a drop in educational aspirations among those who participate in the program. For the group that dropped out of the program there is no change, at pre-test the respective figures are 30 percent and 52 percent relative to 27 percent and 53 percent at post-test.

A higher percentage of the students reported plans to continue with their studies immediately after leaving secondary study at post-test than at pre-test. For those in the comparison group, these figures were 65 percent compared to 69 percent, and for those who participated in the Company Program the figures were 57 percent compared to 73 percent. For the students who dropped out there is a decline, from 79 percent to 61 percent.

3.6.2.4. Motivations for Choosing a Job

We asked students to what extent a range of reasons were important to them in choosing a particular job. The trends in changes from the pre-test to the post-test for the three groups are very similar to those discussed for the full sample in the previous section. The only two exceptions are that the importance of status in selecting a job and of vacation time decline more for the students in the Company Program in the matched sample than for those in the full sample.

Table 3.18. Motivations for Choosing a Job of students in Jordan before and after participating in the company program. (Question: On a scale of 1 to 5, to what extent are the following reasons important to you in choosing a particular job? Percentage who answer 4 and 5)

	Control		Participant		Dropout	
	Before	*After*	*Before*	*After*	*Before*	*After*
Status	82%	76%	93%	64%	70%	67%
Money	60%	62%	73%	71%	74%	65%
Career	94%	72%	87%	86%	86%	77%
Uses skills	97%	91%	100%	79%	86%	82%
Job security	97%	76%	100%	93%	89%	78%
Role deciding	88%	82%	93%	85%	95%	82%
Ample vacation	48%	64%	67%	43%	52%	44%
Easy pace	74%	65%	62%	62%	57%	62%
Autonomy	59%	68%	73%	69%	72%	70%
Family friendly	71%	65%	87%	50%	74%	64%
Jobcolleagues	.	87%	.	71%	.	72%
Confidence interview	94%	85%	93%	80%	93%	78%
Confidence hired	82%	71%	73%	87%	77%	71%

Notes:
Status	High status of job
MoneyAbility to earn a lot of money
Career	Good promotion prospects, clear career path
Uses skills	Uses my skills and abilities
Job security	Job security
Role deciding	Gives me a role in decision making
Ample vacation	Has a lot of vacation time
Easy pace	Easy pace of work
Autonomy	Ability to work independently without supervision
Family friendly	Job that is family friendly
Confidence interview	How much confidence do you have that you could successfully complete a job interview?
Confidence hired	How much confidence do you have that you could be hired to work in the private sector?

3.6.2.5. Interest in Starting a Business and Motivations for Business Creation

As a way to establish the exposure students had to real entrepreneurs, we asked them who among a series of categories of people they knew who had started their own business. There are no differences between both groups in most referent groups mentioned: 15 percent siblings, 85 percent relatives, 65 percent neighbors, 40 percent friends, 26 percent teachers, 67 percent someone else. Those participating in the Company Program are more likely to have parents who are entrepreneurs (71 percent) than those in the comparison group (59 percent).

Students were asked for their views on the ease of starting a business and their interest in starting one. The results for the matched group follow the same trends observed for the full sample and discussed earlier. The percentage of students who thought it was easy to start a business declined significantly in the group that participated in the Company Program and that dropped out, but not in the comparison group. Interest in starting a business declined in the three groups. The percentage of students who had an idea for a business declined among those who participated in the Company Program (Table 3.19).

Table 3.19. Interest in opening a business among students in Jordan before and after participating in the Company Program. (Question: On a scale of 1 to 5. Table includes percentage who answer 4 or 5)

	Control		Participant		Dropout	
	Before	*After*	*Before*	*After*	*Before*	*After*
Easy start	60%	68%	67%	33%	49%	42%
Interest	86%	76%	87%	73%	89%	60%
Joininterest	.	41%	.	27%	.	31%
Idea	9%	19%	40%	14%	13%	17%

Easy start	In general, how easy is it to start a business in your country today?
Interest	How interested are you in someday starting your own business?
Joininterest	How interested are you in someday joining somebody else's business?
Idea	Do you have an idea for a business you would like to start?

A number of questions in the survey explored the motivations students had to start a business. These are summarized in table 3.20. There are no consistent differences between the group who participated and those who did not participate in the Company Program, or between the responses in the pre- and post-survey.

Table 3.20. Importance of various factors in eventual decision to open a business among students in Jordan before and after participating in the Company Program. (Question: If you were to start your own business in the future, indicate on a scale of 1-5 how important each of the following is in your decision to start a business. Percentage who answer 4 or 5)

	Control		Participant		Dropout	
	Before	*After*	*Before*	*After*	*Before*	*After*
Work for self	75%	73%	80%	79%	77%	56%
Use skills	94%	84%	93%	86%	84%	71%
Create new ideas	91%	73%	85%	85%	83%	75%
Solve problems	83%	71%	86%	71%	75%	71%
Earn more	80%	70%	86%	86%	82%	67%
Create jobs	70%	82%	93%	79%	75%	72%
Fame	79%	70%	93%	93%	72%	58%
Friends	60%	64%	69%	57%	60%	47%

Notes:

Work for self	Prefer to work for yourself rather than someone else
Use skills	To use your skills effectively
Create new ideas	To be able to create and develop new ideas
Solve problems	To resolve important social problems
Earn more	You can earn more money running your own business
Create jobs	To create jobs and foster economic growth
Fame	To become a famous entrepreneur
Friends	Your friends want to start a business

3.6.2.6. Financial Management

Students were asked about their financial management habits in terms of whether they planned how to spend money, used a budget and saved regularly. Table 3.21 summarizes these results. Most students report planning how to spend and budget money and save, and students in the

168

Company Program report these practices at very high levels. There are no changes for them after participating in the Company Program. A slightly smaller percentage of students in the control group report these financial management habits, and there is a slight increase over time. For the students who dropped out, there is a decrease in the percentage of students who report these financial management habits.

Table 3.21. Financial management habits among students in Jordan before and after participating in the Company Program. (0=no, 1=yes)

	Control		Participant		Dropout	
	Before	*After*	*Before*	*After*	*Before*	*After*
Plan finances	69%	70%	93%	93%	91%	80%
Budget	74%	73%	93%	93%	74%	78%
Save	74%	70%	79%	80%	89%	77%

Notes:

Plan finances When you have money, do you plan ahead for how to spend it?

Budget Do you use a budget to manage your spending?

Save Do you regularly save money?

3.6.2.7. Attitudes towards Entrepreneurs and Business

With regards to the views students had towards entrepreneurs, business and related social issues, the same trends observed for the full sample are observed for the matched sample, but some of them are accentuated. The percentage of students who believe that entrepreneurs only think about their own gain declines in all groups, but significantly more so among those who participate in the Company Program where it declines from 73 percent to 33 percent. And the percentage who thinks that entrepreneurs contribute to the economic development of the country increases for the group that participates in the Company Program, from 60 percent to 67 percent, and in the control group, from 62 percent to 70 percent, but declines in the group that drops out.

The percentage of students who have gender equitable views is high for all groups. For instance, the percentage who thinks that women can play an important role in the success of a business is 87 percent for the students who participate in the Company Program, and does not change after program participation. In the other groups, this figure declines, from 86 percent to 78 percent for the control group and from 81 percent to 76 percent in the group that dropped out. Similarly, the percentage of students who thinks that men are better qualified than women to be leaders declines in the group that participates in the Company Program from 40 percent to 27 percent, whereas it increases in the other two groups. The percentage who thinks that men should have priority for jobs when they are scarce declines for the students in the Company Program from 40 percent to 27 percent; it increases for the control group and declines only slightly for the group that drops out.

Trust in other people increases significantly in the group that participates in the Company Program, from 13 percent to 27 percent. About half of the students in the control group think that most people in Jordan can get ahead by working hard, and this does not change in the pre- and post-survey. A higher percentage feel this way among the students who participate in the Company Program and among those who dropped out of the program, but these figures decline between the pre- and post-survey.

Paradoxically, the percentage of students who think that people in Jordan can get ahead by working hard declines among the three groups, the percentage who think that there is potential in Jordan for an entrepreneur to be successful decline in all groups – although less so among the students who participate in the Company Program, and the percentage who thinks that entrepreneurs create jobs for others declines among students in the Company Program.

Table 3.22. Attitudes towards entrepreneurship in Jordan. (Question: On a scale of 1-5, to what extent do you agree or disagree with the following statements)

	Control		Participant		Dropout	
	Before	After	Before	After	Before	After
Hard work	52%	52%	67%	60%	65%	51%
Entrepreneurs selfish	63%	52%	73%	33%	67%	44%
Women lead	86%	78%	87%	87%	81%	76%
Trust	40%	55%	13%	27%	44%	34%
Entrepreneurs succeed	70%	58%	79%	73%	65%	44%
Men lead better	46%	52%	40%	27%	39%	45%
Entr. create jobs	47%	58%	53%	47%	48%	48%
Men more rights	47%	64%	40%	27%	43%	40%
Entrepreneurs contribute	62%	70%	60%	67%	65%	51%

Notes:

Hard work   People in your country can get ahead by working hard.

Entrepreneurs selfish Entrepreneurs only think about their own gain.

Women lead   Women can play an important role in the success of a business.

Trust   Most people can be trusted.

Entrepreneurs succeed There is potential in your country for an entrepreneur to become successful.

Men lead better Men are better qualified than women to be business leaders.

Entr. create jobs Entrepreneurs create jobs for others.

Men more rights When jobs are scarce, men should have more rights to a job than women.

Entrepreneurs contribute Entrepreneurs contribute to the economic development of the country.

In addition, students were asked whether they knew someone who was an entrepreneur. There are no systematic differences between the three groups in this respect at pre-test.

Table 3.23. Knowledge of entrepreneurs in Jordan. (Q: Who among the following people do you know who have started their own business?)

	Control	Participant	Dropout
Parent	40%	33%	19%
Sibling	77%	67%	79%
Family	42%	23%	35%
Neighbor	33%	50%	40%
Friend	63%	83%	66%
Teacher	67%	55%	58%
Someone else	26%	33%	18%

Furthermore, the group of students who participated in the program and those who did not are very similar in terms of where they imagine they could access funds to create a business as shown in table 3.24.

Table 3.24. Sources of funding in Jordan. (Q: If you were to start a business, to what extent would you be able to depend on the following financing sources to support your new business? On scale 1-5. Table reports percentage who answered 4 or 5)

	Control	Participant	Dropout
Nuclear family	61%	57%	58%
Extended family	33%	38%	39%
Friends	25%	17%	29%
Bank	47%	46%	40%
Grant	52%	25%	40%

Notes:

Nuclear family	Nuclear family
Extended family	Extended family
Friends	Friend
Bank	Bank loans
Grant	Government grants

3.6.2.8. Knowledge about Entrepreneurship in Jordan

A few questions in the survey assessed student knowledge of basic concepts of entrepreneurship and business. A significantly greater percentage of students who participated in the Company Program answered these questions correctly after the program than before and these gains were greater than gains that took place for students in the comparison group or in the group that dropped out. For instance, the definition of capitalization was correctly identified by 7 percent of students in the company program at pre-test, compared to 33 percent at the post-test. The vision of a company was correctly defined by 33 percent of the students at pre-test, increasing to 73 percent at post-test. The correct definition of marketing decreased from 87 percent to 53 percent. The correct definition of liquidation increased form 7 percent of the students at pre-test to 33 percent at post-test. The percentage of students who could correctly define a company increased from 47 percent to 67 percent. Percentages of students who answered correctly are reported in Table 3.25.

Table 3.25. Knowledge about entrepreneurship in Jordan. (Multiple choice questions)

	Control		Participant		Dropout	
	Before	*After*	*Before*	*After*	*Before*	*After*
Entrepredefine	49%	Only in baseline	60%	Only in baseline	48%	Only in baseline
Sell shares	3%	6%	7%	33%	17%	11%
Vision	34%	31%	33%	73%	28%	37%
Marketing	63%	40%	87%	53%	67%	48%
Liquidation	9%	20%	7%	33%	7%	17%
Company	34%	31%	47%	67%	39%	33%

Notes:

Entrepredefine	An entrepreneur is someone who
Sell shares	Selling shares of stock to get start-up money for a new company is called:

Vision	A _____ represents a company's dream of where it wants to go and what it wants to be.
Marketing	The work you completed in this scenario above is an example of which of the following:
Liquidation	When a company liquidates, it does which of the following:
Company	By definition, a company must have which of the following:

3.7. How Do Company Program Participants Describe the Effects of the Program?

When asked to rate themselves in a series of questions about possible effects of the program, most participants who were surveyed after the program are very favorable about the changes they observe in themselves. To further examine the effects that students who participated in the Company Program attribute to their participation, during the final competition students were asked a series of additional questions. This section focuses on these retrospective questions.

The first set of questions was asked not only of participants but also non-participants and dropouts. These questions asked the students to compare themselves at the end of the school year to where they were at the beginning of the school year and to assess their capabilities in a variety of areas. Table 3.26. reports answers from matched participants (those for whom we have specific results both from pre- and post-surveys).

Table 3.26. Retrospective experience in Jordan (Compare yourself now to where you were at the beginning of the school year. On a scale of 1-5, to what extent do you agree with the following statements about yourself. Table reports percentage who answered 4 or 5.)

	Control	Participants	Dropouts
Leadership	77%	87%	72%
Finances	73%	86%	47%
Education goals	67%	67%	59%
Career goals	65%	87%	44%
Competitive	79%	67%	67%
Know entrepreneurship	59%	93%	55%
Start business	76%	87%	68%

Notes:

Leadership	I feel more empowered to take a leadership role in the workforce in the future.
Finances	I realize more that knowing how to effectively manage my finances is important.
Education goals	I have developed (or further developed) my educational goals.
Career goals	I have developed (or further developed) my career goals.
Competitive	I am more confident in my ability to successfully compete in the workforce in the future.
Know entrepreneurship	I know more about entrepreneurship.
Start business	I am more interested in starting my own business.

Participating students were likely to report high rates in many of the considered areas, especially feeling empowered to take a leadership role in the workforce (87%), realizing the importance of managing finances (86%), having developed their career goals (87%), having more knowledge about entrepreneurship (93%) and being more interested in starting a business (87%). In each of these areas, positive participant responses where fairly high when compared with those of non-participants or dropouts. Only 67 percent of participants felt that they had developed their educational goals, a figure on par with non-participants and higher than dropouts. Perhaps paradoxically, 67 percent of participants felt more confident about their ability to compete in the workforce, compared with 79 percent of non-participants. (Responses from a comparison of all participants, non-participants and dropouts – rather than matched individuals – where generally consistent with responses from the matched group.)

When asked specifically about the effect of the Injaz Company Program on their own abilities in specific areas, 86 percent of the participating students found the Company Program experience valuable or very valuable (80 percent for matched individuals). Table 3.27. reports participant responses about the specific effect of the Company Program on various aspects of their personal development and worldviews.

Table 3.27. Contribution of the Company Program in Jordan. (In your opinion, on a scale of 1-5, to what extent did your participation in the Injaz Company Program help you with the following:)

	All Participants	Matched Participants
Valuable	86%	80%
Empathy	71%	73%
Team work	95%	93%
Citizenship	95%	100%
Innovation	85%	86%
Critical thinking	89%	86%
Business	79%	86%
Initiative	100%	100%
Leadership	86%	93%
Budgeting	80%	87%
Problem solve	90%	87%
Decide	90%	93%
Communicate	90%	93%
Negotiate	75%	73%
Sell	90%	93%
Speak	90%	87%
Creativity	75%	73%

Empathy — It helped me develop understanding of other people's views.
Team work — It helped me develop the ability to work with others as a team.
Citizenship — It helped me develop citizenship skills.
Innovation — It helped me develop the capacity to innovate.
Critical thinking It taught me critical thinking skills.
Business — It taught me useful business skills.
Initiative — It helped me development initiative and self-motivation.
Leadership — It helped me develop my abilities as a leader.
Budgeting — It taught me how to manage a budget.
Problem solve It helped me learn to solve problems.
Decide — It helped me to become a better decision maker.
Communicate It helped me learn to communicate with others.
Negotiate — It helped me learn to negotiate differences with people.
Sell — It helped me learn to sell ideas or products.
Speak — It helped me learn to speak in public more easily.

Creativity   It inspired me to think more creatively about problems.

The strongest impact of the Company Program, from the perspective of participants, seems to be related to the development of initiative and self-motivation, where 100 percent of participants attribute personal improvement to participation in the program. Similarly, 95 percent of participants (100 percent of matched participants) reported that the program helped them to develop citizenship skills (perhaps striking as it is not a priority area for the Company Program's curriculum). Strong responses from participants, at or above 90 percent reporting agreement or strong agreement, are also found in the areas of teamwork, problem solving, decision making, communicating with others, selling ideas or products, and public speaking. While there are differences between the total population of participants and the matched group, reported rates are fairly consistent. Moreover, while findings are weaker in other areas noted in the table above, the vast majority of participants find that the program aided them in each of the measured areas.

Finally, students were also asked to evaluate some of the components of the program (Table 3.28). Most of them say that lectures aroused their interest in the topics discussed and that the volunteer presented the content clearly, held lectures in an interactive way, and was helpful and responsive to questions. Most of them found the Student Guide useful or very useful. Finally, all participants would recommend the Company Program to friends or family.

Table 3.28. Evaluation of the Components of the Program in Jordan. (On a scale of 1-5, to what extent do you agree with the following comments about the Injaz Company Program)

	All participants	Matched participants
Lecture	94%	100%
Volunclear	95%	93%
Volunrespond	94%	92%
Studguide	95%	93%
Volunlecture	89%	93%
Recommend	100%	100%

Notes:

Lecture	Company Program lectures aroused my interest for the topics being discussed.
Volunclear	The volunteer presented the program's content in a clear way.
Volunrespond	The volunteer was helpful and responsive to our questions.
Studyguide	The Student Guide was useful.
Volunlecture	The volunteer held lectures in an interactive way.
Recommend	Would you recommend participating in the Injaz Company Program to friends or family members? (1=YES, 0=NO)

3.8. A Qualitative Analysis of Student Descriptions of Program Effects

Student Perspectives

Within the follow-up survey, students were provided the opportunity to answer an open-ended question regarding their experience with the Company Program: *"Use the following space to provide any comments – positive or negative – about your experience in the Injaz Company Program."* Regrettably, only 10 of the 22 participants took advantage of the opportunity to provide feedback on the program. Still, the comments were provided provide valuable information regarding the program, its impact on participants and areas in which Injaz can take steps to improve the effectiveness of program operations.

First, it should be noted that the comments provided by participants were largely positive. In fact, of the 10, all provided positive views of the program and the learning experience that it provided. Surveyed participants noted, generally, that they appreciated the knowledge that the program provided them in how to start a business or new project, or that they were, more broadly, pleased with the unique learning experience provided by the Company Program.

Other students were more specific: several students noted, in particular, that the program had enabled them to improve their sense of self-confidence, their ability to express themselves, and their leadership abilities. They expressed satisfaction in how the program enabled them to improve their interpersonal skills, to better plan for their futures, and to develop their own ideas into successful projects. Notably, several students emphasized that the experience allowed them to realize skills and abilities that they did not know themselves to have.

Example 1: "Injaz's Company Program helped us in all of life's aspects. It made us think about future more seriously and made us insist on achieving what we dream about."

Example 2: "It helped us in building our personalities and self-confidence, and taught us how to express our ideas clearly."

Example 3: "Through Injaz, I have full confidence that I am going to reach my future goals."

The only negative critique – but one provided by several participants – was the timing of the program. Given a fairly tight delivery schedule, many students did not feel that they had enough time to develop their student company while dealing with other school-related demands. They suggested that the program be offered over a longer time period to allow them to manage their academic needs.

Perspectives from Volunteers and Faculty Members

To supplement our findings, we were able to secure interview with three volunteers from the private sector who served as program instructors. As with the student open-ended responses, the feedback from these interviews is limited but provides an interesting source of information on the program that rounds out our understanding of its potential impact and should inform future actions by the Injaz management team.

Overall, volunteer reactions to the program are highly positive. Asked to reflect on their experiences as instructors, the volunteers spoke largely about the transformational experience that Injaz provides for young people (and the volunteers). As one volunteer stated, "This was the best experience in my life. When I saw students show their products in front of the judges, I was so proud. I felt the change." Another stated, "It was a unique experience, and it is very valuable as an educational tool. I guess I learned more from the students than they learned from me. The relationship between students and the volunteer will never be forgotten... [During one of the meetings,] someone asked how useful the course was and what he had learned so far. He answered that the volunteer had taught us everything, even how to talk."

In hindsight, the volunteers agreed, the program could benefit from greater integration of the training and initial advice given to volunteers with expected outcomes from the students during the competition. That is, they suggested that volunteers not only receive stronger training in the beginning, but that during that training, they meet with previous volunteers and competition judges in order to get a better idea of what they should be reinforcing as volunteers.

The volunteers had considerable concerns about the student guide. Students were provided the student guide in Arabic and English. The volunteers state that the Arabic version did not have sufficient information for the students to draw upon, while the English guide was not well understood by most students. One volunteer suggested providing specific instruction briefs for each department in the student company would help the students move forward more quickly and confidently in developing their companies.

The volunteers were unanimous in another bit of advice: involving parents in the program. They strongly encouraged Injaz to reach out to parents in order to engage them in the overall experience. As one volunteer stated, "It is important to let students' parents live this experience too, especially ... the competition, because it is important [for them] to see the change that took place in their kids' lives." At least, one volunteer noted, Injaz should give a parents a briefing on the program so that they understand the program and the activities in which their children will be involved. This would encourage parents to help their children more and to be more open towards their children spending so much time on the program.

Finally, one volunteer strongly echoed the criticisms coming from students, stating that care should be given to choosing a suitable time for students to participate in the program. He emphasized that the comprehensive examinations for graduating Jordanian students are a "critical point of their education," and as such requires their full attention.

3.9. Discussion

The results highlighted above must be viewed with caution when one is assessing the program effects of Injaz's Company Program, given the potential for various selection effects that bias the results. With this caveat in mind, the results do suggest that the Company Program offers a learning environment that provides Jordanian youth with valuable experiences and skills that they are not getting through the traditional school curriculum. The students who complete the program end up with valuable soft skills, knowledge about business and entrepreneurship, and more inclusive worldviews, if not demonstrating a decidedly bolstered interest in starting their own businesses in the future.

In regard to Injaz's primary goal of encouraging more youth to become entrepreneurs, results are mixed. In fact, in both our overall analysis of the data and our refined analysis of matched surveys, Injaz Company Program participants were slightly less inclined at the conclusion of the program to want to start a business of their own and saw starting a business in Jordan as more difficult than they had originally envisioned. Moreover, fewer participants had ideas for a business they would like to start after the program than at its initiation. However, it is noteworthy that similar declines were measured among both control groups in regard to desire to start a business. Moreover, when students were asked whether they were more inclined to start their own businesses when looking back at themselves at the beginning of the year, participant responses were fairly strong and more positive than those of non-participants.

While these mixed results, overall, could be read as an inability of Injaz to meet its primary goal of encouraging youth to pursue entrepreneurship, it might be more correctly read as Injaz helping youth understand the challenges of starting a business. Beyond the rhetoric behind the promotion of youth entrepreneurship in Jordan and the Arab world as a whole, starting one's own business poses a daunting challenge in the best environments. It is more difficult in environments, like that of Jordan, that pose particular regulatory burdens to new start-ups. Working with a volunteer with private sector experience to develop their own fictitious companies may actually ensure that Company Program participants are opening their eyes in this regard. This can, in the long term, have significant benefits as young people leave school and consider starting their own businesses, ensuring that they do so with full knowledge of the challenges they face and commitment to developing sustainable enterprises.

Data also suggest that Injaz has a mixed impact in regard to showing youth a more positive image of entrepreneurs or appreciation for their role in the economy. When asked about their impressions of entrepreneurs having a role in economic development, favorable responses from students increased after program participation, but only as much as those of non-participants, and participant agreement that entrepreneurs created jobs for others went down in contrast with the views of non-participants. At the same time, participants were much more likely to view entrepreneurs as focusing on outcomes other than their own gain, which is positive.

Injaz participants in Jordan *do* demonstrate a greater knowledge of basic business concepts. They are also more prone to believe that they can get ahead through hard work and that entrepreneurs have the opportunity to succeed in Jordan. Moreover, they demonstrate rates of trust in others that, while lower than comparison groups, climb much higher after program participation. Such perceptions not only reflect a greater openness to the potential of entrepreneurship, but are a basic building block for developing the sense of empowerment needed to motivate youth to take on the risks as they enter the economy, whether as entrepreneurs or when seeking employment and starting their careers.

While Injaz's Company Program may have mixed results in regard to encouraging actual business start-up and promoting a more favorable impression of entrepreneurship more generally, our analysis suggests that it has a direct, tangible bearing on student development in regard to soft skills development and self-efficacy. In both the overall analysis and refined analysis of participant views, they voiced considerable gains in regard to their self-perceived abilities to work with teams, to resolve differences peacefully and to negotiate conflict, to adapt to new situations, to solve problems and to lead a team. Whether or not they intended to

184

start a business, they felt more that they were better able to run a business successfully and to research potential markets effectively. Moreover, a large share of participants felt that they were better able to compete for jobs. In each of these areas, participants demonstrated marked improvements over the course of the program, with improvements being significantly stronger than those observed among non-participating groups.

Finally, while the qualitative responses from students to the open-ended question and volunteer feedback are not quantifiable, they provide overall a passionate argument in favor of the Injaz Company Program. While feedback on specific impacts is limited, both student responses and volunteer responses paint a picture of the Injaz Company Program as a unique and transformative learning experience, a picture that is reinforced by positive quantitative responses to questions about the direct impact that program participation has had on them. Importantly, the student-centered, experiential nature of the program ensures that students are not only receiving bodies, but are engaged in practicing the skills they are intended to learn. Learning by doing is the only effective way to develop many of these skills, particularly those known collectively as soft skills, and for many of these students, Injaz is the sole opportunity to engage in this type of learning.

3.10. Policy and Program Implications

Although our results must be viewed with caution given potential bias, the data – and participant feedback on the experience provided by the program – strongly suggest that it has significant benefits in exposing youth to entrepreneurship and, more importantly, in regard to soft skills development, job-relevant skills and self-efficacy. The experiential learning opportunity provided by the Company Program is a unique learning experience for many youth, one that provides tangible skill development and makes students aware of skills they already possess but are not aware that they have. As such, there would be significant gains for Jordanian youth were the program to be expanded.

While Injaz Jordan has been established for some time now and offers a range of programs across the country, the Company Program – at least during the 2010-2011 school year – was only offered in four schools to a total of 50 participants, all of which are located in the greater Amman area. As such, there is ample room for expanding the program within the country. Importantly, Injaz should consider providing the program to youth in more disadvantaged and more rural areas, where youth do not have the educational opportunities or access to formal sector public and private jobs that youth in Amman have and where self-employment can provide immediate means by which youth can leverage themselves out of poverty or economic vulnerability.

Expanding the delivery of the program will impose elevated costs for Injaz, but more importantly will impose logistical challenges. First among these is identifying and engaging a larger number of (quality) volunteers to deliver the program to a growing number of young participants. To date, Injaz Jordan has been able to work with a small but highly engaged number of volunteers from the private sector. In expanding the program, Injaz Jordan may face growing difficulty in securing volunteers and particularly volunteers that have the significant private sector experience and personal dynamism that make them effective instructors for this program. As such, expansion of the program – as with all programs – must be done carefully to avoid diminishing returns to scale.

In a related note, expanding the services provided through Injaz would require support from the Ministry of Education and local school administrators, all of whom are already facing challenges related to the administration of school calendars and curriculum demands. Injaz should begin to strategically engage representatives of the Ministry of Education and, particularly important, local school administrators to begin developing plans for expansion in the future. Working on an expanded timeline will help ensure that education planners understand the merits of the Company Program and are providing space in the school calendar for the Company Program.

At the same time, our analysis raises some program process issues that Injaz Morocco should address as it works to expand its offerings within Jordan. First, in the future, Injaz must work more closely with the Ministry of Education to ensure that it has early access to school at the beginning of the school year and is able to implement the Company Program in a way that imposes less stress on student participants. According to feedback from students, this means extending the course over a longer time period and holding the national competition at a time when it does not conflict with comprehensive examinations. Injaz might consider offering the Company Program to youth prior to their final year in school in order to avoid this conflict.

In Jordan, as opposed to how it is delivered in most other Arab countries, the Company Program is delivered as an extra-curricular activity. As such, it attracts only those students who are most engaged and committed to completing the program. While this means that fewer students might participate, evidence from other countries in this study suggests that the extra-curricular approach ensures that those who do participate get more out of the program because all of their peers are similarly engaged. At the same time, however, Injaz needs to find a way to attract more students to want to participate and who are willing to stick with the program over time. Discussions with Injaz program managers suggest the parental support is particularly important in this regard. As such, Injaz must find a way to engage parents, informing them of the merits of program participation for their children and ensuring that they understand what activities students will be involved in during the overall program. In garnering parental support, Injaz will not only secure more students, but participating students will have more leeway in going out into the community to work with service and material providers needed to manufacture products and with potential consumers.

187

On this last note, it must also be understood that the Company Program activity, in as much as it requires participants to engage with manufacturers and consumers outside of school, requires students to leave school grounds. Given Ministry of Education regulations, students cannot leave school grounds during the day. Providing some creative way to allow students access to the market either after school hours (transportation support), bringing materials suppliers to school, or working with Ministry officials to allow special permissions, perhaps as a part of a structured field trip, would improve student access to the marketplace.

Finally, while our results strongly point to a significant impact of the program on student self-efficacy, soft skills development and interest in business (both self-employment and private sector employment), it should be noted that the results herein should not be taken to represent the causal evidence of impact that would be provided in the context of a more rigorous impact evaluation. The team suggests that Injaz engage in an experimental evaluation that is able both to determine the exact causal relationship between participation in the program and outcomes in regard to entrepreneurial activity, job-relevant skills development, and employment. Moreover, such an evaluation should take place over a longer time span, allowing for an assessment of actual outcomes within the labor market after youth leave school.

Chapter 4. An exploratory study of the Injaz Company Program in Lebanon

4.1. Introduction

In many ways, Lebanon differs significantly from the rest of the region in terms of the situation of young people. First, Lebanon led the region in its demographic transition. As such, it saw its youth population peak in the late 1980s, when those ages 15-24 made up 20 percent of the population. It has since declined, with the country's 15-24-year-old population currently making up 18.1 percent of the population. Overall, those under the age of 25 make up 43 percent of the Lebanese population compared to 54 percent in the Arab world. This gradual decline in the scale of the youth population has translated into lower pressures in regard to needed job creation. At the same time, the private sector plays a more prominent role in the Lebanese economy that is true of most Arab countries. Only 12.3 percent of the employed in Lebanon work for the public sector, and, as such, there is not the queuing for such jobs among Lebanese youth that one observes in other Arab countries. The Lebanese economy consists in large part of small and medium enterprises: in fact, according to recent estimates, two-thirds of employed Lebanese youth working for the private sector were employed in small firms and of these 38 percent were running their own companies or were self-employed.[6]

Still, the Lebanese economy has failed to create the jobs necessary to absorb the growing numbers of young workers into the ranks of the employed. In 2009, the youth unemployment rate (ages 15-24) in Lebanon was nearly 17 percent, lower than the regional average of 24 percent but

---

[6] Chaaban, Jad, "Instability, Migration and Lebanon's Human Capital" in Navtej Dhillon and Tarik Yousef, eds., *Generation in Waiting: The Unfulfilled Promise of Young People in the Middle East* (Washington, DC: Brookings Institution Press, 2009)

still higher than the international average of 12 percent. Youth make up at least half of Lebanon's total unemployed. On the other hand, many of those that are able to work complain of low wages and informality. This is particularly true for those youth without university degrees: only half of employed youth with less than a university education hold a permanent job (compared with 74 percent of university graduates), while average monthly salaries for youth without university degrees is US$308 (compared with US$657 for university graduates).[7] Poverty is also a pressing issue for some youth, particularly outside of Lebanon's major urban centers, as is Lebanon's legacy of conflict and political instability.

These economic pressures on youth are partially responsible for another factor that makes the Lebanese economy stand out: migration. Poverty, unemployment and low wages, as well as Lebanon's susceptibility to political insecurity, serve as important push factors for youth seeking to emigrate. Nearly a third of Lebanese youth indicate a desire to leave the country, while 17 percent of these want to leave permanently.[8] While migration has been a relative boon to the Lebanese economy, in terms of decreasing labor market pressures and increasing remittances, it represents an overall loss to the country in regard to human capital and the economic outcomes that could result if more of Lebanon's educated youth put their skills to use in the local economy.

In this regard, it is important to highlight the relative successes that Lebanon has had in regard to education when compared with other Arab countries. While Lebanon continues to struggle with enrollment among youth, particularly at the secondary and university level, basic indicators of educational outcomes are positive. For example, literacy among youth (ages 15-24) is estimated at nearly 99 percent. Moreover, in international examinations of student performance, such as Trends in International Mathematics and Sciences Study (TIMSS), Lebanese students score

---

[7] Chaaban, 2009
[8] Chaaban, 2009

relatively well. In 2007, the performance of eight-grade students in Lebanon on the TIMSS examinations earned an average of 449 in mathematics and 414 in sciences. While these average scores put Lebanese students below the international scale average of 500, they put Lebanon at the top of the Arab world.[9]

The challenge for Lebanon, while bolstering educational outcomes for a larger share of its youth, is creating an atmosphere wherein more educated Lebanese youth are finding employment opportunities at home and thus, deploying their talents for the development and growth of the Lebanese economy more directly. In this regard, efforts must be taken on the demand side to stimulate private sector job growth, including efforts to encourage more youth to take up entrepreneurial activity and self-employment. However, there is also an important need for preparing youth to take on these positions through training and education that more directly provide them with business-relevant knowledge and skills that do not hold a position of particular importance in the Lebanese curricula, as well as softer life skills, such as teamwork, leadership, and personal skills that are not readily taught in Lebanese schools.

4.2. Injaz Lebanon and the Company Program

Towards this end, Injaz Lebanon has been working with the Lebanese Ministry of Education and local schools, both private and public, to deliver a broad base of entrepreneurship training opportunities to

---

[9] Mullis, I.V.S., Martin, M.O., & Foy, P. (with Olson, J.F., Preuschoff, C., Erberber, E., Arora, A., & Galia, J.), *TIMSS 2007 International Mathematics Report: Findings from IEA's Trends in International Mathematics and Science Study at the Fourth and Eighth Grades* (Chestnut Hill, MA: TIMSS & PIRLS International Study Center, Boston College, 2008); Martin, M.O., Mullis, I.V.S., & Foy, P. (with Olson, J.F., Erberber, E., Preuschoff, C., & Galia, J.), *TIMSS 2007 International Science Report: Findings from IEA's Trends in International Mathematics and Science Study at the Fourth and Eighth Grades* (Chestnut Hill, MA: TIMSS & PIRLS International Study Center, Boston College, 2008)

Lebanese youth through the school system. By working with local volunteers from the business community, Injaz seeks to provide young Lebanese with opportunities to develop the basic business skills and the financial literacy they need to start and run their own businesses, while developing the softer job-ready skills that are in increasing demand by the private sector through an experiential learning environment.

As such, Injaz Lebanon offers intermediate, secondary and university students a number of programs in which they are able to participate as part of their school curriculum (see table 4.1). For each of these programs, Injaz provides instructional materials, secures and trains volunteers to run the programs, and works with local school administrators to arrange for program delivery within schools. Programs range from day-long interventions like Innovation Camp to programs carried out over the course of the academic year, like the Company Program. The *Company Program* is the lead program among Injaz's offerings in Lebanon.

Table 4.1: Injaz Programs Offered in Lebanon

Program name	Duration	Age group	Purpose
Banks in Action	8 sessions	Secondary/ university	Promotes understanding of banking fundamentals and operations of competitive banks.
Be Entrepreneurial	Variable	Secondary	Interactive classroom activities aimed to encourage youth to start their own businesses before leaving school.
Business Ethics	7-12 sessions	Secondary	Fosters student's ethical decision-making as they prepare to enter the workforce
Success Skills	7 sessions	Secondary	Works with students to prepare them for job search and interview skills.
Job Shadow	4 sessions	Secondary/ university	Prepares students for careers with 3 classroom sessions and an on-site orientation in the workplace.
Economics for Success	6 sessions	Secondary	Introduces students to personal finance and educational and career options.
More than Money	6 sessions	Grades 3-5	Teaches students about earning, saving and spending money responsibly.
Entrepreneurship Master Class	1 day	Grades 10-12	Introduction to entrepreneurship and self-employment
Community Citizenship	Variable	Secondary/ university	Class participates in a community service project
Innovation Camp	1 day	Secondary/ university	Participants discuss a particular business challenge and develop potential solutions.
Company Program	4-6 months	Secondary/ university	Participants develop a business plan, launch a business, market and sell their product and then liquidate the business for first-hand experience in entrepreneurship.

4.3. Evaluating Injaz's Impact on Participants

In Lebanon, as in the rest of the countries, we had planned to design a study in which students who participated in the Company Program would fill out a questionnaire before and after participating. A group of students not participating in the program from comparable classes within the same schools would also complete a pre-post survey. While the assignment of students to participation in the program would not be random, we had expected that the pre-post comparison and the existence of a quasi-comparison group would have allowed us to reach conclusions about plausible program effects.

In Lebanon, the team faced difficulty in securing significant numbers of follow-up surveys from participants due to these concerns. At baseline, 189 students who did not participate in the program completed the survey, as did 222 students who participated in the Company Program. After the completion of the program, 61 students who did not participate completed the follow up survey, and 43 of those who participated in the program did so. It should be noted that the follow up surveys were only secured by the Injaz team for two schools (St. Joseph's and Jesus and Mary); this may have skewed the sample towards parochial schools with largely Christian student populations. It was only possible to match pre- and post-surveys for 70 students, 34 who did not participate in the Company Program and 36 who did. In this analysis, we focus on the responses provided by both groups of students at pre-test, and subsequently analyze the differences observed for the matched students. Because the sample size of each of the matched groups is too small, we do not estimate the statistical significance of the observed differences.

Table 4.2. Number of students surveyed in Lebanon for control and participant groups

	Control		Participants	
	Before	*After*	*Before*	*After*
Full Sample	189	61	222	43
Females	120		140	
Matched Sample	34	34	36	36

4.4. Who Participates in the Company Program?

In this section of the report, we characterize the 411 students who completed the questionnaire before participating in the Company Program. Sixty-three percent of these students are girls, in both groups: those who participated in the Company Program and the comparison group. Ninety-five percent of the students are between 15 and 17 years old, and the ages of students range from 15 to 19. Students in the comparison group are slightly older, as 89 percent are between the ages of 15 and 17 and 11 percent are 18 or older, relative to 95 percent and 5 percent respectively among those who participated in the Company Program. The level of parental education varies. Over half of the students' fathers have a post-secondary degree or more, and almost half have secondary education or less. The educational level of mothers is similar. Whereas 44 percent of the mothers have a secondary education or less, 10 percent have a post-secondary degree, 26 percent have a university degree and 14 percent have a post-graduate degree. There are no differences with the comparison group.

Fathers of the students who participate in the program have a range of occupations. Sixteen percent work as government employees, police or armed forces, or in a public sector company. A fifth of them work in a large private sector company and 7 percent in a small private sector company. A small percentage of them work in a family business (8%), and a third (34%) are self-employed. None define their work as housework, and under 2 percent are unemployed. Less than 5 percent are outside the labor force or retired. The occupational profile of mothers is different. Only 11 percent work as government employees, police or armed forces or in a public sector company. Only 13 percent work in a large or small private company. Only 9 percent work in a family business or are self-employed. Almost half (49%) define their work as housework, and 4 percent are unemployed and 5 percent outside the labor force.

The students come from homes which vary with regards to how much literacy is valued. When asked how many books were in their homes, 2 percent said less than 10 books, 9 percent reported having 11-25 books, 42 percent reported having 26-100 books, 21 percent had 101-200 books, and 25 percent had more than 200.

Finally, we asked the students how satisfied they were with their standard of living, and the majority of them were either very satisfied (40%) or satisfied (38%), and only 3 percent were not satisfied or barely satisfied. Among the non-participants, 34 percent reported being very satisfied and 39 percent satisfied.

4.5. How Do Participants Their Time and How Do They Differ from the Comparison Group?

There are no differences in the way that students who participate in the program and those who do not participate spend their time. Most students report spending much time watching TV and radio, chatting with friends, in various forms of entertainment, talking to their parents and studying. Less than a third of the students spend time thinking about their career, researching business opportunities or following the news. These figures are summarized in table 4.3.

Table 4.3. How much time do students in Lebanon spend on the following activities in a typical week? Responses before participating in the Company Program (Question: On a scale of 1-5, how much time to you spend on the following activities. Table includes percentage who answer that they spent *much time* or a *lot of time*)

	Control	Participant
Careers	21%	22%
Research	25%	28%
News	26%	31%
Talk parents	50%	62%
Studying	64%	69%
Entertainment	64%	66%
Chatting friends	69%	74%
TV and Radio	81%	79%

Careers	Investigating career possibilities
Research	Research potential ideas for a new business
News	Following the news
Talk parents	Talking to your parents about career possibilities
Studying	Studying or working on school-related activities
Entertainment	Keeping up-to-date on entertainment, fashion or sports
Chatting friends	Chatting with friends
TV and Radio	Watching TV or listening to music

4.6. How Do Participants and Non-Participants Differ before and after the Program?

In this section, we compare four groups: the students in the comparison group who did not participate in the Company Program before (189 students) and after (61 students) the program, and those who participated in the Company Program, both before the program (222 students) and after the program (43 students).[10]

---

[10] Fewer participants were surveyed after the Program partly due to logistical reasons tracking down students. For these reason the differences observed in this section should not be attributed to the program, they could also be the result of

Because this section of the analysis does not match baseline questionnaires to those after the program per students, the differences identified in this section could be the result of program effects, the result of differences between the students who completed the survey after program completion from those who abandoned the program or did not fill out the follow-up survey (selection effects), or the result of an interaction between program effects and selection effects (i.e., the program may have effects on the kind of students who remain in the program). A subsequent section performs the same analysis only for the much smaller sample for which we are able to match students before and after the program.

4.6.1. Aspirations, Views of Self and Worldviews

Overall, students have high aspirations and worldviews in both groups. There are for the most part no differences between the students who participate in the Company Program and those who don't before or after participation. One exception is that students who participate in the Company Program are more likely to trust that in the future they will achieve their goals than those who do not participate in the program. Students in both groups are more likely to see challenges as opportunities and to believe that what they learn now will help them in the future in the post-questionnaire.

Each of these aspirations and worldviews was measured with a five-point scale in which students were asked to rate themselves from completely disagree (1) with completely agree (5). In table 4.4, we have calculated the percentages for each item represented by the students who selected agree or completely agree (points 4 and 5 in the scale).

---

differences between the students who did not take the post-questionnaire and those who took the pre- questionnaire.

Table 4.4. Aspirations and worldviews towards future and self of students in Lebanon before and after participating in the Company Program. (Question: On a scale of 1-5, to what extent do you agree or disagree with the following statements about yourself. Table includes percentage who answer 4 or 5)

	Control		Participant	
	Before	*After*	*Before*	*After*
Achieve goals	69%	69%	86%	91%
Learn from failure	84%	83%	89%	86%
Challenges opport.	62%	72%	69%	81%
Outside school	49%	57%	59%	62%
Studying matters	79%		84%	
Educ matters	83%	63%	82%	82%
Learnfuture	73%		86%	
Negotiate	67%	64%	78%	74%
Leadership	63%	73%	73%	65%
Set goals	78%	72%	86%	84%
Creativity		75%		72%

Achieve goals	I trust that in the future, I will achieve my goals.
Learn from failure	If I fail at something, I try to figure out why so that I can succeed the next time.
Challenges opport.	I see challenges as opportunities.
Outside school	I participate in activities outside of school to prepare for my future.
Studying matters	Studying is important to me
Educ matters	I go to school because education is important for getting a job later.
Learnfuture	The things that I am learning now will help me in the future.
Negotiate	I believe that achieving my goals requires negotiating with others.
Leadership	I can see myself in a leadership position in the future.
Set goals	I set goals for myself in order to attain the things I want.
Creativity	I try to find creative solutions to problems.

With regards to trust in their own capacity to achieve their goals in the future, there are differences between the control group and the group who participated in the Company Program. In the control group, 69 percent of the students are confident that they will achieve their goals. In the group that participated in the Company Program, this figure is about 90 percent. Over 80 percent of the students in both groups report that, faced with failure, they try to figure out the reasons in order to succeed the next time. The percentage of students who come to see challenges as opportunities is over 80 percent for those participating in the Company Program and 70 percent among those not participating.

About 60 percent of the students in this study participate in out of school activities to prepare for their future. Over 80 percent of the students included in this study believe that studying is important. This figure is 100 percent for those who participate in the Company Program after participation. Along similar lines, the percentage of students who believe that education is important in order to obtain a job in the future is very high, about 80 percent. Similarly, students had very favorable views towards learning before and after the program, over 70 percent. This percentage is much higher for those students who took the post-questionnaire. When asked to what extent there was a clear connection between what they learned in school and the real world, after the program, 36 percent of those in the comparison group saw a connection, compared to 44 percent of those who participated in the program.

Students understand that achieving their goals requires negotiating with others, more so for those who participate in the program. For those who did not participate these figures are about 60 percent whereas they are about 75 percent for those who participate in the Company Program. Most of the students (over 60 percent) see themselves as leaders in the future.

Most students set goals for themselves, more so among those who participate in the Company Program than among those who do not. For those who do not participate in the program the percentage of students who set goals for themselves is over 70 percent, whereas it is over 80 percent for those who do participate in the program. Most students, over 70 percent, report an interest in finding creative solutions to problems.

To sum up, most students who completed the questionnaires score on the high end of the various dimensions explored in this section. There are a few differences in these various aspects of worldviews and views of themselves between students who did not participate in the program and those who did prior to participation.

4.6.2.   Perceived Self-Efficacy

Students were asked to what extent they felt capable of performing a series of tasks. Table 4.5 summarizes the percentage of those students who felt capable of doing them to a great extent –values 4 and 5 in the 5-point scale. In the majority of the dimensions evaluated, there are no differences between the students who participated in the Company Program and those who did not or in the views expressed in the pre- and post-tests. Those who participate in the Company Program are more likely to see themselves as capable to work in a team to accomplish a result, and to present a topic to a group of peers or adults and to understand the role of business owners in the economy.

Table 4.5. Perception of Self-Efficacy of students in Lebanon before and after participating in the Company Program. (Question: On a scale of 1-5, to what extent do you feel that you are able to. Table includes percentage who answer 4 or 5)

	Control		Participant	
	Before	*After*	*Before*	*After*
Teamwork	67%	66%	84%	74%
Adapt	67%	79%	75%	71%
Problemsolve	74%	70%	78%	84%
Presentpeers	60%	62%	71%	77%
Presentadult	61%	58%	74%	74%
Resolvediff	63%	67%	80%	69%
Purpose	69%		77%	
Commproblem	55%	42%	57%	55%
Persuade	76%	68%	74%	69%
Negconflict	69%	66%	75%	67%
Competejob	80%	74%	86%	79%
Startbusiness	64%	69%	76%	67%
Rolebusiness	50%	36%	63%	51%
Leadteam	66%	57%	77%	60%
Research	63%	42%	70%	54%
Learnrealworld	53%	36%	55%	44%

Teamwork	Work with a team to accomplish a result
Adapt	Adapt to new situations
Problemsolve	Solve problems
Presentpeers	Present a topic to a group of classmates
Presentadult	Present a topic to a group of adults
Resolvediff	Resolve differences within a group to reach a solution satisfactory to most
Purpose	Understand your purpose in life
Commproblem	Solve community problems
Persuade	Persuade a group of people about an idea
Negconflict	Negotiate personal conflicts in a peaceful way
Competejob	Be competitive in securing a good job
Startbusiness	Start and run your own business someday
Rolebusiness	Understand the role of business owners in our economy
Leadteam	Lead the members of a group to meet a deadline in

	producing a result
Research	Research the potential market for a company
Learnrealworld	To what extent is there a clear connection between what you are learning in school and the real world?

When asked whether they feel capable of working with a team to accomplish a result, over 66 percent in the comparison group did, relative to 74 percent in the Company Program group. In terms of their ability to adapt to new situations, about 70 percent see themselves as capable to do this. About 80 percent of the students see themselves as able to solve problems. When asked whether they were able to solve community problems and about half of them said they were.

We asked students about their ability to persuade a group of people about their ideas. About 70 percent reported they were able to do this. When asked about their ability to present to a group of peers about 60 percent of those in the comparison group and 70 percent of those in the Company Program participants group feel capable to do this. Similar differences are reported with regard to ability to present to a group of adults, 60 percent of those in the comparison group feel capable of doing it, relative to 75 percent of those in the Company Program.

About 70 percent of the students felt capable of resolving differences within a group to reach a solution satisfactory to most group members. We asked students, before participating in the program, whether they understood their purpose in life, and about 70 percent of them said they did. Students were asked whether they were able to negotiate conflicts in a peaceful way. About 70 percent said they were.

When asked whether they felt competitive in securing a good job about three quarters did. We also asked students whether they could start and run their own business someday. About 70 percent said they could. We asked whether they understood the role of business owners in the economy. About a third of those who did not participate in the program did, compared to about half of those who did.

Students were asked whether they felt capable of leading the members of a group to meet a deadline in producing a result, about 60 percent did. We asked students whether they could research the potential market for a company. For those who did not participate in the Company Program 42 percent did, compared to 54 percent of those who participated in the program.

4.6.3.   Educational Aspirations

There are pronounced differences in the educational aspirations of the students who took the post-questionnaire and those who took the pre-questionnaire. For those in the control group, at pre-test, 34 percent aspired to complete university and 58 percent aspired to complete post-graduate studies. At post-test, the respective figures were 5 percent and 93 percent. For those in the Company Program, these figures were 24 percent who aspired to completed university and 72 percent who aspired to complete graduate studies at pre-test, vs. 14 percent and 81 percent after participating in the program.

A higher percentage of the students reported plans to continue with their studies immediately after leaving secondary study at post-test than at pre-test. For those in the comparison group these figures were 74 percent vs. 89 percent, and for those who participated in the Company Program the figures were 79 percent vs. 88 percent.

4.6.4.   Motivations for Choosing a Job

We asked students to what extent a range of reasons were important to them in choosing a particular job. There were few differences between those students who participated in the Company Program and those in the comparison group: before the program, high status of a job was important to 74 percent of the students; ability to earn a lot of money was important to 75 percent of the students; good promotion prospects were important to 90 percent of the students; the opportunity to use their skills and abilities was a motivation for over 90 percent of the students; and job security was important to 90 percent of the students before the program; autonomy to have a role in decision making was important to 77 percent of the students; having a lot of vacation time was mentioned by 44 percent of the students; easy pace of work was mentioned by about half of the students; ability to work independently without supervision was mentioned by about 60 percent of the students; a job that is family friendly was mentioned by 70 percent of the students. About 60 percent mentioned the kind of people they would work with as an important factor (this question was not asked of students before the program).

When asked how confident they were that they could complete successfully a job interview, about 70 percent of the students before participating in the Company Program felt confident. Confidence was higher (79%) after the program among those who participated. We also asked students how much confidence they had that they would be hired to work in the private sector. Before participating in the program, 65 percent in the comparison group felt very confident in the pre-test, compared to 76 percent in the post-test, the respective figures for the students who participated in the Company Program were 76 percent vs. 93 percent.

Table 4.6. Motivations for choosing a job in Lebanon before and after participating in the Company Program. (Question: On a scale of 1 to 5, to what extent are the following reasons important to you in choosing a particular job? Percentage who answer 4 and 5)

	Control		Participant	
	Before	*After*	*Before*	*After*
Status	74%	64%	73%	84%
Money	75%	65%	73%	81%
Career	87%	82%	90%	90%
Uses skills	92%	95%	96%	88%
Job security	87%	66%	92%	74%
Role deciding	77%	64%	78%	81%
Ample vacation	44%	28%	39%	33%
Easy pace	49%	42%	47%	44%
Autonomy	63%	67%	58%	79%
Family friendly	70%	42%	72%	51%
Jobcolleagues Confidence		62%		65%
interview	73%	72%	76%	79%
Confidence hired	65%	76%	73%	93%

Status	High status of job
Money	Ability to earn a lot of money
Career	Good promotion prospects, clear career path
Uses skills	Uses my skills and abilities
Job security	Job security
Role deciding	Gives me a role in decision making
Ample vacation	Has a lot of vacation time
Easy pace	Easy pace of work
Autonomy	Ability to work independently without supervision
Family friendly	Job that is family friendly
Confidence interview	How much confidence do you have that you could successfully complete a job interview?
Confidence hired	How much confidence do you have that you could be hired to work in the private sector?

4.6.5. Interest in starting a business and motivations for business creation

Students were asked for their views on the ease of starting a business and their interest in starting one. When asked how easy they thought it was to start a business in their country today, 53 percent said it was easy or very easy before participating in the Company Program (Table 4.7).

In response to the question of how interested they were in starting a business someday in the country, over 70 percent of them said they were interested or very interested before participating in the Company Program.

After participation in the Company Program, we asked how interested participants were in someday joining somebody else's business. Over a third said that they were interested or very interested.

Before the Company Program, we asked students whether they had an idea for a business they would like to start. About a third in the control and a fourth of the participants replied yes. The percentages having an idea was lower in the follow-up survey.

Table 4.7. Interest in opening a business among students in Lebanon before and after participating in the Company Program. (Question: On a scale of 1 to 5. Table includes percentage who answer 4 or 5)

	Control		Participant	
	Before	*After*	*Before*	*After*
Easy start	51%		53%	
Interest	73%	60%	77%	67%
Joininterest		33%		40%
Idea	34%	27%	20%	12%
Easy start	In general, how easy is it to start a business in your country today?			
Interest	How interested are you in someday starting your own business?			
Joininterest	How interested are you in someday joining somebody else's business?			
Idea	Do you have an idea for a business you would like to start			

A number of questions in the survey explored the motivations students had to start a business. These are summarized in table 4.8.

Table 4.8. Importance of various factors in eventual decision to open a business among students in Lebanon before and after participating in the Company Program. (Question: If you were to start your own business in the future, indicate on a scale of 1-5 how important each of the following is in your decision to start a business. Percentage who answer 4 or 5)

| | Control | | Participant | |
	Before	After	Before	After
Work for self	67%	74%	73%	67%
Use skills	88%	95%	94%	86%
Create new ideas	86%	86%	92%	93%
Solve problems	59%	61%	66%	72%
Earn more	70%	81%	70%	79%
Create jobs	61%	64%	64%	74%
Fame	56%	43%	56%	53%
Friends	28%	27%	38%	28%

Work for self   Prefer to work for yourself rather than someone else
Use skills   To use your skills effectively
Create new ideas To be able to create and develop new ideas
Solve problems   To resolve important social problems
Earn more   You can earn more money running your own business
Create jobs   To create jobs and foster economic growth
Fame   To become a famous entrepreneur
Friends   Your friends want to start a business

There are no consistent differences between the group who participated and those who did not participate in the Company Program, or between the responses in the pre- and post- survey. Before participating in the Company Program, the percentage who preferred to work for themselves rather than someone else was 73 percent. The percentage who indicated that they would want to do this to use their skills effectively was 94 percent. Those who indicated that this would allow them to create and develop new ideas were 92 percent. Those who mentioned the ability to resolve important problems were 66 percent. Those who reported that they could earn more money running their own business were 70 percent. Those who mentioned the ability to create jobs and foster economic growth increased from 64 percent. The figures for becoming a famous entrepreneur were 56 percent. To have friends who want to start a business 38 percent.

4.6.6.   Financial Management

Students were asked about their financial management habits in terms of whether they planned how to spend money, used a budget and saved regularly. Table 4.9 summarizes these results. Students participating in the Company Program are more likely to plan how to spend money, to budget and to save than those in the comparison group, even before participating in the program. These differences are greater in the follow-up survey.

Table 4.9. Financial management habits among students in Lebanon before and after participating in the Company Program. (0=no, 1=yes)

	Control		Participant	
	Before	*After*	*Before*	*After*
Plan finances	76%	75%	83%	86%
Budget	65%	69%	75%	84%
Save	56%	54%	64%	70%

Plan finances   When you have money, do you plan ahead for how to spend it?
Budget   Do you use a budget to manage your spending?
Save   Do you regularly save money?

4.6.7.   Attitudes towards Entrepreneurship and Business

Students who participated in the Company Program and those who did not differed in some of their attitudes towards entrepreneurship. For example, those participating were more likely to think that people can get ahead by working hard, more likely to think that entrepreneurs only think about their own gain, more likely to think that most people can be trusted, and more likely to think that entrepreneurs contribute to the economic development of the country.

As shown in table 4.10, about two in five students believe that people in the country can get ahead by working hard. A similar percentage thinks that entrepreneurs only care about their own gain. Four in five believe that women can play an important role in the success of a business. A very small percentage of students –less than 10 percent - believe that most people can be trusted. About one in three believe that there is potential in Lebanon for an entrepreneur to become successful. One in four students believe that men are better qualified than women to be business leaders in the pre-survey, but this figures declines below 10 percent in the post-survey. The percentage of students who believe that entrepreneurs create jobs for others is about one in three at the pre-survey and over half in the post-survey. About one in four students think that when jobs are scarce men should have more rights to jobs than women, this figure declines to about 10 percent in the post-survey. About 68 percent of the students believe that entrepreneurs contribute to the economic development of the country.

Table 4.10. Attitudes towards Entrepreneurship in Lebanon. (Question: On a scale of 1-5, to what extent do you agree or disagree with the following statements)

	Control		Participant	
	Before	*After*	*Before*	*After*
Hard work	36%	41%	44%	42%
Entrepreneurs selfish	59%	42%	64%	37%
Women lead	85%	83%	84%	86%
Trust	8%	7%	12%	5%
Entrepreneurs succeed	35%	34%	37%	40%
Men lead better	27%	8%	27%	9%
Entr. create jobs	30%	58%	39%	56%
Men more rights	27%	10%	28%	9%
Entrepreneurs contribute	37%	68%	53%	67%

Hard work   People in your country can get ahead by working hard.
Entrepreneurs selfish Entrepreneurs only think about their own gain.
Women lead   Women can play an important role in the success of a business.
Trust   Most people can be trusted.
Entrepreneurs succeed There is potential in your country for an
                entrepreneur to become successful.
Men lead better Men are better qualified than women to be business
                leaders.
Entr. create jobs Entrepreneurs create jobs for others.
Men more rights When jobs are scarce, men should have more rights to a
                job than women.
Entrepreneurs contribute Entrepreneurs contribute to the economic
                development of the country.

In addition, students were asked whether they knew someone who was an entrepreneur. Most students know entrepreneurs who are relatives, family members or friends. There are no differences in this respect between the students who participate in the Company Program and those who do not. Over 70 percent of the students have a sibling or a teacher who is an entrepreneur, and about 60 percent have a friend who is an entrepreneur. About one in three has a parent or knows someone who is an entrepreneur.

Table 4.11. Knowledge of Entrepreneurs in Lebanon. (Q: Who among the following people do you know who have started their own business?)

	Control	Participant
Parent	36%	32%
Sibling	77%	81%
Family	21%	15%
Neighbor	41%	39%
Friend	59%	57%
Teacher	72%	60%
Someone else	32%	30%

Furthermore, the group of students who participated in the program and those who did not are very similar in terms of where they imagine they could access funds to create a business. About half of them expect that they could find support within their nuclear family or from a bank, and about one in five from their extended family or government grant.

Table 4.12. Sources of funding in Lebanon. (Q: If you were to start a business, to what extent would you be able to depend on the following financing sources to support your new business? On scale 1-5. Table reports percentage who answered 4 or 5)

	Control	Participant
Nuclear family	49%	48%
Extended family	22%	22%
Friends	12%	10%
Bank	45%	55%
Grant	23%	27%

Nuclear family	Nuclear family
Extended family	Extended family
Friends	Friend
Bank	Bank loans
Grant	Government grants

4.6.8. Knowledge about Entrepreneurship

A few questions in the survey assessed student knowledge of basic concepts of entrepreneurship and business. While there are clear and sizeable differences with the group who had participated in the Company Program demonstrating greater knowledge, this group is far from achieving mastery of these basic knowledge concepts. Percentages of students who answered correctly are reported in Table 4.13.

Table 4.13. Knowledge about entrepreneurship in Lebanon. (Multiple choice questions)

	Control		Participant	
	Before	*After*	*Before*	*After*
Entrepredefine	32%		52%	
Sell shares	13%	41%	21%	65%
Vision	19%	26%	21%	58%
Marketing	46%	56%	73%	88%
Liquidation	12%	38%	27%	49%
Company	17%	43%	37%	58%

Entrepredefine An entrepreneur is someone who
Sell shares   Selling shares of stock to get start-up money for a new company is called:
Vision   A _____ represents a company's dream of where it wants to go and what it wants to be.
Marketing   The work you completed in this scenario above is an example of which of the following:
Liquidation   When a company liquidates, it does which of the following:
Company   By definition, a company must have which of the following

Before participation in the Company Program, students were asked to define an entrepreneur. Only about a third in the comparison group, compared to over half in the group that participated in the Company Program correctly identified 'creates a business' as the correct answer. This question was not asked in the follow up.

When asked to identify the term for selling shares of stock to get start-up money for a new company, only 13 percent in the comparison group and 21 percent in the participant group identified the correct option capitalization before the program. After the program these figures increased to 41 percent and 65 percent respectively.

When asked to fill in the term for the definition of a vision statement only 19 percent of the comparison students and 21 percent of the participant students did so correctly before participating in the program, compared to 26 percent and 58 percent respectively after participating in the program.

When asked to recognize a scenario representing a marketing strategy, 46 percent of the students in the comparison group and 73 percent in the participant group did so correctly before participating in the Company Program, compared to 56 percent and 88 percent respectively after program participation.

When asked to recognize the definition of liquidation, 12 percent in the comparison group and 27 percent in the participant group did so correctly before participating in the Company Program, vs. 38 percent and 49 percent respectively after program participation.

Lastly, when asked to identify that a company must have stockholders, 17 percent of the comparison students and 37 percent of the participant group did so before participating in the program, compared to 43 percent and 58 percent respectively of those who had participated in the program.

4.7. Analysis of Differences between Participants and Non-Participants with Matched Pre- and Post- Questionnaires

As mentioned earlier we were only able to match the pre- and the post-questionnaires of 34 students in the comparison group and 36 students who participated in the Company Program. These students differ in a number of dimensions from the original sample of students, as will become evident in the following section. However, they represent the best group on which to draw conclusions about possible program effects because there is information for all students before and after the Company Program –unlike the previous section, which was based on data for the students who began the study, and for those who completed it, and therefore some of the differences might be simply due to a selection effect, as students who took the post-questionnaire differed, even in the pre-test, from those who did not complete the post-questionnaire.

4.7.1. How Do Participants Spend Their Time and How Do They Differ from the Comparison Group?

There are no differences in the way that students who participate in the program and those who don't spend their time. Most students report spending much time watching TV and radio, chatting with friends, in various forms of entertainment, talking to their parents and studying. Less than a third of the students spend time thinking about their career, researching business opportunities or following the news. These figures are summarized in the table 4.14.

Table 4.14. How much time do students in Lebanon spend on the following activities in a typical week? Responses before participating in the Company Program (Question: On a scale of 1-5, how much time to you spend on the following activities. Table includes percentage who answer that they spent *much time* or a *lot of time*)

	Control	*Participant*
Careers	3%	9%
Research	21%	11%
News	22%	19%
Talk parents	61%	47%
Studying	70%	74%
Entertainment	67%	67%
Chatting friends	70%	83%
TV and Radio	81%	88%

Careers	Investigating career possibilities
Research	Research potential ideas for a new business
News	Following the news
Talk parents	Talking to your parents about career possibilities
Studying	Studying or working on school-related activities
Entertainment	Keeping up-to-date on entertainment, fashion or sports
Chatting friends	Chatting with friends
TV and Radio	Watching TV or listening to music

4.7.2.   How Do Participants and Non-Participants Differ before and after Participation?

In this section, we compare two matched groups: the 34 students in the comparison group who did not participate in the Company Program and the 36 students who participated in the Company Program, both before and after the program.[11]

4.7.2.1. Aspirations, Views of Self and Worldviews

Overall, students have high aspirations and fairly dynamic worldviews in both groups. There are no apparent differences in the changes before and after of both groups, suggesting that participation in the Company Program does not influence them for the matched students.

Each of these aspirations and worldviews was measured with a five-point scale in which students were asked to rate themselves from completely disagree (1) with completely agree (5). In table 4.15, we have calculated the percentages for each item represented by the students who selected agree or completely agree (points 4 and 5 in the scale).

---

[11] Fewer participants were surveyed after the Program partly due to logistical reasons tracking down students.

Table 4.15. Aspirations and worldviews towards future and self of students in Lebanon before and after participating in the Company Program. (Question: On a scale of 1-5, to what extent do you agree or disagree with the following statements about yourself. Table includes percentage who answer 4 or 5)

	Control		Participant	
	Before	*After*	*Before*	*After*
Achieve goals	71%	65%	89%	92%
Learn from failure	91%	85%	86%	83%
Challenges opport.	62%	74%	75%	83%
Outside school	48%	53%	50%	61%
Studying matters	70%		75%	
Educ matters	85%	68%	86%	77%
Learnfuture	71%		67%	
Negotiate	82%	71%	89%	77%
Leadership	58%	74%	78%	69%
Set goals	82%	71%	81%	81%
Creativity		76%		72%

Achieve goals	I trust that in the future, I will achieve my goals.
Learn from failure	If I fail at something, I try to figure out why so that I can succeed the next time.
Challenges opport.	I see challenges as opportunities.
Outside school	Participate in activities outside of school to prepare for my future.
Studying matters	Studying is important to me
Educ matters	I go to school because education is important for getting a job later.
Learnfuture	The things that I am learning now will help me in the future
Negotiate	I believe that achieving my goals requires negotiating with others.
Leadership	I can see myself in a leadership position in the future.
Set goals	I set goals for myself in order to attain the things I want..
Creativity	I try to find creative solutions to problems

4.7.2.2. Perceived Self-Efficacy

Students were asked to what extent they felt capable of performing a series of tasks. Table 4.16 summarizes the percentage of those students who felt capable of doing them to a great extent –values 4 and 5 in the 5-point scale. In the majority of the dimensions evaluated, there are no differences between the students who participated in the Company Program and those who did not or in the changes observed between the pre- and the post-tests for each group. The only differences are a greater ability to present in front of peers and adults for both groups in the post-survey, and greater clarity about purpose in life for students in the Company Program.

A greater percentage of the students who participate in the Company Program feel more prepared to compete for a job after the program than before and find that what they learn is relevant to the real world. Paradoxically, in both group a lower percentage feels prepared to conduct research in the post-survey than in the pre-survey.

Table 4.16. Perception of Self-Efficacy of students in Lebanon before and after participating in the Company Program. (Question: On a scale of 1-5, to what extent do you feel that you are able to. Table includes percentage who answer 4 or 5)

	Control		Participant	
	Before	*After*	*Before*	*After*
Teamwork	67%	74%	89%	72%
Adapt	79%	76%	81%	69%
Problemsolve	73%	85%	89%	86%
Presentpeers	55%	68%	69%	81%
Presentadult	58%	65%	66%	78%
Resolvediff	64%	70%	74%	71%
Purpose	58%		60%	
Commproblem	45%	48%	57%	57%
Persuade	66%	68%	83%	71%
Negconflict	70%	74%	81%	67%
Competejob	91%	74%	86%	91%
Startbusiness	66%	65%	75%	72%
Rolebusiness	45%	37%	58%	53%
Leadteam	64%	56%	83%	60%
Research	67%	50%	77%	53%
Learnrealworld	41%	41%	37%	44%

Teamwork	Work with a team to accomplish a result
Adapt	Adapt to new situations
Problemsolve	Solve problems
Presentpeers	Present a topic to a group of classmates
Presentadult	Present a topic to a group of adults
Resolvediff	Resolve differences within a group to reach a solution satisfactory to most
Purpose	Understand your purpose in life
Commproblem	Solve community problems
Persuade	Persuade a group of people about an idea
Negconflict	Negotiate personal conflicts in a peaceful way
Competejob	Be competitive in securing a good job
Startbusiness	Start and run your own business someday
Rolebusiness	Understand the role of business owners in our economy
Leadteam	Lead the members of a group to meet a deadline in producing a

result
Research   Research the potential market for a company
Learnrealworld To what extent is there a clear connection between what you
                are learning in school and the real world?

4.7.2.3. Educational Aspirations

There are significant differences between the educational aspirations of the students who took the post-questionnaire and those who took the pre-questionnaire for both groups. For those in the control group, at pre-test, 15 percent aspired to complete university and 85 percent aspired to complete post-graduate studies. At post-test, the respective figures were 6 percent and 91 percent. For those in the Company Program, these figures were 17 percent who aspired to completed university and 81 percent who aspired to complete graduate studies at pre-test, vs. 17 percent and 77 percent after participating in the program. This suggests that for the matched sample there is a drop in educational aspirations among those who participate in the program.

A higher percentage of the students reported plans to continue with their studies immediately after leaving secondary study at post-test than at pre-test. For those in the comparison group these figures were 84 percent vs. 91 percent, and for those who participated in the Company Program the figures were 74 percent vs. 89 percent.

4.7.2.4. Motivations for Choosing a Job

We asked students to what extent a range of reasons were important to them in choosing a particular job. There were very few differences between those students who participated in the Company Program and those in the comparison group, although there were increases in the percentage selecting some of these motivations in both groups. Before and after the program, students who participated in the program were more likely to select a job based on its status, income or career possibilities than those who did not participate. The percentage who indicated that they would select a job based on its status among those students who participated in the Company Program increased from 71 percent to 83 percent. While the percentage of students who indicated that they would chose a job based on the ability to work without supervision increased for those in the comparison group as well as those participating in the Company Program, the increase was almost three times greater for those participating, from 50 percent at pre-test to 77 percent at post-test, compared to 58 percent versus 67 percent in the comparison group. Also the percentage of students participating in the Company Program who expressed confidence in successfully completing a job interview and in being hired in the private sector increased significantly from 69 percent to 83 percent for confidence to complete an interview successfully, and from 81 percent to 94 percent for confidence of being hired in the private sector.

Table 4.17. Motivations for Choosing a Job of students in Lebanon before and after participating in the Company Program. (Question: On a scale of 1 to 5, to what extent are the following reasons important to you in choosing a particular job? Percentage who answer 4 and 5)

	Control		Participant	
	Before	*After*	*Before*	*After*
Status	69%	64%	71%	83%
Money	71%	74%	83%	81%
Career	85%	82%	94%	89%
Uses skills	94%	97%	94%	89%
Job security	79%	74%	80%	75%
Role deciding	73%	67%	75%	81%
Ample vacation	42%	24%	42%	39%
Easy pace	47%	38%	44%	47%
Autonomy	58%	67%	50%	77%
Family friendly	61%	42%	51%	56%
Jobcolleagues		65%		61%
Confidence interview	74%	70%	69%	83%
Confidence hired	66%	76%	81%	94%

Status   High status of job
Money   Ability to earn a lot of money
Career   Good promotion prospects, clear career path
Uses skills   Uses my skills and abilities
Job security Job security
Role deciding Gives me a role in decision making
Ample vacation Has a lot of vacation time
Easy pace   Easy pace of work
Autonomy   Ability to work independently without supervision
Family friendly Job that is family friendly
Confidence interview How much confidence do you have that you could successfully complete a job interview?
Confidence hired How much confidence do you have that you could be hired to work in the private sector?

4.7.2.5. Interest in Starting a Business and Motivations for Business Creation

Students were asked for their views on the ease of starting a business and their interest in starting one. At baseline, about 35 percent thought it was easy to start a business (Table 4.18).

In response to the question of how interested they were in starting a business someday in the country, about two thirds of them said they were interested or very interested, and this did not change much after participation in the program.

To the group after participation in the Company Program, we asked how interested they were in someday joining somebody else's business. Over a third said that they were interested or very interested.

We asked students whether they had an idea for a business they would like to start. A greater percentage replied yes in the comparison group than in the Company Program group.

Table 4.18. Interest in opening a business among students in Lebanon before and after participating in the Company Program. (Question: On a scale of 1 to 5. Table includes percentage who answer 4 or 5)

| | Control | | Participant | |
	Before	*After*	*Before*	*After*
Easy start	36%		44%	
Interest	62%	61%	69%	64%
Joininterest		42%		36%
Idea	38%	24%	11%	14%

Easy start	In general, how easy is it to start a business in your country today?
Interest	How interested are you in someday starting your own business?
Joininterest	How interested are you in someday joining somebody else's business?
Idea	Do you have an idea for a business you would like to start

A number of questions in the survey explored the motivations students had to start a business. These are summarized in table 4.19.

Table 4.19. Importance of various factors in eventual decision to open a business among students in Lebanon before and after participating in the Company Program. (Question: If you were to start your own business in the future, indicate on a scale of 1-5 how important each of the following is in your decision to start a business. Percentage who answer 4 or 5)

	Control		Participant	
	Before	*After*	*Before*	*After*
Work for self	52%	75%	72%	64%
Use skills	94%	100%	92%	83%
Create new ideas	87%	91%	94%	92%
Solve problems	56%	66%	64%	72%
Earn more	72%	88%	72%	81%
Create jobs	63%	66%	72%	72%
Fame	55%	50%	50%	58%
Friends	23%	28%	20%	31%

Work for self Prefer to work for yourself rather than someone else
Use skills   To use your skills effectively
Create new ideas To be able to create and develop new ideas
Solve problems To resolve important social problems
Earn more   You can earn more money running your own business
Create jobs   To create jobs and foster economic growth
Fame   To become a famous entrepreneur
Friends   Your friends want to start a business

There are no consistent differences between the group who participated and those who did not participate in the Company Program, or between the responses in the pre- and post-survey.

4.7.2.6. Financial Management

Students were asked about their financial management habits in terms of whether they planned how to spend money, used a budget, and saved regularly. Table 4.20 summarizes these results. Students participating in the Company Program report modest increases in planning how to spend money, to budget although similar increases are observed in the comparison group.

Table 4.20. Financial management habits among students in Lebanon before and after participating in the Company Program. (0=no, 1=yes)

	Control		Participant	
	Before	*After*	*Before*	*After*
Plan finances	85%	82%	75%	83%
Budget	55%	76%	72%	81%
Save	59%	53%	67%	69%

Plan finances When you have money, do you plan ahead for how to spend it?
Budget   Do you use a budget to manage your spending?
Save   Do you regularly save money?

4.7.2.7. Attitudes towards Entrepreneurship and Business

More students expressed favorable views towards entrepreneurship in the post-test than in the pre-test, for both groups. More believed that people in Lebanon can get ahead by working hard, that there is potential in Lebanon for an entrepreneur to succeed, that entrepreneurs create jobs for others and that entrepreneurs contribute to the economic development of the country.

Table 4.21. Attitudes towards entrepreneurship in Lebanon. (Question: On a scale of 1-5, to what extent do you agree or disagree with the following statements)

	Control		Participant	
	Before	*After*	*Before*	*After*
Hard work	39%	59%	35%	42%
Entrepreneurs selfish	66%	53%	58%	39%
Women lead	88%	88%	86%	83%
Trust	6%	3%	0%	6%
Entrepreneurs succeed	40%	41%	29%	36%
Men lead better	22%	12%	9%	11%
Entr. create jobs	29%	65%	16%	50%
Men more rights	19%	12%	12%	11%
Entrepreneurs contribute	26%	68%	44%	64%

Hard work   People in your country can get ahead by working hard.
Entrepreneurs selfish   Entrepreneurs only think about their own gain.
Women lead   Women can play an important role in the success of a business.
Trust   Most people can be trusted.
Entrepreneurs succeed There is potential in your country for an
            entrepreneur to become successful.
Men lead better Men are better qualified than women to be business leaders.
Entr. create jobs Entrepreneurs create jobs for others.
Men more rights When jobs are scarce, men should have more rights to a job
            than women.
Entrepreneurs contribute Entrepreneurs contribute to the economic
            development of the country.

In addition, students were asked whether they knew someone who was an entrepreneur. There are no differences between both groups in this respect at pre-test.

Table 4.22. Knowledge of Entrepreneurs in Lebanon. (Q: Who among the following people do you know who have started their own business?)

	Control	Participant
Parent	41%	29%
Sibling	85%	85%
Family	15%	17%
Neighbor	34%	41%
Friend	61%	50%
Teacher	74%	74%
Someone else	30%	29%

Furthermore, the group of students who participated in the program and those who did not are very similar in terms of where they imagine they could access funds to create a business.

Table 4.23. Sources of funding in Lebanon. (Q: If you were to start a business, to what extent would you be able to depend on the following financing sources to support your new business? On scale 1-5. Table reports percentage who answered 4 or 5)

	Control	Participant
Nuclear family	42%	50%
Extended family	24%	17%
Friends	13%	11%
Bank	48%	58%
Grant	32%	24%

Nuclear family	Nuclear family
Extended family	Extended family
Friends	Friend
Bank	Bank loans
Grant	Government grants

4.7.2.8. Knowledge about Entrepreneurship

A few questions in the survey assessed student knowledge of basic concepts of entrepreneurship and business. A significantly greater percentage of students who participated in the Company Program answered these questions correctly after the program than before and these gains were greater than gains that took place for students in the comparison group. For instance the definition of capitalization was correctly identified by 6 percent of students in the Company Program at pre-test, compared to 61 percent at the post-test. The vision of a company was correctly defined by 31 percent of the students at pre-test, increasing to 56 percent at post-test. The correct definition of marketing increased from 61 percent to 86 percent. The correct definition of liquidation increased form 11 percent of the students at pre-test to 50 percent at post-test. The percentage of students who could correctly define a company increased from 31 percent to 61 percent. Percentages of students who answered correctly are reported in Table 4.24.

Table 4.24. Knowledge about entrepreneurship in Lebanon. (Multiple choice questions)

	Control		Participant	
	Before	*After*	*Before*	*After*
Entrepredefine	29%		47%	
Sell shares	9%	50%	6%	61%
Vision	32%	29%	31%	56%
Marketing	47%	71%	61%	86%
Liquidation	12%	50%	11%	50%
Company	24%	56%	31%	61%

Entrepredefine An entrepreneur is someone who

Sell shares   Selling shares of stock to get start-up money for a new company
is called:

Vision   A _____ represents a company's dream of where it wants to go and what it wants to be.

Marketing   The work you completed in this scenario above is an example of which of the following:

Liquidation   When a company liquidates, it does which of the following:

Company   By definition, a company must have which of the following

4.8. How Do Students Who Participated in the Company Program Describe Its Effects?

When asked to rate themselves in a series of questions about possible effects of the program, most participants who were surveyed after the program are favorable about the changes they observe in themselves; however, results are not as strong as one might suspect given a comparison both with non-participating Lebanese students and to participants in other countries that we have surveyed. To further examine the effects that students who participated in the Company Program attribute to their participation, during the final competition students were asked a series of additional questions. This section focuses on these retrospective questions.

The first set of questions was asked not only of participants but also non-participants and dropouts. These questions asked the students to compare themselves at the end of the school year to where they were at the beginning of the school year and to assess their capabilities in a variety of areas. Table 4.25 reports answers from matched participants (those for whom we have specific results both from pre- and post-surveys).

Table 4.25. Retrospective experience in Lebanon (Compare yourself now to where you were at the beginning of the school year. On a scale of 1-5, to what extent do you agree with the following statements about yourself. Table reports percentage who answered 4 or 5.)

	Control	Participant
	After	*After*
Leadership	69%	69%
Finances	56%	77%
Education goals	71%	60%
Career goals	69%	61%
Competitive	75%	78%
Know entrepreneurship	34%	58%
Start business	41%	56%

Leadership	I feel more empowered to take a leadership role in the workforce in the future.
Finances	I realize more that knowing how to effectively manage my finances is important.
Education goals	I have developed (or further developed) my educational goals.
Career goals	I have developed (or further developed) my career goals.
Competitive	I am more confident in my ability to successfully compete in the workforce in the future.
Know entrepreneurship	I know more about entrepreneurship.
Start business	I am more interested in starting my own business.

Overall, positive feelings reported about empowerment in the areas under analysis by participants are not extremely high. The most positive responses received regarded realization of importance of managing finances, with 77 percent of Injaz participants agreeing that they were more aware of this importance at the end of the school year than non-participants. Also, in terms of confidence in ability to compete in the workforce in the future, 78 percent of Injaz participants were more confident, although this compares to a nearly equal 75 percent among non-participants. Barely a majority of participants felt that they knew more about entrepreneurship (58%) and were more interested in starting a business (56%) than they were at the beginning of the year; however, it should be noted that these rates are much higher than those for non-participants at 34 percent and 41 percent respectively.

Still, when asked specifically about the effect of the Injaz Company Program on their own abilities in specific areas, 91 percent of the participating students found the Company Program experience valuable or very valuable. Table 4.26 reports participant responses about the specific effect of the Company Program on various aspects of their personal development and worldviews.

Table 4.26. Contribution of the Company Program in Lebanon. (In your opinion, on a scale of 1-5, to what extent did your participation in the Injaz Company Program help you with the following:)

	Participant			Participant
	After			*After*
Valuable	91%		Budgeting	84%
Empathy	73%		Problem solve	82%
Team work	88%		Decide	85%
Citizenship	74%		Communicate	67%
Innovation	81%		Negotiate	82%
Critical thinking	82%		Sell	79%
Business	79%		Speak	76%
Initiative	91%		Creativity	76%
Leadership	75%			

Valuable	In general, how valuable did you find participating in the Injaz company program
Empathy	It helped me develop understanding of other people's views.
Team work	It helped me develop the ability to work with others as a team.
Citizenship	It helped me develop citizenship skills.
Innovation	It helped me develop the capacity to innovate.
Critical thinking	It taught me critical thinking skills.
Business	It taught me useful business skills.
Initiative	It helped me development initiative and self-motivation.
Leadership	It helped me develop my abilities as a leader.
Budgeting	It taught me how to manage a budget.
Problem solve	It helped me learn to solve problems.
Decide	It helped me to become a better decision maker.
Communicate	It helped me learn to communicate with others.
Negotiate	It helped me learn to negotiate differences with people.
Sell	It helped me learn to sell ideas or products.
Speak	It helped me learn to speak in public more easily.
Creativity	It inspired me to think more creatively about problems.

The strongest effect of the Company Program, from the perspective of participants, seems to be related to the development of initiative and self-motivation, where 91 percent of participants attribute personal improvement to participation in the program. Similarly, 88 percent of participants reported that the program helped them to develop teamwork skills. Strong responses from participants, at or above 80 percent reporting agreement or strong agreement, are also found in the areas of innovation thinking, critical thinking, managing a budget, decision making skills, negotiation skills, problem solving.

Finally, students were also asked to evaluate some of the components of the program (Table 4.27). Most of them say lectures aroused their interest in the topics, that the volunteer presented the content clearly, held lectures in an interactive way, and was helpful and responsive to questions. However, overall, reported rates suggest that a sizeable population of participants did not feel positively about how these aspects of the program were delivered. Importantly, only half of participants found the Student Guide useful or very useful. Finally, all participants would recommend the Company Program to friends or family.

Table 4.27. Evaluation of the Components of the Program in Lebanon. (On a scale of 1-5, to what extent do you agree with the following comments about the Injaz Company Program)

	Participant
	After
Lecture	63%
Volunclear	75%
Volunrespond	75%
Studguide	50%
Volunlecture	69%
Recommend	100%

4.9. A Qualitative Analysis of Student Descriptions of Program Effects

Within the follow-up survey, students were provided the opportunity to answer an open-ended question regarding their experience with the Company Program: *"Use the following space to provide any comments –*

positive or negative – about your experience in the Injaz Company Program." Of the 43 participants for whom we secured follow-up surveys, only 16 used this opportunity to express views –either positive or negative – about the program. Moreover, the majority of responses were not detailed. However, a review of these responses provides an opportunity to round out our understanding of the outcomes most important to the program's participants while providing some critiques for Injaz to use in revising operational approaches in coming years.

By and large, the responses from students were positive. In fact, 13 respondents (81%) used this question only to provide positive reactions to their participation. Two individuals critiqued aspects of the program but in the context of an overall positive response, while one individual used the space solely to critique the program. Regarding positive feedback, the majority of individuals stated generally that the program had been a positive experience without detailing ways in which they benefitted from the program. (In fact, some are absolutely glowing in their appreciation for the program.) However, several students highlighted how program participation had empowered them to speak or express themselves in public (3), improved their knowledge of how to run a business (2), bolstered their self-confidence (1) and sense of character (2), improved their ability to make decisions in a rational way (1), helped them with personal interactions (1), and encouraged them to act and think creatively (1). One student emphasized that the program had helped him change his career goals. Provided critiques focused largely on logistical issues (see below).

Positive Responses

"It helped me become a stronger person who is not afraid to express her opinion in public. I can express myself in a more creative way."

"It was a positive experience. :)"

"One of the best experiences in my life."

"A really nice experience! And a useful one: I won't forget it and I will use it as a tool for my future."

"The Injaz program helped me a lot: in a business manner (how to sell), how to talk with people. It gave me more self-confidence [when] interacting with my friends."

"The Injaz program was great, although I was dismissed couple of times!"

"It is such a great experience. It changed me a lot. It built a part of my character and allowed me to see the other part of life: work and reality. It is hard and it takes <u>a lot</u> of time, but it is worth it! I'm so proud of this program. It's amazing. And I wish my company the best of luck. Thank you, Injaz. I am hoping to live up to all your expectations."

"I learned a lot from this experience! It helped me make some changes about my future career."

"Helpful – improves public speaking."

"It is very helpful; it developed our character."

"Very helpful and a great experience, full of good times and knowledge. I enjoyed it greatly and I now have a clearer idea about the business world."

"Useful. [The program] helps in making decisions and rational thinking."

"It was 'a walk to remember...!'"

Mixed Responses

"We had a great experience, but I think the Company Program is somehow not close to reality."

"It has been an unbelievable experience; however, if the final report and competition could have been rescheduled until after exams, it would have been much easier."

Critiques

"There should be more coordination and follow up from Injaz. Our school didn't get the materials CD-ROM until the last day, which means we worked hard to find the documents on our own while others had them on the CD."

4.10. Discussion

While the results highlighted above must be viewed with caution, given the potential for selection bias and the attrition we faced in collecting data, they suggest that Injaz's Company Program provides a learning environment that offers Lebanese youth with valuable experiences and skills that they are not getting through the traditional school curriculum. Participating students end up with valuable soft skills and skills and knowledge about entrepreneurship. They also have positive views of what they learned as a result of participating in the Company Program. There is no apparent impact of the program in student aspirations and worldviews, in perceived self-efficacy in a range of soft skills, in educational aspirations, or motivations to choose a job.

In regard to Injaz's primary goal of encouraging more youth to become entrepreneurs, our results do not suggest that the Company Program has effects in this regard. About two-thirds of the students before and after the program are interested in starting a business, and a very small proportion of students have an actual idea for a business. Student participants also do not differ from non-participants in terms of the motivations that would lead them to open a business. Tangible evidence of efforts to start a business is not found in the data, which is natural given both that the students surveyed are still in school, and the vast majority of them plan to go on to university or higher education before entering the labor market as well as the fact that the follow-up survey was carried out only a few months after the conclusion of the program. However, one would expect participating students to show an increase in their interest in starting a business of their own. Instead, student interest remains stagnant, and in fact declines slightly, after participation in the program.

Along similar lines, Injaz participants have mixed feelings about business and entrepreneurship more generally. Following participation, participants are highly likely to see entrepreneurs as playing an important part in job creation and economic growth, but similar increases are seen among the control group. This is perhaps reflective of the public attention that entrepreneurship has received in Lebanon and the region as a whole in the past few years. Overall, participants are more likely to have a positive view of entrepreneurs as contributors to the greater good. Moreover, they demonstrate a (slightly) better grasp of basic business concepts than non-participants. However, this does not translate into a perception that entering into business is an easy thing. When asked whether people can get ahead in Lebanon by working hard, participants registered a particular drop when compared with views of non-participants and, notably, no participants at the close of the program agreed that starting a business in Lebanon was easy to do. While on the surface, this might seem a negative outcome from the program, it is also possible that participation ensured that participants were cured of the perception that starting one's own business is a simple task. As such, they may do so with eyes wide open, ensuring greater long-term success. There are gains in knowledge of basic concepts of entrepreneurship for students in the participant, as well as in the comparison, group.

What factors could account for the mixed results we have observed in our analysis of the Company Program in Lebanon? First and foremost, the high rates of attrition from the study and even in the selection of initial treatment and control groups could be giving us a biased sample. Secondly, the sample of parochial schools survey might not generalize to students attending other type of schools. Thirdly, a factor in which Injaz should look into in more depth, is whether the program is being carried out within Lebanon in an ineffective way. In their open-ended remarks, students did not criticize the program's operation extensively, but several reflected on issues related to organization, late delivery of materials, etc. This suggests that there are logistical problems that might also affect the quality of instruction during the program.

In addition, one should consider the Lebanese context on a more macro level: as perhaps the most dynamic country in the Arab world in regard to small business, entrepreneurship and educational outcomes, it is arguable that Lebanese students, compared with peers elsewhere in the Arab world, are able to develop the business knowledge and life skills taught through Injaz through other sources. As such, Injaz's Company Program might not provide the unique example of education that it does in other countries and may not have the impact that it would have were students to have less exposure to business and job-relevant skills that they do through alternative sources.

In parallel, entrepreneurship in Lebanon is a much more highly competitive environment than it is in other parts of the Arab world. As such, Injaz's Company Program may actually be opening the eyes of participants in regard to the complexities of doing business in this competitive environment. This may be reinforced by volunteers who, while well intended, may be painting an accurate picture of the challenges of entrepreneurship while students outside of the program are more than likely pulling in an unfiltered picture of entrepreneurship as it is promoted in the media as a solution to youth unemployment challenges in the country. This is conjecture, with no results from our study to support it. However, it should be considered when one is assessing the mixed quantitative results of our study.

However inconclusive the quantitative results are, the feedback from students to the open-ended question should not be discounted. As noted above, student reactions to Injaz are extremely positive. However general these student comments are, they reflect a learning opportunity that is unique, exciting and plays a strong role in shifting mindsets about education, careers, and the transition from school to work in a positive way.

4.11.   Policy and Program Implications

Overall, the findings suggest that Injaz Lebanon creates a positive experience on student participants. However, our results are mixed and suggest, at least on the surface, that the impact of the program is limited in the Lebanese context. To explore this further, it is suggested that Injaz undertake a detailed study of the logistics and operations of the program as it is carried out in Lebanon in an effort to ensure that materials are reaching students, that volunteers are effectively teaching and leading the program (and sending the messages to students).

Currently, Injaz Lebanon works with the Ministry of Education to provide its programs, including the Company Program, in a relatively small sample of Lebanese schools in major urban areas like Beirut and Tripoli. As pointed before, we cannot forget that data analyzed in this document comes from parochial schools with largely Christian student populations (even though the program itself is delivered to a more diverse range of schools). The positive results would suggest that there would be benefit to offering the program to students in a larger number of schools across the country. Nevertheless, expanding the services provided through Injaz would require support from the Ministry of Education and local school administrators, all of whom are already facing challenges related to the administration of school calendars and curriculum demands.

At the same time, expanding the program would require additional support from the private sector, both in terms of the provision of volunteers who serve as instructors and financial support needed to cover costs related to instructional materials and the national competition. Part of the power of the Injaz approach is its engagement with volunteers from the private sector, who bring tremendous experience with them and are able to contextualize student learning in a way that trainers with no private sector experience could not. By depending on volunteers in this regard, however, Injaz will occasionally engage a volunteer whose business obligations conflict with commitments to the program or who do not communicate well with students, as noted in our qualitative analysis. In this context, it is important to realize that expansion of the program might come at the cost of dimensioning returns, if for no other reason than it would strain Injaz's logistical capacities and that, as Injaz depends on a growing number of volunteers, the program might have to be less selective in its identification of volunteers.

At the same time, our analysis raises some program process issues that Injaz Lebanon should address as it works to expand its offerings within Lebanon:

First, the way in which the program is offered in most schools – as a class during school hours in which participants are selected rather than opting in – means that students are not there by choice and that some will, in this context, not fully engage with or get much out of the program. Data from these students may not be reflected in our results due to selection bias. In this case, Injaz – and more engaged students – may benefit from more selectivity in participant selection. Running the Company Program as an extra-curricular activity that participants must sign up for would ensure that participants are more engaged in the course. At the same time, Injaz's other programs – which provide shorter, more focused interventions than the Company Program – can serve as a means of introducing a wider group of youth through classroom activities to entrepreneurial concepts, building the number of youth who would seek out the experience provided by the Company Program.

In the future, Injaz must work more closely with the Ministry of Education to ensure that it has early access to school at the beginning of the school year and is able to implement the Company Program in a way that imposes less stress on student participants. According to feedback from students, this means extending the course over a longer time period and spreading out the time cost of participation. Importantly, holding the national competition at a time when it does not conflict with comprehensive examinations would ensure that students are better able to focus on the program and improving their student companies for competition. Injaz might also consider offering the Company Program to youth prior to their final year in school in order to avoid this conflict. At the same time, however, there is something to the argument that by running the competition at the same time as comprehensive examinations provides students with an important experience with managing time constraints that would benefit them in the future.

Finally, while our analysis strongly point to a change on student self-efficacy, soft skills development and interest in business (both self-employment and private sector employment), it should be noted that the results herein should not be taken to represent the causal evidence of impact that would be provided in the context of a more rigorous impact evaluation. The team suggests that Injaz should engage in an experimental evaluation that is able both to determine the exact causal relationship between participation in the program and outcomes in regard to entrepreneurial activity, job-relevant skills development, and employment. Moreover, such an evaluation should take place over a longer time span, allowing for an assessment of actual outcomes within the labor market after youth leave school.

Chapter 5. An exploratory study of the Injaz Company Program in Morocco

5.1. Introduction

Over the past two decades, Morocco has undergone a demographic transition. As a result, the country has experienced a tremendous surge in its youth population. Currently, over 19 percent of the country's population is between the ages of 15 and 24, and 29 percent is between the ages of 15 and 29. This "youth bulge" has put led to tremendous pressures on the country's labor markets, as such a large share of the population is concurrently seeking to make the transition from school to work. In this context, the Moroccan economy has failed to create the jobs necessary to absorb the growing number of young workers into the ranks of the employed. In 2010, the youth unemployment rate (ages 15-24) in Morocco reached 17.6 percent. Moreover, in urban areas, it was as high as 31.3 percent, a number that must be understood in the context of poor economic outcomes in rural areas and high rates of migration to urban centers by those seeking employment.[12]

The reasons behind the poor economic outcomes for Moroccan youth are complex. One important issue that has been put forward is the gap between the skills that youth leaving the school system bring to the labor market and the needs of current employers. Despite relatively high educational spending and continuous efforts at reform, Morocco's school system continues to struggle in meeting its basic goals. Youth literacy remains at a low 79 percent. Moreover, in international examinations of student performance, such as the Trends in International Mathematics and Sciences Study (TIMSS), Moroccan students scored poorly in the application of mathematics and science knowledge: in 2007, the

---

[12] Between 2005-2010, the urban population in Morocco grew by 1.9% a year, while the rural population grew by 0.05%.

performance of eight-grade students in Morocco on the TIMSS examinations earned an average of 381 in mathematics and 303 in sciences, compared with the international scale average of 500.[13]

In addition to the results of these quantitative assessments of skills, Moroccan private sector leaders routinely decry the lack of more intangible soft skills among young job seekers. Recently, when Moroccan CEOs were asked whether the school system provided people with adequate skills and sufficient qualities to the economy, only 53 percent reported affirmatively that they were able to find those with the skills they needed and 48 percent affirmed that they were able to find those with other qualities for which they were looking.[14] In particular, the report notes a demand for communications skills, teamwork, self-motivation and initiative, creative and innovative thinking, flexibility and leadership. These soft skills are not developed adequately by an educational system that continues to favor rote memorization and theoretical knowledge.

5.2. Injaz Morocco and the Company Program

With these skills gaps in mind, Injaz Morocco has been working with the Ministry of Education and local schools to deliver a broad base of entrepreneurship training opportunities to Moroccan youth through the school system. By working with local volunteers from the business

---

[13] Mullis, I.V.S., Martin, M.O., & Foy, P. (with Olson, J.F., Preuschoff, C., Erberber, E., Arora, A., & Galia, J.), *TIMSS 2007 International Mathematics Report: Findings from IEA's Trends in International Mathematics and Science Study at the Fourth and Eighth Grades* (Chestnut Hill, MA: TIMSS & PIRLS International Study Center, Boston College, 2008); Martin, M.O., Mullis, I.V.S., & Foy, P. (with Olson, J.F., Erberber, E., Preuschoff, C., & Galia, J.), *TIMSS 2007 International Science Report: Findings from IEA's Trends in International Mathematics and Science Study at the Fourth and Eighth Grades* (Chestnut Hill, MA: TIMSS & PIRLS International Study Center, Boston College, 2008)

[14] Mohammed bin Rashid Foundation, *Arab Human Capital Challenge: The Voice of CEOs* (Dubai: Mohammed bin Rashid Foundation, 2009).

community, Injaz seeks to provide young Moroccans with opportunities to develop the basic business skills and financial literacy they need to start and run their own businesses, while developing the softer job-ready skills that are in increasing demand by the private sector through an experiential learning environment.

Towards this end, Injaz Morocco provides intermediate, secondary and university students with a number of programs in which they are able to participate as part of their school curriculum (see table 5.1). For each of these programs, Injaz provides instructional materials, secures and trains volunteers to run the programs, and works with local school administrators to arrange for program delivery within schools. Particular programs range from day-long interventions like Innovation Camp to programs carried out over the course of the academic year, like the Company Program. The *Company Program* is the banner program among Injaz's offerings in Morocco.

Table 5.1: Injaz Programs Offered in Morocco

Program name	Duration	Age group	Purpose
Banks in Action	8 sessions	Secondary/ university	Promotes understanding of banking fundamentals and operations of competitive banks.
Be Entrepreneurial	Variable	Secondary	Interactive classroom activities aimed to encourage youth to start their own businesses before leaving school.
Business Ethics	7-12 sessions	Secondary	Fosters student's ethical decision-making as they prepare to enter the workforce
Success Skills	7 sessions	Secondary	Works with students to prepare them for job search and interview skills.
Job Shadow	4 sessions	Secondary/ university	Prepares students for careers with 3 classroom sessions and an on-site orientation in the workplace.
Economics for Success	6 sessions	Secondary	Introduces students to personal finance and educational and career options.
More than Money	6 sessions	Grades 3-5	Teaches students about earning, saving and spending money responsibly.
Entrepreneurship Master Class	1 day	Grades 10-12	Introduction to entrepreneurship and self-employment
Community Citizenship	Variable	Secondary/ university	Class participates in a community service project
Innovation Camp	1 day	Secondary/ university	Participants discuss a particular business challenge and develop potential solutions.
Company Program	4-6 months	Secondary/ university	Participants develop a business plan, launch a business, market and sell their product and then liquidate the business for first-hand experience in entrepreneurship.

In Morocco, as in the rest of the countries, we had planned to design a study in which students who participated in the Company Program would fill out a questionnaire before and after participating. A group of students not participating in the program from comparable schools or classes within the same schools would also complete a pre-post survey. While the assignment of students to participation in the program would not be random, we had expected that the pre-post comparison and the existence of a quasi-comparison group would have allowed us to reach conclusions about plausible program effects.

In practice, however, the data in Morocco were collected in ways that differed significantly from these intended plans. At baseline, 267 students from 14 schools completed the questionnaire before starting the program. In the follow-up phase, 113 students from 15 schools were added to the study. These were students who participated in the program but were not administered the baseline questionnaire. If these 15 schools are excluded from the analysis, we have post-data for 75 students from 10 schools who participated in the Company Program. In addition, we were not able to directly link the post-data for these 75 students with their pre-questionnaire. In the following section of this report, we focus only on the 267 students who participated in the pre-questionnaire, and compare them with the 75 students who took the post-questionnaire and at times also with the 219 students in the intended control group also at pre-test. Because no post-data are available for the control group, some of the planned comparisons are not possible.

5.3. Who Participates in the Company Program?

In this section of the report, we characterize the 267 students who completed the questionnaire before participating in the Company Program.

In terms of broad demographics, girls are significantly more likely to participate than males, as 63 percent of the students are female. The students range in age from 15 to 21 years old, while most students (84%) are between the ages of 15 and 17.

The level of parental education varies, with fathers having higher levels of education than mothers. Whereas 32 percent of the fathers have only secondary education or less, 16 percent have a post-secondary diploma, 26 percent have a university degree and 23 percent have a post-graduate degree. In contrast, 51 percent of the mothers have a secondary education or less, 17 percent have a post-secondary degree, 20 percent have a university degree and 11 percent have a post-graduate degree.

Fathers of the students who participate in the program have a range of occupations. A third work as government employees, police or armed forces, or in a public sector company. A fifth of them work in a large private sector company and 8 percent in a small private sector company. A small percentage of them work in a family business (4%) or are self-employed (17%). None define their work as housework, and only 3 percent are unemployed. Less than 1 percent are outside the labor force or retired.

The occupational profile of mothers is very different. One in four work as government employees, police or armed forces or in a public sector company. Only one in ten mothers work in a large or small private company. Only 6 percent work in a family business or are self-employed. Almost half (47%) define their work as housework, and 3 percent are unemployed and 2 percent outside the labor force.

The students come from homes which vary with regards to how much literacy is valued. When asked how many books were in their homes, 7 percent said less than 10 books, 28 percent reported having 11-25 books, 27 percent reported having 26-100 books, 21 percent had 101-200 books, and 17 percent had more than 200.

We asked the students how satisfied they were with their standard of living, and the majority of them were either very satisfied (48%) or satisfied (33%), and only 6 percent were not satisfied or barely satisfied.

Students participate in the program for a diversity of reasons. About 36 percent noted that they were assigned by their teachers, 6 percent were encouraged by their parents and 56 percent chose to participate. The vast majority of the students in this study had not participated in other Injaz programs or entrepreneurship programs, as well as any other training courses outside of school.

5.4. How Do Participants Spend Their Time and How Do They Differ from the Comparison Group?

The activity that most students report as spending much time is studying. More students who participate in the Company Program report studying much (80%) than students in the comparison group (65%). About three in five students report that they spend much time talking to their parents, in various forms of entertainment, chatting with friends or watching TV and radio. There are no differences between students who participate in the Company Program and the comparison group in this regard. Relatively fewer students, about two in five, report that they spend time researching opportunities for a business, and one in five students spends time thinking about their career. These figures are summarized in the table 5.2.

Table 5.2. How much time do you spend doing the following activities in a typical week in Morocco? (Question: On a scale of 1-5, how much time to you spend on the following activities. Table includes percentage who answer that they spent *much time* or a *lot of time*)

	Control	Participant	
		Before	*After*
Careers	34%	21%	
Research	41%	37%	
News	44%	47%	
Talk parents	63%	58%	
Studying	65%	80%	
Entertainment	59%	65%	
Chatting friends	62%	61%	
TV and Radio	65%	61%	

Careers   Investigating career possibilities
Research   Research potential ideas for a new business
News   Following the news
Talk parents   Talking to your parents about career possibilities
Studying   Studying or working on school-related activities
Entertainment Keeping up-to-date on entertainment, fashion or sports
Chatting friends Chatting with friends
TV and Radio Watching TV or listening to music

Table 5.3 shows the results of the tests of statistical significance of those differences. Only in the time devoted to thinking about careers, time spent researching market opportunities and time spent following the news are there significant differences between both groups. In all these differences, the control group has higher scores than the participant group.

Table 5.3. How much time do students in Morocco spend on the following activities in a typical week?

	Control	Participant		Difference		
		Before	After	PB - C		PA - PB
Careers	2.51	2.22		-0.29	**	
	(1.51)	(1.51)		-2.10		
Research	3.11	2.70		-0.40	***	
	(1.39)	(1.51)		-3.00		
News	3.37	3.05		-0.32	**	
	(1.35)	(1.43)		-2.49		
Talk parents	3.70	3.52		-0.19		
	(1.32)	(1.52)		-1.42		
Studying	4.04	4.14		0.10		
	(1.01)	(1.06)		1.06		
Entertainment	3.68	3.75		0.07		
	(1.27)	(1.22)		0.64		
Chatting friends	3.74	3.58		-0.16		
	(1.28)	(1.27)		-1.42		
TV and Radio	3.76	3.72		-0.04		
	(1.17)	(1.12)		-0.38		

*** significant at 1% level, ** at 5% level, * at 10% level.
Standard deviations in parentheses, t-statistics in italics.
C=Control, PB= Participant Before, PA=Participant After

5.5. How Do Participants Differ before and after Participation in the Program?

In this section, we compare three groups: the students in the comparison group who did not participate in the Company Program (219 students), and those who participated in the Company Program, both before the program (267 students) and after the program (75 students).[15] The first part of each section describes the views of students in the various knowledge and attitude measurements in the questionnaire. This is followed by a statistical analysis of the significance of these differences. In each case, we compare those who participated in the program, before participation (before), with those who did not participate (control). We then compare those who participated before and after participation.

Because we do not have information on basic demographic characteristics of the students who took the post-questionnaire, we are unable to establish in what ways this group of student is similar or different to all those who took the pre-questionnaire. As a result, the differences identified in this section could be the result of program effects, the result of differences between the students who completed the survey after program completion from those who abandoned the program or did not fill out the follow-up survey (selection effects), or the result of an interaction between program effects and selection effects (i.e., the program may have effects on the kind of students who remain in the program).

5.5.1. Aspirations, Views of Self and Worldviews

There are consistent differences in the aspirations and worldviews of students before and after the program and most of these are statistically significant, as show in table 5.4. Of eight dimensions surveyed, these views were more favorable after the program than before; seven of these differences were statistically significant at 5% level. Notice that these changes take place in a context where students have quite high aspirations even before participation in the Company Program.

Each of these aspirations and worldviews was measured with a five-point scale in which students were asked to rate themselves from completely

---

[15] Fewer participants were surveyed after the Program partly due to logistical reasons tracking down students.

disagree (1) with completely agree (5). In table 5.4, we have calculated the percentages for each item represented by the students who selected agree or completely agree (points 4 and 5 in the scale).

Table 5.4. Aspirations and worldviews towards future and self of students in Morocco before and after participating in the Company Program. (Question: On a scale of 1-5, to what extent do you agree or disagree with the following statements about yourself. Table includes percentage who answer 4 or 5)

	Control	Participant	
		Before	*After*
Achieve goals	74%	74%	95%
Learn from failure	89%	80%	97%
Challenges opport.	67%	66%	88%
Outside school	66%	55%	82%
Studying matters	96%	92%	
Educ matters	85%	79%	85%
Learnfuture	83%	80%	
Negotiate	66%	64%	92%
Leadership	64%	62%	88%
Set goals	82%	76%	96%
Creativity			84%

Achieve goals I trust that in the future, I will achieve my goals.

Learn from failure If I fail at something, I try to figure out why so that I can succeed the next time.

Challenges opport.   I see challenges as opportunities.

Outside school Participate in activities outside of school to prepare for my future.

Studying matters   Studying is important to me.

Educ matters I go to school because education is important for getting a job later.

Negotiate   I believe that achieving my goals requires negotiating with others.

Leadership   I can see myself in a leadership position in the future.

Set goals   I set goals for myself in order to attain the things I want.

Creativity   I try to find creative solutions to problems.

As shown, with regards to trust in their own capacity to achieve their goals in the future, there are no differences between the control group and the group who participated in the Company Program. In both of them, three-fourths of the students are confident that they will achieve their goals. After participation in the program, however, this figure increases to 95 percent.

With regards to the idea that, faced with failure, they try to figure out the reasons in order to succeed the next time, whereas 89 percent of the students in the comparison group indicated that they did so, only 80 percent of the students who would participate in the program did. After participation, however, most (97%) of the students surveyed were inclined to figure out the reasons for their failures in order to succeed in the future. The percentage who 'agreed a lot' increased from 58 percent to 82 percent.

There is also a sizeable increase in the percentage of students who come to see challenges as opportunities. The percentage of students who agreed a lot or agreed with this view increased from 66 percent before participating in the Company Program – no different to the comparison group – to 88 percent after the program.

There is a very important difference in the percentage of students who participate in out of school activities to prepare for their future. Before participating in the Company Program, the percentage of agreed a lot or agreed was 55 percent, whereas it was 66 percent in the comparison group. After the program, this percentage had increased to 82 percent for those surveyed.

The students included in this study believe that studying is important. 92 percent of those participating in the program agreed or agreed a lot with this statement before participating in the Company Program, compared to 96 percent of those who did not participate. We did not ask this question after participation in the program.

Along similar lines, the percentage of students who believe that education is important in order to obtain a job in the future is very high. Before participation in the program, 79 percent of the students agreed or agreed a lot with that statement, compared to 85 percent in the comparison group. After participation in the Company Program, 85 percent of them did.

Similarly, students had very favorable views towards learning before the program. 80 percent of the students who participated in the program believe that they are learning now will help them in the future. This figure is very similar to the 83 percent for those who did not participate in the program. This question was not asked of students after program participation.

Students understand that achieving their goals requires negotiating with others. Before participation in the program, 64 percent agreed or agreed a lot with this statement. This figure increased to 92 percent after the program.

When asked whether they saw themselves as leaders in the future, 62 percent of them did before participating in the program, whereas after the program 88 percent did.

Most students set goals for themselves. Before the program, 76 percent of those who participated in the program did, compared to 82 percent of those who did not participate. After the program, this figure increased to 96 percent.

Students who participated in the program also report an interest in finding creative solutions to problems: 84 percent of them do. We did not ask this question to students prior to participation in the program.

To sum up, most students who were surveyed after their participation in the program score on the high end of the various dimensions explored in this section. There are few differences in these various aspects of worldviews and views of themselves between students who did not participate in the program and those who did prior to participation. When there were differences, they were in favor of those students who did not participate. However, after participation in the program, there are sizeable increases in the percentage of students who are at the high end of the scales measuring these dimensions.

We then carried out a formal test of the statistical significance of these differences, summarized in table 5.5. The summary of these tests is that, at the end of the program, students have greater trust in their ability to achieve their goals in the future, are more likely to learn from failure and to persevere, are more likely to see challenges as opportunities, are more likely to participate in extra-curricular activities to prepare for their future, are more likely to believe that negotiation with others is essential to achieving their goals, are more likely to see themselves in a leadership position in the future, and are more likely to set goals for themselves. The differences in these dimensions are statistically significant at 5 percent level. A dimension in which there is also apparent difference, but that is not statistically significant in favor of the students at the end of the program, is that students after the program are more likely to believe that education is important to obtain a job in the future.

The average means in the scales used to measure these dimensions, the difference and the t-statistics are presented in table 5.6.

Table 5.6. Aspirations and worldviews towards future and self of students in Morocco before and after participating in the Company Program. (Question: On a scale of 1-5, to what extent do you agree or disagree with the following statements about yourself)

	Control	Participant		Difference				
		Before	After	PB - C		PA – PB		
Achieve goals	4.05	4.12	4.37	0.07		0.25	**	
	(0.94)	(0.84)	(0.74)	0.84		-2.47		
Learn from failure	4.48	4.32	4.79	-0.17	**	0.48	***	
	(0.85)	(0.95)	(0.47)	-1.99		-5.90		
Challenges opport.	3.97	3.87	4.46	-0.10		0.59	***	
	(1.18)	(1.17)	(0.92)	-0.93		-4.52		
Outside school	3.84	3.61	4.39	-0.24	**	0.79	***	
	(1.24)	(1.22)	(0.96)	-2.05		-5.71		
Studying matters	4.70	4.56		-0.14	**			
	(0.68)	(0.67)		2.16				
Educ matters	4.38	4.19	4.44	-0.19	*	0.24	*	
	(1.01)	(1.05)	(1.04)	-1.94		-1.77		
Learnfuture	4.39	4.38		-0.01				
	(0.95)	(0.95)		-0.07				
Negotiate	4.00	3.89	4.45	-0.11		0.56	***	
	(1.09)	(1.07)	(0.76)	-1.07		-4.99		
Leadership	3.76	3.84	4.41	0.07		0.57	***	
	(1.19)	(1.04)	(0.78)	0.69		-5.11		
Set goals	4.23	4.22	4.71	-0.01		0.49	***	
	(1.05)	(0.99)	(0.54)	-0.08		-5.51		

*** significant at 1% level, ** at 5% level, * at 10% level.
Standard deviations in parentheses, t-statistics in italics.
C=Control, PB= Participant Before, PA=Participant After

5.5.2. Perceived Self-Efficacy

Students were asked to what extent they felt capable of performing a series of tasks. Table 5.7 summarizes the percentage of those students who felt capable of doing them to a great extent –values 4 and 5 in the 5-point scale. In the majority of the dimensions evaluated, students who were surveyed after participating in the program felt more efficacious than before. There were some differences between program participants and students in the comparison group.

Table 5.7. Perception of Self-Efficacy of students in Morocco before and after participating in the Company Program. (Question: On a scale of 1-5, to what extent do you feel that you are able to. Table includes percentage who answer 4 or 5)

	Control	Participant	
		Before	After
Teamwork	70%	78%	93%
Adapt	66%	74%	90%
Problemsolve	68%	60%	82%
Presentpeers	58%	64%	85%
Presentadult	58%	64%	70%
Resolvediff	68%	66%	93%
Purpose	71%	66%	
Commproblem	52%	47%	73%
Persuade	66%	60%	88%
Negconflict	79%	71%	88%
Competejob	85%	83%	93%
Startbusiness	78%	71%	90%
Rolebusiness	58%	62%	64%
Leadteam	66%	64%	86%
Research	69%	67%	71%
Learnrealworld	53%	54%	63%

Teamwork	Work with a team to accomplish a result
Adapt	Adapt to new situations
Problemsolve	Solve problems
Presentpeers	Present a topic to a group of classmates
Presentadult	Present a topic to a group of adults
Resolvediff	Resolve differences within a group to reach a solution satisfactory to most
Commproblem	Solve community problems
Persuade	Persuade a group of people about an idea
Negconflict	Negotiate personal conflicts in a peaceful way
Competejob	Be competitive in securing a good job
Startbusiness	Start and run your own business someday

Rolebusiness   Understand the role of business owners in our economy
Leadteam   Lead the members of a group to meet a deadline in producing a
                result
Research   Research the potential market for a company
Learnrealworld To what extent is there a clear connection between what you
                Are learning in school and the real world?

When asked whether they feel capable of working with a team to accomplish a result, 78 percent of them did before participating in the program, compared to 70 percent in the comparison group. This figure increased to 93 percent for students after participating in the program.

In terms of their ability to adapt to new situations, 74 percent of those participating in the program and 66 percent of those in the comparison group reported that they were able to do this, compared to 90 percent after the program.

Before participating in the program, 60 percent reported that they were able to solve problems. This figure increased to 82 percent after participation. Similarly, before the program, 64 percent feel capable of presenting a topic to a group of classmates. After the program 85 percent of them do.

When asked about their ability to present to a group of adults, 58 percent of the students in the comparison group and 64 percent of those in the company program felt capable before the program, in comparison to 70 percent after the program. Paradoxically, the percentage who felt capable 'to a large degree' decreased from 41 percent before the program, to 27 percent after the program.

Students were asked whether they were capable of resolving differences within a group to reach a solution satisfactory to most group members. Before participation in the program, 66 percent of them felt capable to do so. After program participation, this figure increased to 93 percent.

We asked students, before participating in the program, whether they understood their purpose in life, and 66 percent of them said they did, compared to 71 percent of those in the comparison group. We did not ask this question after program participation.

When asked whether they were able to solve community problems, 47 percent of them said they did before program participation. After participating in the Company Program, 73 percent of them did.

We asked students about their ability to persuade a group of people about their ideas. Before participation in the program, 60 percent of them felt able to do this. This figure increased to 88 percent after program participation.

Students were asked whether they were able to negotiate conflicts in a peaceful way. Before program participation, 71 percent of them did, less than 79 percent in the comparison group. After program participation, 88 percent of the students felt capable of negotiating conflicts in a peaceful way.

When asked whether they felt competitive in securing a good job, 83 percent did so before the program, compared to 93 percent after the program.

We also asked students whether they could start and run their own business someday. Before participation in the program, 71 percent felt capable of doing this. This figure increased to 90 percent after program participation.

We asked whether they understood the role of business owners in the economy. Before the program, 62 percent of them did. After program participation, 64 percent did.

Students were asked whether they felt capable of leading the members of a group to meet a deadline in producing a result. Before program participation, 64 percent did. After program participation, this figure increased to 86 percent.

We asked students whether they could research the potential market for a company. Before program participation, 67 percent of them did; a figure that rose to 71 percent for those who completed the program.

When asked to what extent there was a clear connection between what they learned in school and the real world, 54 percent of them before participation in the program said there was one. This figure increased to 63 percent after program participation.

The differences before and after the program on self-efficacy are less consistent than for aspirations and worldviews. Of 15 dimensions evaluated, there are statistically significant differences for ten of them.

The results of the statistical analysis of these differences show that students after the program are more likely to feel that they are able to working in teams to accomplish a result, adapt to new situations, solve problems, present a topic to a group of classmates, resolve differences within a group to reach a solution that satisfies most group members, persuade a group about an idea, negotiate personal conflicts in a peaceful way, start and run their own business someday, and lead a team to meet a deadline to produce a result.

For the following dimensions, the differences are not statistically significant although the direction of the differences is the same, with students having more confidence in their skills after participation in the program: present a topic to a group of adults, be competitive in securing a job, understand the role of business owners in the economy, research the potential market for a company, and find a connection between what they learn in school and the real world.

Table 5.8 summarizes the average means in the scales for each group, the difference and the t-statistics are presented in table 5.

Table 5.8. Perception of Self-Efficacy of students in Morocco before and after participating in the company program. (Question: On a scale of 1-5, to what extent do you feel that you are able to:)

| | Control | Participant | | Difference | | | |
		Before	After	PB - C		PA - PB	
Teamwork	3.93	4.22	4.60	0.29	***	0.38	***
	(1.03)	(0.91)	(0.66)	3.26		-3.95	
Adapt	3.84	4.09	4.36	0.25	***	0.26	***
	(1.12)	(0.88)	(0.65)	2.69		-2.78	
Problemsolve	3.86	3.65	4.22	-0.21	**	0.57	***
	(1.02)	(1.03)	(0.77)	-2.18		-5.08	
Presentpeers	3.56	3.85	4.25	0.29	***	0.40	***
	(1.28)	(1.09)	(0.82)	2.63		-3.36	
Presentadult	3.63	3.85	3.84	0.22	*	-0.01	
	(1.34)	(1.18)	(0.97)	1.81		0.06	
Resolvediff	3.94	3.85	4.38	-0.09		0.54	***
	(1.05)	(1.13)	(0.86)	-0.91		-4.34	
Purpose	3.43	3.85		-0.19			
	(1.23)	(1.13)		-1.57			
Commproblem	3.92	3.24	3.89	-0.28	***	0.65	***
	(1.06)	(1.29)	(1.10)	-2.60		-4.23	
Persuade	4.22	3.64	4.34	-0.29	***	0.70	***
	(0.94)	(1.23)	(0.85)	-2.93		-5.53	
Negconflict	4.46	3.92	4.36	-0.10		0.43	***
	(0.91)	(1.20)	(0.96)	-1.20		-3.18	
Competejob	4.16	4.36	4.51	-0.10		0.16	
	(1.11)	(0.95)	(0.63)	-0.95		-1.60	
Startbusiness	3.72	4.06	4.47	-0.01		0.41	***
	(1.11)	(1.06)	(0.85)	-0.11		-3.34	
Rolebusiness	3.81	3.70	3.69	0.01		-0.01	
	(1.14)	(1.20)	(0.91)	0.10		0.08	
Leadteam	3.87	3.82	4.44	-0.09		0.62	***
	(1.26)	(1.11)	(0.82)	-0.73		-5.16	
Research	3.55	3.78	3.90	0.01		0.12	
	(1.05)	(1.26)	(0.86)	0.09		-0.93	
Learnrealworld	3.51	3.56	3.59	0.11		0.03	
	(0.99)	(1.04)	(1.27)	1.09		-0.18	

*** significant at 1% level, ** at 5% level, * at 10% level.
Standard deviations in parentheses, t-statistics in italics.
C=Control, PB= Participant Before, PA=Participant After

5.5.3.   Educational Aspirations

When asked about their educational aspirations before program participation, 15 percent hope to complete university while 68 percent of the students hope to achieve post-graduate studies (Masters or above). After program participation, the respective figures are 8 percent and 86 percent.

When asked about their immediate plans after leaving secondary school, most (74%) of the students before participating in the program said they planned to continue with their studies. The same was true for those students (82%) after participating in the program. The percentage of students who planned to work immediately after their studies, declined from 7 percent before program participation, to 3 percent after program participation.

Students had higher educational aspirations after participating in the Company Program than before, but there were no significant differences in their immediate plans after leaving secondary school, as seen in table 5.9.

Table 5.9. Educational Aspirations and Plans in Morocco

| | Control | Participant | | Difference | | | |
		Before	After	PB - C		PA - PB	
Education	4.02	4.55	4.83	0.53	***	0.28	**
	(1.03)	(0.89)	(0.56)	5.89		-3.29	
Plans	2.45	2.49	2.51	0.04		0.02	
	(1.29)	(1.38)	(1.39)	0.36		-0.09	

Education   What is the highest level of education that you would like to complete?

    1=will not finish secondary school
    2=will finish secondary
    3=post-secondary training program or diploma
    4= University (Bachelor)
    5= Post-graduate degree (Masters or PhD)
    6= Other (please specify)

Plans   Immediately after leaving secondary school, I plan to:

    1=Work or look for a job
    2=Continue with my formal education (post-secondary diploma or university)
    3=Participate in additional training programs
    4=Establish my own business
    5=Stay at home
    6=To study and work at same time
    7=To study and start own business at same time

5.5.4.   Motivations for Choosing a Job

We asked students to what extent a range of reasons were important to them in choosing a particular job. The differences here are smaller than in the previous two domains. The largest differences seem to be that students who participate in the Company Program have more confidence in their ability to successfully complete a job interview and to work in the private sector than before participation. They also seem to have greater appreciation for a job that would allow them the opportunity to use their skills and abilities and that would give them a role in decision making. They also seem to value more freedom in their work schedule.

Before the program, high status of a job was important to 71 percent of the students of participated in the Company Program, relative to 81 percent of those in the comparison group. This figure increases, after program

264

participation, to 84 percent. Ability to earn a lot of money was important to 73 percent of the students before the program and did not change after participation. Good promotion prospects were important to 82 percent of the students before the program, and did not change after program participation. The opportunity to use their skills and abilities was a motivation for 88 percent of the students before the program and to 97 percent of them after the program. Job security was important to 90 percent of the students before the program, and to 82 percent after the program.

The autonomy to have a role in decision making was important to 71 percent of the students before the program, and to 84 percent of the students after participating in the program. Having a lot of vacation time was mentioned by 47 percent of the students before the program, and by 54 percent of the students after the program. Easy pace of work was mentioned by 37 percent of the students before the program and did not change after program participation. Ability to work independently without supervision was mentioned by 58 percent of the students before the program, and by 61 percent of the students after the program. A job that is family friendly was mentioned by 57 percent of the students before the program and by 79 percent of the students after the program. For the group of students who had participated in the program, 63 percent mentioned the kind of people they would work with as an important factor (this question was not asked of students before the program).

When asked how confident they were that they could complete successfully a job interview, 65 percent of the students before participating in the company program felt confident, compared to 90 percent after participating in the program. We also asked students how much confidence they had that they would be hired to work in the private sector. Before participating in the program, 55 percent felt very confident, compared to 83 percent after program participation.

Table 5.10. Motivations for Choosing a Job of students in Morocco before and after participating in the company program. (Question: On a scale of 1 to 5, to what extent are the following reasons important to you in choosing a particular job? Percentage who answer 4 and 5)

	Control	Participant	
		Before	*After*
Status	81%	71%	84%
Money	77%	73%	73%
Career	83%	82%	82%
Uses skills	82%	88%	97%
Job security	88%	90%	82%
Role deciding	81%	71%	84%
Ample vacation	57%	47%	54%
Easy pace	53%	37%	38%
Autonomy	64%	58%	61%
Family friendly	73%	57%	79%
Jobcolleagues			63%
Confd. interview	64%	65%	90%
Confidence hired	54%	55%	83%

Status   High status of job
Money   Ability to earn a lot of money
Career   Good promotion prospects, clear career path
Uses skills   Uses my skills and abilities
Job security   Job security
Role deciding   Gives me a role in decision making
Ample vacation   Has a lot of vacation time
Easy pace   Easy pace of work
Autonomy Ability to work independently without supervision
Family friendly   Job that is family friendly
Confidence interview   How much confidence do you could successfully complete a job interview?
Confidence hired   How much confidence do you have that you could be hired to work in the private sector?

In testing these differences among students before and after participating in the Company Program in terms of their motives to choose a job, we found that only six of the twelve dimensions explored were statistically significant at 5 percent level. Students after the program are more interested in a job that uses their skills and abilities, to value a job that values their role in decision making, want a job with more vacation time, want a job that is family friendly, and are more confident that they can be complete a job interview and be hired to work in the private sector.

There are no statistically significant differences before and after participation in the Company Program in terms of valuing a job for the status it confers, ability to earn a lot of money, clear career path, job security, or easiness of work pace, ability to work independent. Table 5.11. summarizes those differences.

Table 5.11. Motivations for Choosing a Job of students in Morocco before and after participating in the company program. (Question: On a scale of 1 to 5, to what extent are the following reasons important to you in choosing a particular job?)

	Control	Participant		Difference				
		Before	After	PB - C		PA - PB		
Status	4.16	4.05	4.23	-0.10		0.18		
	(1.12)	(1.07)	(1.01)	-1.01		-1.27		
Money	4.06	3.98	3.97	-0.08		0.00		
	(1.04)	(0.97)	(1.02)	-0.86		0.03		
Career	4.27	4.26	4.44	-0.01		0.18		
	(0.95)	(0.80)	(0.87)	-0.16		-1.55		
Uses skills	4.44	4.54	4.75	0.10		0.21	**	
	(0.96)	(0.74)	(0.56)	1.20		-2.57		
Job security	4.55	4.54	4.31	-0.01		-0.23	*	
	(0.84)	(0.71)	(0.96)	-0.10		1.81		
Role deciding	4.19	4.03	4.30	-0.16		0.28	**	
	(0.97)	(1.08)	(0.85)	-1.64		-2.25		
Ample vacation	3.58	3.17	3.55	-0.41	***	0.38	**	
	(1.23)	(1.43)	(1.10)	-3.24		-2.35		
Easy pace	3.46	2.96	3.17	-0.50	***	0.20		
	(1.38)	(1.38)	(1.25)	-3.75		-1.15		
Autonomy	3.73	3.65	3.75	-0.08		0.09		
	(1.29)	(1.21)	(1.16)	-0.63		-0.58		
Family friendly	4.03	3.72	4.19	-0.31	**	0.47	***	
	(1.26)	(1.32)	(1.16)	-2.45		-2.86		
Confidence interview	3.76	3.72	4.35	-0.04		0.63	***	
	(0.90)	(1.06)	(0.85)	-0.43		-5.14		
Confidence hired	3.53	3.42	4.06	-0.11		0.64	***	
	(0.95)	(1.11)	(1.00)	-1.15		-4.58		

*** significant at 1% level, ** at 5% level, * at 10% level.
Standard deviations in parentheses, t-statistics in italics.
C=Control, PB= Participant Before, PA=Participant After

5.5.5. Interest in Starting a Business and Motivations for Business Creation

Before participation in the program we asked students if they thought there was more job security owning their own business vs. working for the private sector. 42 percent replied that owning their own business, 20 percent replied that working for the private sector, and 35 percent did not know. We did not ask this question of the group after participation in the program.

As a way to establish the exposure students had to real entrepreneurs, we asked them who among a series of categories of people they knew who had started their own business. The following groups were mentioned: 34 percent parents, 17 percent siblings, 72 percent relatives, 48 percent neighbors, 30 percent friends, 21 percent teachers, 57 percent someone else.

Students were asked for their views on the ease of starting a business and their interest in starting one. When asked how easy they thought it was to start a business in their country today, 46 percent said it was easy or very easy before participating in the company program. After participating in the company program the figure remained 46 percent (Table 5.12).

In response to the question of how interested they were in starting a business someday in the country, 67 percent of them said they were interested or very interested before participating in the company program. After participation in the program this figure increased to 81 percent.

To the group after participation in the Company Program, we asked how interested they were in someday joining somebody else's business. Less than half, 47 percent, said that they were interested or very interested.

Table 5.12. Interest in opening a business among students in Morocco before and after participating in the company program. (Question: On a scale of 1 to 5. Table includes percentage who answer 4 or 5)

	Control	Participant	
		Before	*After*
Easy start	54%	46%	46%
Interest	69%	67%	81%
Joininterest			47%

Easy start today?	In general, how easy is it to start a business in your country
Interest	How interested are you in someday starting your own business?
Joininterest	How interested are you in someday joining somebody else's business?

We asked students whether they had an idea for a business they would like to start. Before program participation 51 percent replied yes, 14 percent replied no, and 34 percent did not know. After program participation the respective figures were 78 percent, 11 percent and 8 percent.

Before participation in the program students were also asked to what extent they could obtain financing from various sources. The following sources were mentioned as to an extent or large extent: nuclear family 47 percent, extended family 34 percent, friends 13 percent, bank loans 55 percent, government grants 26 percent.

There were no differences between both groups in terms of how easy they thought opening a business was. Students were significantly more interested in one day starting a business at the end of the program than before the program. Table 5.13 summarizes those differences.

Table 5.13. Interest in opening a business among students in Morocco before and after participating in the Company Program. (Question: On a scale of 1 to 5)

	Control	Participant		Difference			
		Before	After	PB - C		PA - PB	
Easy start	0.54	0.46	0.46	-0.09	*	0.01	
	(0.50)	(0.50)	(0.50)	0.06		0.11	
Interest	0.69	0.67	0.81	-0.02		0.14	**
	(0.46)	(0.47)	(0.40)	0.66		2.48	
Idea	0.17	0.18	0.11	0.01		-0.07	
	(0.38)	(0.55)	(0.32)	0.84		-1.36	

*** significant at 1% level, ** at 5% level, * at 10% level.
Standard deviations in parentheses, t-statistics in italics.
C=Control, PB= Participant Before, PA=Participant After

A number of questions in the survey explored the motivations students had to start a business. These are summarized in table 5.14.

Table 5.14. Importance of various factors in eventual decision to open a business among students in Morocco before and after participating in the Company Program. (Question: If you were to start your own business in the future, indicate on a scale of 1-5 how important each of the following is in your decision to start a business. Percentage who answer 4 or 5)

	Control	Participant	
		Before	After
Work for self	65%	63%	68%
Use skills	84%	84%	97%
Create new ideas	81%	80%	96%
Solve problems	53%	59%	85%
Earn more	64%	64%	73%
Create jobs	66%	68%	90%
Fame	44%	58%	69%
Friends	35%	38%	63%

Work for self   Prefer to work for yourself rather than someone else
Use skills   To use your skills effectively
Create new ideas To be able to create and develop new ideas
Solve problemsTo resolve important social problems

Earn more	You can earn more money running your own business
Create jobs	To create jobs and foster economic growth
Fame	To become a famous entrepreneur
Friends	Your friends want to start a business

Before participating in the Company Program, the percentage who preferred to work for themselves rather than someone else was 63 percent. This figure was 68 percent after the program. The percentage who indicated that they would want to do this to use their skills effectively was 84 percent before the program, and 97 percent after the program. Those who indicated that this would allow them to create and develop new ideas were 80 percent before the program, and 95 percent after the program. Those who mentioned the ability to resolve important problems were 59 percent before the program, and 85 percent after the program. Those who mentioned that they could earn more money running their own business were 64 percent before the program and 73 percent after the program. Those who mentioned the ability to create jobs and foster economic growth increased from 68 percent before the program, to 90 percent after the program. The figures for becoming a famous entrepreneur were 58 percent before and 69 percent after. To have friends who want to start a business 38 percent before the program and 63 percent after the program.

When asked to rate the importance of various factors in their eventual decision to start a business students were more likely after participating in the Company Program to say that their motivation would be to use their skills effectively, to create and develop new ideas, to resolve important social problems, to create jobs and foster economic growth and to have friends who also want to start a business. There were no differences after participation in the company program and before with regards to preferring to work for someone else vs. self, or in terms of earning more money with a business or to become a famous entrepreneur. Table 5.15. summarizes these differences.

Table 5.15. Importance of various factors in eventual decision to open a business among students in Morocco before and after participating in the Company Program.(Question: If you were to start your own business in the future, indicate on a scale of 1-5 how important each of the following is in your decision to start a business)

	Control	Participant		Difference		
		Before	After	PB - C		PA - PB
Work for self	3.78	3.93	3.83	0.15		-0.09
	(1.37)	(1.16)	(1.07)	1.19		0.64
Use skills	4.40	4.49	4.85	0.09		0.35 ***
	(1.05)	(0.82)	(0.44)	0.98		-4.81
Create new ideas	4.23	4.36	4.81	0.13		0.45 ***
	(1.20)	(0.95)	(0.49)	1.18		-5.33
Solve problems	3.55	3.59	4.27	0.04		0.68 ***
	(1.08)	(1.24)	(0.94)	0.33		-4.93
Earn more	3.82	3.84	4.04	0.02		0.20
	(1.19)	(1.20)	(0.95)	0.19		-1.48
Create jobs	3.75	3.94	4.53	0.19	*	0.59 ***
	(1.15)	(1.10)	(0.80)	1.70		-4.98
Fame	3.23	3.69	3.79	0.46	***	0.09
	(1.43)	(1.23)	(1.22)	3.56		-0.57
Friends	2.88	3.18	3.67	0.30	**	0.49 ***
	(1.39)	(1.27)	(1.05)	2.29		-3.20

*** significant at 1% level, ** at 5% level, * at 10% level.
Standard deviations in parentheses, t-statistics in italics.
C=Control, PB= Participant Before, PA=Participant After

5.5.6. Financial Management

Students were asked about their financial management habits in terms of whether they planned how to spend money, used a budget and saved regularly. Table 5.16. summarizes these results.

Table 5.16. Financial management habits among students in Morocco before and after participating in the Company Program. (0=no, 1=yes)

	Control	Participant	
		Before	After
Plan finances	79%	70%	92%
Budget	58%	55%	73%
Save	66%	56%	77%

Plan finances   When you have money, do you plan ahead for how to spend it?
Budget   Do you use a budget to manage your spending?
Save   Do you regularly save money?

Students after participating in the Company Program were significantly more likely to do these things than before participating in the Company Program. Before the program, 70 percent planned ahead how to spend their money, compared to 92 percent after the program. Those reporting the use of a budget to manage spending increased from 55 percent before the program to 73 percent after the program. Saving regularly increased from 56 percent before the program to 77 percent after the program.

The statistical test of these differences is summarized in Table 5.17.

Table 5.17. Financial Management habits among students in Morocco before and after participating in the Company Program. (no=0, yes=1)

	Control	Participant		Difference			
		Before	After	PB - C		PA - PB	
Plan finances	0.79	0.70	0.92	-0.09	***	0.22	***
	(0.41)	(0.46)	(0.27)	-2.21		5.20	
Budget	0.58	0.55	0.73	-0.03		0.18	***
	(0.49)	(0.50)	(0.45)	-0.67		2.95	
Save	0.66	0.56	0.77	-0.09		0.21	***
	(0.57)	(0.50)	(0.42)	-1.87	*	3.54	

*** significant at 1% level, ** at 5% level, * at 10% level.
Standard deviations in parentheses, t-statistics in italics.
C=Control, PB= Participant Before, PA=Participant After

5.5.7.   Attitudes towards Entrepreneurship and Business

Students who participated in the Company Program and those who did not differed in some of their attitudes towards entrepreneurship. For example, those participating where less likely to think that entrepreneurs only think about their own gain, more likely to believe that entrepreneurs can succeed in Morocco, less likely to believe that men are more qualified than women to be leaders and less likely to believe that if jobs were scarce men should have priority. After participating in the program, a greater percentage of students believed that hard work leads to progress, believed that women can play an important role in the success of a business, believed that entrepreneurs can succeed in the country and believed that entrepreneurs can contribute to the economic development of the country. After the program, a smaller percentage of students believed men are more qualified than women to be leaders and that when jobs are scarce men should have priority in accessing them.

According to table 5.18, the percentage of students who agreed that people in the country can get ahead by working hard increased from 56 percent before participating in the Company Program to 86 percent after the Company Program. Those who think that entrepreneurs only think about their own gain declined slightly from 53 percent to 49 percent. Those who believe that women can play an important role in the success of a business increased from 87 percent to 95 percent after participating in the Company Program. There was no difference in the percentage of those who believed that most people should be trusted, only one in five students. Those who believe that there is potential in the country for an entrepreneur to become successful increased from 54 percent to 68 percent. Those who think that men are better qualified than women to be business leaders decreased from 24 percent to 18 percent. There was a significant increase in the percentage of those who think that entrepreneurs create jobs for others from 37 percent to 66 percent. The percentage who thinks that when jobs are scarce men should have more rights to a job than women was 23 percent before the program vs. 18

percent after the program. Those who think that entrepreneurs contribute to the economic development of the country represent 52 percent before the program vs. 70 percent after the program.

Table 5.18. Attitudes towards Entrepreneurship in Morocco. (Question: On a scale of 1-5, to what extent do you agree or disagree with the following statements)

	Control	Participant	
		Before	After
Hard work	58%	56%	86%
Entrepreneurs selfish	68%	53%	49%
Women lead	85%	87%	95%
Trust	21%	18%	19%
Entrepreneurs succeed	48%	54%	68%
Men lead better	40%	24%	18%
Entr. create jobs	30%	37%	66%
Men more rights	44%	23%	18%
Entrepreneurs contribute	55%	52%	70%

Hard work   People in your country can get ahead by working hard.
Entrepreneurs selfish Entrepreneurs only think about their own gain.
Women lead Women can play an important role in the success of a business.
Trust   Most people can be trusted.
Entrepreneurs succeed There is potential in your country for an entrepreneur to become successful.
Men lead better Men are better qualified than women to be business leaders.
Entr. create jobs Entrepreneurs create jobs for others.
Men more rights When jobs are scarce, men should have more rights to a job than women.
Entrepreneurs contribute Entrepreneurs contribute to the economic development of the country.

The statistical analysis of the differences in attitudes towards entrepreneurship is summarized in table 5.19.

Table 5.19. Attitudes towards Entrepreneurship in Morocco. (Q: On a scale of 1-5, to what extent do you agree or disagree with the following statements)

	Control	Participant		Difference			
		Before	After	PB - C		PA - PB	
Hard work	3.59	3.77	4.36	0.18		0.59	**
	(1.31)	(1.12)	(0.82)	1.54		4.97	
Entrepreneurs selfish	3.93	3.63	3.22	-0.30	***	-0.41	**
	(1.29)	(1.16)	(1.26)	-2.59		-2.47	
Women lead	4.50	4.42	4.66	-0.08		0.24	**
	(0.95)	(0.89)	(0.63)	-0.90		2.58	
Trust	2.50	2.43	2.49	-0.07		0.07	
	(1.27)	(1.18)	(1.19)	-0.60		0.42	
Entrepreneurs succeed	3.36	3.61	4.00	0.25	**	0.39	**
	(1.18)	(1.03)	(1.02)	2.32		2.87	
Men lead better	2.76	2.56	2.26	-0.20		-0.30	
	(1.51)	(1.36)	(1.27)	-1.49		-1.76	
Entr. create jobs	2.85	3.26	3.84	0.41	***	0.57	**
	(1.20)	(1.05)	(1.07)	3.82		4.03	
Men more rights	2.93	2.50	2.11	-0.43	***	-0.39	**
	(1.61)	(1.33)	(1.37)	-3.07		-2.17	
Entrepreneurs contribute	3.48	3.57	4.01	0.09		0.44	**
	(1.24)	(1.15)	(1.16)	0.83		2.86	

*** significant at 1% level, ** at 5% level, * at 10% level.
Standard deviations in parentheses, t-statistics in italics.
C=Control, PB= Participant Before, PA=Participant After

In addition, students were asked whether they knew someone who was an entrepreneur. Most students know entrepreneurs who are relatives, family members or friends. There are no differences in this respect between the students who participate in the Company Program and those who do not, except for having a sibling who is an entrepreneur.

Table 5.20. Knowledge of Entrepreneurs in Morocco. (Q: Who among the following people to you know who have started their own business?)

	Control	Participant	
		Before	After
Parent	65%	59%	
Sibling	76%	83%	
Family	20%	33%	
Neighbor	56%	52%	
Friend	68%	70%	
Teacher	74%	79%	
Someone else	35%	43%	

Furthermore, the group of students who participated in the program and those who did not are very similar in terms of where they imagine they could access funds to create a business.

Table 5.21. Sources of funding in Morocco. (Q: If you were to start a business, to what extent would you be able to depend on the following financing sources to support your new business? On scale 1-5. Table reports percentage who answered 4 or 5))

	Control	Participant	
		Before	After
Nuclear family	63%	47%	
Extended family	24%	24%	
Friends	12%	13%	
Bank	35%	55%	
Grant	21%	27%	

Nuclear family	Nuclear family
Extended family	Extended family
Friends	Friend
Bank	Bank loans
Grant	Government grants

As shown in the following table, there are no statistically significant differences for most of these sources between the comparison group and those participating in the Company Program.

Table 5. 22. Sources of funding in Morocco

| | Control | Participant | | Difference | |
		Before	After	PB - C	PA - PB
Nuclear family	3.43	3.38		-0.05	
	(1.44)	(1.51)		-0.37	
Extended family	2.53	2.26		-0.27	**
	(1.43)	(1.39)		-2.00	
Friends	1.91	1.89		-0.02	
	(1.17)	(1.27)		-0.20	
Bank	3.14	3.32		0.19	
	(1.33)	(1.41)		1.44	
Grant	2.37	2.28		-0.08	
	(1.39)	(1.46)		-0.57	
Finsuppother	2.47	2.21		-0.25	
	(1.69)	(1.60)		-1.00	

*** significant at 1% level, ** at 5% level, * at 10% level.
Standard deviations in parentheses, t-statistics in italics.
C=Control, PB= Participant Before, PA=Participant After

5.5.8. Knowledge about Entrepreneurship

A few questions in the survey assessed student knowledge of basic concepts of entrepreneurship and business. While there are clear and sizeable differences with the group who had participated in the Company Program demonstrating greater knowledge, this group is far from achieving mastery of these basic knowledge concepts. Percentages of students who answered correctly are reported in Table 5.23.

Table 5.23. Knowledge about entrepreneurship in Morocco. (Multiple choice questions)

	Control	Participant	
		Before	After
Entrepredefine	32%	29%	
Sell shares	5%	10%	36%
Vision	11%	9%	29%
Marketing	43%	53%	92%
Liquidation	7%	14%	45%
Company	14%	18%	60%

Entrepredefine An entrepreneur is someone who
Sell shares   Selling shares of stock to get start-up money for a new company is called:
Vision   A _____ represents a company's dream of where it wants to go and what it wants to be.
Marketing   The work you completed in this scenario above is an example of which of the following:
Liquidation   When a company liquidates, it does which of the following:
Company   By definition, a company must have which of the following

Before participation in the Company Program, students were asked to define an entrepreneur. Only 29 percent correctly identified 'creates a business' as the correct answer. This question was not asked in the follow up.

When asked to identify the term for selling shares of stock to get start-up money for a new company, only 10 percent identified the correct option capitalization before the program, and 36 percent did so after the program.

When asked to fill in the term for the definition of a vision statement only 9 percent of the students did so correctly before participating in the program, compared to 29 percent after participating in the program. It is noteworthy that most students, before and after the program, selected 'a business plan' as the correct definition of 'a company's dream of where it wants to go and what it wants to be'.

When asked to recognize a scenario representing a marketing strategy, 53 percent of the students did so correctly before participating in the Company Program, compared to 92 percent after program participation.

When asked to recognize the definition of liquidation, 14 percent did so correctly before participating in the Company Program, vs. 45 percent after program participation.

Lastly, when asked to identify that a company must have stockholders, 18 percent of the students did so before participating in the program, compared to 60 percent of those who had participated in the program.

5.6. How Do Students in the Company Program Describe the Effects of the Program?

When asked to rate themselves in a series of questions about possible effects of the program, most participants who were survey after the program are very favorable about the changes they observe in themselves. To further examine the effects that students who participated in the Company Program attribute to their participation, during the final competition students were asked a series of additional questions. This section focuses on these questions and compares the reported 'effects' for the 75 students in the original sample and for the all the students who participated in the program and attended the national competition. Percentages between both groups about their program experience are very consistent. However, there is a plausible upward bias as these are the students who completed the program and attended the competition. Students who abandon the program or did not attend the national competition may have different views of the Company Program.

After participating in the Company Program and attending the national competition, nine in ten students feel more empowered to take a leadership role in the workforce in the future (Table 5.24). 86 percent of the students say they understand the importance of managing their finances. 86 percent say that they have further developed their educational goals. Between 90 percent and 96 percent of participants say they have developed their career goals. Almost 90 percent say that they now feel more confident about their ability to successfully compete in the workforce in the future. About 77 percent say they now know more about entrepreneurship, and 88 percent say they are now more interested in starting their own business.

Table 5.24. Retrospective experience in Morocco (Compare yourself now to where you were at the beginning of the school year. On a scale of 1-5, to what extent do you agree with the following statements about yourself.)

	Participant After	
	Original sample (n=75)	All surveyed (n=208)
Leadership	89%	90%
Finances	86%	86%
Education goals	96%	90%
Career goals	89%	88%
Competitive	89%	92%
Know entrepreneurship	77%	79%
Start business	88%	88%

Leadership	I feel more empowered to take a leadership role in the workforce in the future.
Finances	I realize more that knowing how to effectively manage my finances is important.
Education goals	I have developed (or further developed) my educational goals.
Career goals	I have developed (or further developed) my career goals.
Competitive	I am more confident in my ability to successfully compete in the workforce in the future.
Know entrepreneurship	I know more about entrepreneurship.
Start business	I am more interested in starting my own business.

When asked specifically about the Injaz Company Program to participants, 96 percent of the students found it valuable or very valuable, 87 percent attribute to the program an enhanced understanding of other people's views, and 96 percent of the students say that the program helped them develop the ability to work with others as a team. Also, 83 percent say that it helped them develop citizenship skills, 91 percent say that the program helped them develop the capacity to innovate, 87 percent say that the program taught them critical thinking skills, and 95 percent say that the program taught them useful business skills.

About 94 percent say that it helped them develop initiative and self-motivation, 84 percent say that the program helped them develop their abilities as a leader, 85 percent say that it taught them how to manage a budget. 88 percent say that it helped them learn to solve problems, 92 percent say that it helped them to become a better decision maker, 94 percent say that it helped them learn to communicate with others, 88 percent say that it helped them learn to negotiate differences with people, 91 percent say that it helped them learn to sell ideas or products, 84 percent say that it helped them learn to speak in public more easily, 91 percent say that it inspired them to think more creatively about problems.

Table 5.25. Contribution of the Company Program in Morocco. (n your opinion, on a scale of 1-5, to what extent did your participation in the Injaz Company Program help you with the following)

| | Participant After | |
	Original sample (n=75)	All surveyed (n=208)
Valuable	93%	96%
Empathy	89%	87%
Team work	93%	96%
Citizenship	85%	83%
Innovation	92%	91%
Critical thinking	89%	87%
Business	94%	95%
Initiative	96%	94%
Leadership	79%	84%
Budgeting	80%	85%
Problem solve	93%	88%
Decide	96%	92%
Communicate	90%	94%
Negotiate	86%	88%
Sell	86%	91%
Speak	80%	84%
Creativity	92%	91%

Valuable   In general, how valuable did you find participating in the Injaz company program
Empathy   It helped me develop understanding of other people's views.
Team work   It helped me develop the ability to work with others as a team.
Citizenship   It helped me develop citizenship skills.
Innovation   It helped me develop the capacity to innovate.
Critical thinking   It taught me critical thinking skills.
Business   It taught me useful business skills.
Initiative   It helped me development initiative and self-motivation.
Leadership   It helped me develop my abilities as a leader.
Budgeting   It taught me how to manage a budget.
Problem solve It helped me learn to solve problems.
Decide   It helped me to become a better decision maker.
Communicate It helped me learn to communicate with others.

Negotiate	It helped me learn to negotiate differences with people.
Sell	It helped me learn to sell ideas or products.
Speak	It helped me learn to speak in public more easily.
Creativity	It inspired me to think more creatively about problems.

Students were also asked to evaluate some of the components of the program (Table 5.26). Most of them say the program aroused their interest in the topics. About nine in ten students say the volunteer presented the content clearly, held lectures in an interactive way, and was helpful and responsive to questions. Most of them found the Student Guide useful or very useful.

Overall, 97 percent of the participants from the original sample and 99 percent of participants surveyed at the national competition would recommend the Company Program to friends or family.

Table 5.26. Evaluation of the Components of the Program in Morocco. (On a scale of 1-5, to what extent do you agree with the following comments about the Injaz Company Program)

	Participant After	
	Original sample (n=75)	All surveyed (n=208)
Lecture	93%	87%
Volunclear	90%	89%
Volunrespond	94%	91%
Studguide	94%	92%
Volunlecture	89%	89%
Recommend	97%	99%

Lecture   Company Program lectures aroused my interest for the topics being discussed.
Volunclear   The volunteer presented the program's content in a clear way.
Volunrespond   The volunteer was helpful and responsive to our questions.
Studyguide   The Student Guide was useful.
Volunlecture   The volunteer held lectures in an interactive way.
Recommend   Would you recommend participating in the Injaz Company Program to friends or family members? (1=YES, 0=NO)

5.7. A Qualitative Analysis of Student Descriptions of Program Effects

Within the follow-up survey, students were provided the opportunity to answer an open-ended question regarding their experience with the Company Program: *"Use the following space to provide any comments – positive or negative – about your experience in the Injaz Company Program."* The question received a significant response both in the numbers of youth that took time to provide comments and the detail provided therein.

The following section provides an overview analysis of the comments provided by participating students. To guide this quantitative analysis, we reviewed the responses provided by survey participants in this section and coded them on the basis of major themes identified within responses, themes that align largely with those presented in the quantitative analysis presented above. While the results cannot be analyzed statistically in the same way that quantitative results can, they are particularly interesting as they come from students without particular prompts.

By and large, the responses from students were extremely positive. In fact, 98 percent of respondents reported positive comments regarding their experiences. Overall, negative comments or critiques were provided by 26.5 percent of respondents, although most of these were provided in the context of otherwise positive reviews.

5.7.1. Student Perceptions on the Benefits of Injaz's Company Program

The experience of working with teams and improved teamwork ability stand out as the benefit of Injaz's Company Program that earns the most appreciation from participants. Nearly 33 percent of student responses focus, at least in part, on teamwork or working within groups in describing what the benefitted from during the program. In addition, 14 percent of respondents noted that the Company Program improved their ability to interact and communicate with others, while nearly 12 percent noted an improved respect for others and their opinions. Slightly more than 5 percent described how the program gave them negotiating skills to deal with conflict and to reach mutually agreeable ends.

Interpersonal communications and teamwork seem to be the benefits most appreciated by participants. However, respondents note other self-efficacy factors that they felt improved after participation in the program. More than 13 percent stated that the Company Program experience had improved their self-confidence, allowing them to overcome shyness and fear. Nearly 13 percent stressed that participation had taught them how to deal with and overcome problems. About 9 percent highlighted a greater sense of responsibility, while 7 percent noted an improved capacity for creativity and innovation. 4 percent of respondents felt that participation had improved their ability to persuade others of their ideas. Fewer respondents noted an improved capacity for public speaking, self-expression, time management, decision making, leadership and adaptability to changing environments.

Nearly 15 percent of participants highlighted that the program taught them about business and the economy more broadly, while 17 percent stated that the experience had taught them how to establish and manage a business. In describing this knowledge of business, respondents are enthusiastic, but only 3 percent specifically state that the Company Program inspired them to want to start their own businesses. Many respondents focused in on very particular aspects of business that participation had drawn them to: buying and selling stocks, developing contracts, marketing, etc. Toward this end, nearly 5 percent of respondents emphasized the benefit of engaging with members of the business community (volunteers, judges, service providers) and clients.

Slightly less than 15 percent of student responses note that Injaz provided them with improved job-relevant skills. Some focused fairly specifically, noting that they improved their abilities in writing and presentations. Others noted an appreciation for how Injaz allowed them to apply their skills, skills that they often were not aware that they had until participating in Injaz. Participation in the Company Program also increased individuals' initiative and perceived ability to achieve future goals (9%). Several youth citing the program's role in helping them define and achieve their goals focused specifically on educational goals (2.3%) and career goals (1.4%).

Several students noted general improvements in their sense of personal wellbeing that resulted from participation. Two students noted that the program made them optimistic. Others noted that they had gained a better understanding of themselves or had been able to develop their characters or personality. The Company Program also allowed an environment in which several students said that they had met new people and gained new friends.

5.7.2. Student Critiques of the Company Program

While the comments provided by students were positive overall, several provided critiques of the program, most of which are useful to informing future program implementation rather than providing general negative feedback on the Company Program experience as a whole. In all, 73 critiques or complaints about the Company Program were provided by participating students, nearly all of which were presented also in the context of positive comments about the program.

The most common issue raised by students was the timing of the program, particularly of the national competition, which was held when most students were preparing for final comprehensive examinations. 23 percent of included critiques of the program focused on this issue. This should be understood in the context that the majority of participants in Morocco are in their final year of secondary school and must complete intensive comprehensive examinations, the results of which will determine their ability to pursue university educations and largely determine what fields they will study therein. A related concern was that the Company Program was not long enough and did not provide enough time for the students to develop and implement their company ideas. 15 students provided this critique, representing 20.5 percent of all negative comments on the program.

Other issues of potential concern were voiced with much less frequency. Several students (9, or 12.3 percent of all critiques) voiced concerns about the tensions that arose at times within their groups, as individuals conflicted with each other over decisions related to the development of their student companies. At the same time, many of these students noted that this initial tension was eventually overcome, providing a lesson in problem solving and conflict resolution. Two students complained that their student company experience was troubled by frequent absenteeism or lack of participation by some students, which should be read in the context of the fact that most student companies in the Morocco program consisted of classes placed in the program rather than being run as extra-curricular activities in which students participate by choice. Three students voiced concerns that the program was often very stressful in general.

Several students complained about the quality of instruction and engagement provided by the volunteers appointed to their student groups (9.6 percent of negative comments). In particular, students expressed concern that the volunteers working with their student companies were frequently late or did not show up as expected (3); that lectures were not presented clearly or that the volunteer did not communicate effectively with students (3); or that the program could benefit from more instructors in general (1). It is important to keep in mind the small number of these cases; however, at the same time, Injaz's dependence on volunteers to provide instruction means that the program is vulnerable to the schedules and demands of these busy professionals. Some problems are thus to be expected, but can have significant reputational costs for the organization. One student complained similarly about interactions with Injaz staff, wherein they felt that there was poor communication between students and staff in general.

Several students voiced complaints about the way in which the national competition was carried out (6, or 8.2 percent of negative comments). Particular complaints were that the rules and assessment criteria were vague, that judges' questions were unclear or disconnected from the experience of the Company Program, that awards should differentiate between technical innovators and cosmetically attractive products, and that the competition – at one day – was too short for the student companies to adequately present their cases.

Finally, several students provided critiques that can be viewed actually as a positive response to program participation. Three students lamented the fact that, having created companies with products that they were proud of, they had to liquidate and close the company as part of the program. Similarly, three students wished that they would be allowed to participate in the Company Program in the future, or a follow up program, but understood that students can only participate in the program once.

5.7.3. Selected Responses from Student Participants

The following are selected responses from student answers to the open-ended question described above. While not drawn randomly, they are chosen to reflect a representative sample of the responses provided. (Responses have been edited for grammar and clarity, but care has been taken to ensure that no change to meaning takes place in doing so.)

"It was an unforgettable experience. It helped me to fulfill my dream of establishing a company. It gave me self-confidence. We learned that the secret to success to believe in what you do and team work."

"It was a unique experience where we learned how to manage a business and that helped us to develop the sense of teamwork, good manners and success. Those were our values in the company."

"Personally, I loved this experience and I wish I could do it next year too. I learned a lot about human resources and accepting the opinions of others. Thanks a lot Injaz."

"In fact, it was an amazing experience. I learned how to take responsibility for my actions, interact with my team, self-confidence, trusting the team, be optimistic, recognition of my mistakes, and thinking about the others before myself."

"The program helped me to improve my communication skills, managing disputes, and respecting the opinion of others. It helped me to be courageous and to be able to confront any one. But I think the program should give others the opportunity to participate and expand the program to the whole country."

"It was very good and exciting program; it introduced us to the corporative field and taught us the basics of corporations. I gained both leadership and communication skills. And I think this experiment should be expanded all over the country."

"It was a great experience for the mind and the soul. I learned a lot and improved my abilities, and it made me more confident. Now I know that the future is in my hands. I didn't see any negative things in this experience."

"The negative part was that some participants didn't pay any attention to the project, even the people who should have. Otherwise I learned a lot from this program. I have started initiating conversations, I am not that shy anymore, and I learned the principles of management and accounting."

"We learned a lot of practical and personal stuff and how to deal with other people. But it came at the same time with exams."

"Positives: Team work. My future is clear now. It opened new dimensions for me, as I started from zero. Negatives: nothing."

"It's a dream came true, it's an adventure that I've always wanted to live. The program taught us a lot of things like working in teams, responsibility, listening to others, solving conflicts in a peaceful way, accepting the others opinion, and that making a company is not a difficult thing , it just needs managing and planning."

"I gained a lot from my experience in Injaz. I learned how to apply the skills I've been taught in the course, but there were coordinating issues."

"Negatives: some difficulties at the beginning, miscommunication between the team members. But by listening to each other and communicating in the right way, we managed to overcome all the obstacles we faced and we managed to reach our goals and a profit we didn't expect. All the team members behaved with lots of responsibility, and acted like part of a big family."

"I'd appreciate it if the volunteers were given lessons in communicating with the students, so they would interact with the students in a quiet environment away from confrontation."

"This experience gave me a lot because I gained team spirit and group work. I also learned to be patient, responsible, helpful and understanding. This experience has served a lot socially, helping me to get rid of my shyness and letting me make a fair business by working in groups."

5.8. Discussion

While the results highlighted above must be viewed with caution, given the potential for selection bias, they suggest that Injaz's Company Program provides a learning environment that offers Moroccan youth with valuable experiences and skills that they are not getting through the traditional school curriculum. The students who finish the competition end up with valuable soft skills and skills and knowledge about entrepreneurship. They also have positive views of what they learned as a result of participating in the Company Program.

In regard to Injaz's primary goal of encouraging more youth to become entrepreneurs, the Company Program seems to greatly improve the interest of participants in starting a business. Tangible evidence of efforts to start a business is not found in the data, which is natural given both that the students surveyed are still in school, and the vast majority of them plan to go on to university or higher education before entering the labor market as well as the fact that the follow-up survey was carried out only a few months after the conclusion of the program. This said, however, participating students show a fairly dramatic increase in their interest in starting a business of their own. Moreover, their motivations for doing so are not out of a particular preference to work for themselves but more to have the opportunity to best use their skills, to develop new ideas, and to create jobs and better economic opportunities for others.

More broadly, Injaz participants report having a greater awareness of business and how private sector enterprises operate. They are also more prone to believe that they can get ahead through hard work, that entrepreneurs have the opportunity to succeed, and that entrepreneurs contribute to the development of the economy. Such beliefs not only reflect a greater openness to the potential of entrepreneurship, but a sense of empowerment needed to motivate youth to take on the risks of starting their own businesses as they enter the economy. All of this suggests the benefit of expanding a program like Injaz's Company Program as Morocco struggles with ways to encourage more youth to initiate efforts to start their own businesses upon leaving school or to seek out employment in the private sector.

Results are arguably more interesting in regard to the potential impact that Injaz's Company Program has on soft skills development and the self-efficacy of students. Our results suggest that the experiential learning that goes on within the Company Program provides students with a means of developing soft skills and capacities that they are not necessarily receiving through the course of their regular classes. They are skills that, while more intangible than the specific business-related skills provided by Injaz, can have a wider effect on youth as they enter the labor force, opening opportunities in the public and private sector in addition to self-employment. In particular, the results suggest that the Company Program experience boosts participant perceptions about their own abilities to work in a team setting, to adapt to new situations, to solve problems, to communicate with others more effectively, to persuade others regarding their ideas, and to resolve differences through communication and negotiation.

While improving outcomes for young participants in this area is of secondary importance to Injaz, this area is an important identified gap for youth in Morocco and the wider Arab region, as noted in the introduction. As such, Injaz's Company Program seems to be filling an important void in skills development and the ability of the school system to provide youth with skills needed to be competitive in the labor market. Again, while our data does not provide tangible evidence that young participants are more successful in securing employment having taken the program, evidence of the need for soft skills within the labor market and student perceptions of the skills attained while in the program suggest that a large number of them will be better positioned once they have completed their educations to find gainful employment in the private sector.

5.9. Policy and Program Implications

Currently, Injaz Morocco works with the Ministry of Education to provide its programs, including the Company Program, in a relatively small sample of Moroccan schools in two major urban areas (Rabat and Casablanca). The positive results would suggest that there would be benefit to offering the program to students in a larger number of schools across the country.

Expanding the services provided through Injaz would require support from the Ministry of Education and local school administrators, all of whom are already facing challenges related to the administration of school calendars and curriculum demands. At the same time, expanding the program would require additional support from the private sector, both in terms of the provision of volunteers who serve as instructors and financial support needed to cover costs related to instructional materials and the national competition.

At the same time, our analysis raises some program process issues that Injaz Morocco should address as it works to expand its offerings within Morocco:

First, the way in which the program is offered in most schools – as a class during school hours in which participants are selected rather than opting in – means that students are not there by choice and that some will, in this context, not fully engage with or get much out of the program. Data from these students may not be reflected in our results due to selection bias. However, our qualitative results indicate that some students were frustrated by having to work with partners who were not committed to their student companies. Injaz – and more engaged students – may benefit from more selectivity in participant selection. Running the Company as an extra-curricular activity that participants must sign up for would ensure that participants are more engaged in the course. At the same time, Injaz's other programs – which provide shorter, more focused interventions than the Company Program – can serve as a means of introducing a wider group of youth through classroom activities to entrepreneurial concepts, building the number of youth who would seek out the experience provided by the Company Program.

In the future, Injaz must work more closely with the Ministry of Education to ensure that it has early access to school at the beginning of the school year and is able to implement the Company Program in a way that imposes less stress on student participants. According to feedback from students, this means extending the course over a longer time period and holding the national competition at a time when it does not conflict with comprehensive examinations. Injaz might also consider offering the Company Program to youth prior to their final year in school in order to avoid this conflict.

Part of the power of the Injaz approach is its engagement with volunteers from the private sector, who bring tremendous experience with them and are able to contextualize student learning in a way that trainers with no private sector experience would not. By depending on volunteers in this regard, Injaz will occasionally engage a volunteer whose business obligations conflict with commitments to the program or who do not communicate well with students, as noted in our qualitative analysis.

Finally, while our results strongly point to a significant impact of the program on student self-efficacy, soft skills development and interest in business (both self-employment and private sector employment), it should be noted that the results herein should not be taken to represent the causal evidence of impact that would be provided in the context of a more rigorous impact evaluation. The team suggests that Injaz should engage in an experimental evaluation that is able both to determine the exact causal relationship between participation in the program and outcomes in regard to entrepreneurial activity, job-relevant skills development, and employment. Moreover, such an evaluation should take place over a longer time span, allowing for an assessment of actual outcomes within the labor market after youth leave school.

How Injaz Al-Arab helps youth develop an entrepreneurial mindset

Chapter 6. An exploratory study of the Injaz Company Program in Saudi Arabia

6.1 Introduction

Saudi Arabia stands as the world's second largest producer of crude oil, producing over 8.8 million barrels a day (10.1 percent of global production). The abundance of Saudi Arabia's oil resources has enabled Saudi Arabia to invest significantly in its infrastructure and economic development. Moreover, it has ensured that Saudi Arabia has been able to provide its citizens with opportunities to vastly improve their quality of life. However, the abundance of oil with which the Saudi population is blessed has also come with costs. The country continues to struggle with efforts to diversify the economy beyond oil, which accounts for nearly 52 percent of GDP.

Moreover, Saudi Arabia has had to depend on importing large numbers of foreign workers, both unskilled and highly skilled, to develop its industrial capacity and growing service economy. There are nearly 6.5 million expatriates residing in Saudi Arabia. They make up nearly 28 percent of the country's total population and 50.2 percent of the labor force. There is also a marked segmentation within the labor market, with the majority of Saudi workers employed within the public sector and the majority of expatriates employed in the private sector. Strikingly, nearly three-quarters of Saudi workers work for the public sector.

This dependence on foreign workers, and the segmentation of workers by nationality and sector, was a rational response to the economic situation in Saudi Arabia during its early development and the first oil boom, when the country arguably did not have the domestic manpower needed for its rapid infrastructure development and where public employment offered a practical means of redistributing oil wealth to Saudi citizens. However, the Saudi population has been transformed in the past decade. Following decades of high population growth, the country is undergoing a demographic transition, and there is now a pronounced youth bulge among the Saudi population. Today, those between the ages of 15 and 24, the age group in which individuals are making the core investments in education and career development that will shape their economic futures, make up over 21 percent of the Saudi population. Those under the age of 25 make up more than 58 percent of the Saudi population.

The scale of the population of young Saudis means that the public sector, despite the country's oil wealth, cannot keep up with the growth of new entrants to the labor force. Overall, the Saudi national labor force has grown at an average annual rate of 4.2 percent over the past decade, while government employment has grown by less than 3 percent a year over the same period (total employment among Saudi nationals has grown by about 3.6 percent a year.). In turn, Saudi Arabia has witnessed increasing rates of youth unemployment. In fact, the unemployment rate for individuals between the ages of 15 and 24 was estimated in 2009 at 29.9 percent. When one considers only the Saudi national population, the rate of youth unemployment jumps up to 40 percent.

As suggested above, the high rate of unemployment is reflective of the unique structure of the Saudi Arabian economy. Given the attractiveness of public sector employment, Saudi youth often queue for jobs in the public sector rather than seeking out employment in the private sector. At the same time, Saudi private sector firms favor the employment of expatriates, who have lower reservation wages and who are easier to dismiss in times of economic downturn or if they should prove to be unproductive workers.

The long-established quota system in Saudi Arabia, which requires Saudi private sector firms to hire 30 percent of employees from the Saudi population, has ensured that private sector firms make efforts to meet their quota requirements by hiring young Saudis; however, most companies in Saudi Arabia have failed to meet their quotas, claiming that there are not enough skilled Saudis to meet their particular skill needs. With the availability of so many trained foreign workers, firms have been loath to take on young Saudi workers and provide them training. Moreover, the system has had perverse results, including disincentivizing productivity among Saudi workers in the private sector (who understand that their positions and salaries often depend more on their national status than productivity) and encouraging the hiring of "ghost workers" to meet quotas (wherein Saudi workers are paid to include their names on employee rolls but are not expected to work).

The lure of public sector employment (and the skewed incentives imposed by quotas) has also shaped the investments that young Saudis are making in education. By and large, youth seek out university degrees that enable them to access public sector jobs rather than degrees that make them competitive in the private sector. Moreover, especially for young men, opportunities in the military and police often disincentivize the pursuit of university education. On top of these labor market drivers, the public education system is troubled by issues of quality. Despite increased efforts to reform the education system, curricula are still dominated by rote memorization and teacher-centered instruction. Students have few opportunities to engage in practical skills application or to develop broader soft skills (teamwork, communication, problem solving, etc.) that would benefit them in their future career development.

Challenges are greater for young Saudi women seeking to enter the marketplace. While young Saudi women are on par with male colleagues in regard to education, they lack the mobility that young men have within the economy. Saudi Arabia's strict conservative social values mean that women have limited access to the public sphere. Public venues are highly segregated, and women must depend on the male family members (or hired drivers) for transportation, since driving is prohibited. Companies hiring women are expected to provide completely segregated working environments (although some industries such as banking are increasingly operating in a mixed gender environment), and they must secure approval of a woman's male guardian before hiring her. Moreover, offered work must be deemed "appropriate" for women and should not impose on the responsibilities of women as caretakers and homemakers.

As such, few Saudi women enter into the labor force at all. Female labor force participation rates are among the lowest in the world at 13.3 percent. Only 6 percent of those women ages 15-24 are in the labor force (12.9 percent of those ages 20-24). Moreover, unemployment rates among young women are extremely high at 71 percent. Most working women are found in education and the medical field, although the number of women working in finance has increased rapidly, filling a niche market of providing financial advisory and banking services to other Saudi women.

In recent years, the Saudi Arabian government has sought to alter the equation for Saudi youth as a whole by promoting privatization and private-led employment creation for Saudi citizens. The government put forward a National Employment Strategy in 2009 to lower unemployment in the short-term through policies aimed at reducing dependency of foreign labor and enhancing competitiveness and productivity of the private sector in the long-run through regulatory reform. Significant steps have been taken regarding easy business start-up regulations. In 2011, the government also deployed the Niqaqat system for regulating foreign worker visas, which incentivizes firms to hire more Saudi workers to renew foreign worker visas and maximize their employment of other foreign workers. Initial results suggest that the system has rapidly increased the hiring of Saudi workers.

Additionally, in the wake of the Arab Spring, the Saudi Arabian government announced a package of financial benefits worth an estimated US$36 billion. The benefits support education, housing, and youth employment. The package also includes, for the first time in Saudi Arabia, unemployment compensation for up to a year for jobless Saudis. Also, the Prince Mohammad bin Fahd Program for Youth Development is providing vocational training and employment to youth in this

302

particularly vulnerable region. The program has provided training to more than 36,000 young Saudis, and reportedly has found employment for more than 39,000 Saudi youths.

Such policy efforts come at significant financial cost to the Saudi government. They also do little to change the long-term incentives for Saudi youth to invest in competitive skills development or to take the risks associated with seeking out employment in the private sector or as business owners. As a result, Saudi Arabia faces the long-term challenge of creating enough jobs on a sustainable basis to meet the needs of Saudi youth while also creating quality jobs that effectively align skill development with the types of jobs that help Saudi Arabia diversify its economy and enabling youth to take on new and emerging opportunities. Moreover, there is a need to create opportunities for Saudi Arabia's increasingly educated young women to contribute their talents to the economic development of their nation.

6.2. Injaz Saudi Arabia and the Company Program

Injaz Saudi Arabia has been working with local schools, both private and public, to deliver a broad base of entrepreneurship training opportunities to Saudi youth. By working with local volunteers from the business community, Injaz seeks to provide youth in Saudi Arabia with opportunities to develop the basic business skills and the financial literacy they need to start and run their own businesses, while developing the softer job-ready skills that are in increasing demand by the private sector through an experiential learning environment.

As such, Injaz Saudia offers intermediate, secondary and university students with programs in which they are able to participate as part of their school curriculum (see Table 6.1). For each of these programs, Injaz provides instructional materials, secures and trains volunteers to run the programs, and works with local school administrators to arrange for program delivery within schools. Programs range from day-long interventions like Innovation Camp to programs carried out over the course of the academic year, like the Company Program. The Company Program is the most important program among Injaz's offerings in Saudi Arabia.

Table 6.1: Injaz Programs Offered in Saudi Arabia

Program name	Duration	Age group	Purpose
Banks in Action	8 sessions	Secondary/ university	Promotes understanding of banking fundamentals and operations of competitive banks.
Be Entrepreneurial	Variable	Secondary	Provides interactive classroom activities aimed to encourage youth to start their own businesses before leaving school.
Business Ethics	7-12 sessions	Secondary	Fosters student's ethical decision-making as they prepare to enter the workforce
Success Skills	7 sessions	Secondary	Works with students to prepare them for job search and interview skills.
Job Shadow	4 sessions	Secondary/ university	Prepares students for careers with 3 classroom sessions and an on-site orientation in the workplace.
Economics for Success	6 sessions	Secondary	Introduces students to personal finance and educational and career options.
More than Money	6 sessions	Grades 3-5	Teaches students about earning, saving and spending money responsibly.
Entrepreneurship Master Class	1 day	Grades 10-12	Provides an introduction to entrepreneurship and self-employment
Community Citizenship	Variable	Secondary/ university	Provides an opportunity to participate in a community service project
Innovation Camp	1 day	Secondary/ university	Provides an opportunity to discuss a particular business challenge and develop potential solutions.
Company Program	4-6 months	Secondary/ university	Provides participants a opportunity to develop a business plan, launch a business, market and sell their product and then liquidate the business for first-hand experience in entrepreneurship.

In Saudi Arabia, as in the rest of the countries, we designed a study in which students who participated in the Company Program would fill out a questionnaire before and after participating. A group of students from comparable classes within the same schools not participating in the Company Program would also complete a pre- and post-survey. While the assignment of students for participation in the program would not be random, we had expected that the pre-post comparison and the existence of a quasi-comparison group would have allowed us to reach conclusions about plausible program effects.

Logistical impediments caused modifications to the original design. In Saudi Arabia, the team identified and surveyed a treatment group of participants and a comparable control group of non-participants. However, due to logistical problems, we were not able to secure names or contact information for these individuals. Therefore, we were not able to match individual results from pre-surveys to results from post-surveys. We also were not able to survey participants in the control group after the program. In total 123 students were surveyed in the control group, 188 in the participant group before the program and 46 students in the participant group after the program. As such, there is no comparative control group with which to compare results after the completion of the program. We report results for the control group's pre-surveys where appropriate to provide descriptive comparisons with the treatment group.

6.3. Who Participates in the Company Program?

In this section of the report, we characterize the students who completed the questionnaire before participating in the Company Program in the control and participant group.

In terms of broad demographics, only 33 percent of the students in the control group are girls, whereas girls represent 61 percent of the students in the participant group before the program and 50 percent of the participants who completed the survey after the program. The students range in age from 16 to 19 years old in the control group, from 15 to 30 in the participant group at pre-test and from 16 to 18 in the participant group at post-test. Most students are between the ages of 16 and 18: 97 percent in the control group, 95 percent in the participant group at pre-test and all of them in the participant group at post-test.

The level of parental education varies, with fathers having higher levels of education than mothers. Education levels are similar across the three groups. About 60 percent of the fathers have a university or a post-graduate degree, and about 40 percent have secondary education or less. In the control group about 60 percent of the mothers have a university or post-graduate degree; this figure is about 45 percent for those in the participant group.

About half of the fathers work for the government administration, the police, or the armed forces. In the control group, 28 percent are farmers and 20 percent work for the private sector. Among the participants in the program, 15 percent of the fathers at pre-test and 27 percent at post-test work for the private sector. The occupational profile of mothers is somewhat different. Under 20 percent work for the government, the police, or the armed forces. About 40 percent are unemployed or define their occupation as housework.

The students come from homes which vary with regards to how much literacy is valued. A quarter of the students live in homes where less than 25 books are owned, a third live in homes with between 26 and 100 books, and more than a third live in homes with more than 100 books.

We asked the students how satisfied they were with their standard of living, and the majority of them, over 80 percent, was either very satisfied or satisfied, with only about 7 percent reporting dissatisfaction.

6.4. How Do Participants Spend Time and How Does This Differ from Non-Participants?

There are no differences in how students who participate in the program and those who do not spend their time. Over half of the student report that they spend much time studying, with their parents, chatting with friends, in entertainment and watching TV or listening to the radio. Only about a third of the students say that they spend much time investigating career possibilities, researching ideas for business or watching the news. These figures are summarized in the table 6.2.

Table 6.2. How much time do students in Saudi Arabia spend on the following activities in a typical week? (Question: On a scale of 1-5, how much time to you spend on the following activities…? Table includes percentage who answer that they spent *much time* or a *lot of time*.)

	Control	Participant	
	Before	*Before*	*After*
Careers	32%	34%	
Research	35%	39%	
News	27%	33%	
Talk parents	53%	51%	
Studying	47%	63%	
Entertainment	62%	51%	
Chatting friends	65%	59%	
TV and Radio	68%	63%	

Careers	Investigating career possibilities
Research	Research potential ideas for a new business
News	Following the news
Talk parents	Talking to your parents about career possibilities
Studying	Studying or working on school-related activities
Entertainment	Keeping up-to-date on entertainment, fashion or sports
Chatting friends	Chatting with friends
TV and Radio	Watching TV or listening to music

6.5. How Do Participants Differ before and after Participation in the Program?

In this section, we compare three groups: the students in the control group who did not participate in the Company Program, and those who participated in the Company Program, both before and after the program. In each case, we compare those who participated in the program, before participation (before), with those who did not participate (control). We then compare those who participated before and after participation.

Because we do not have information on basic demographic characteristics of the students who took the post-questionnaire, and because we cannot match pre- and post-surveys, we are unable to establish in what ways this group of students is similar or different from the group who took the pre-questionnaire. As a result, the differences identified in this section could be the result of program effects, the result of differences between the students who completed the survey after program completion from those who abandoned the program or did not fill out the follow-up survey (selection effects), or the result of an interaction between program effects and selection effects (i.e., the program may have effects on the kind of students who remain in the program).

6.5.1. Aspirations, Views of Self and Worldviews

There are no differences between the aspirations and worldviews of students in the control and participant group before the program, but there are differences in most dimensions for students who participate in the program before and after participation. Of the eight dimensions surveyed, these views were more favorable after the program than before in seven of them. The aspirations of students are high even before participation in the Company Program.

Each of these aspirations and worldviews was measured with a five-point scale in which students were asked to rate themselves from completely disagree (1) with completely agree (5). In Table 6.3, we have calculated the percentages for each item represented by the students who responded agree or completely agree (points 4 and 5 in the scale).

Table 6.3. Aspirations and worldviews towards future and self of students in Saudi Arabia before and after participating in the Company Program. (Question: On a scale of 1-5, to what extent do you agree or disagree with the following statements about yourself...? Table includes percentage who answer 4 or 5 representing high agreement)

	Control	Participant	
	Before	*Before*	*After*
Achieve goals	81%	82%	93%
Learn from failure	83%	87%	93%
Challenges opport.	65%	62%	75%
Outside school	57%	54%	88%
Studying matters	85%	81%	.
Educ matters	86%	82%	84%
Learnfuture	81%	86%	.
Negotiate	78%	71%	93%
Leadership	74%	73%	82%
Set goals	78%	81%	88%
Creativity	.	.	84%

Achieve goals	I trust that in the future, I will achieve my goals.
Learn from failure	If I fail at something, I try to figure out why so that I can succeed the next time.
Challenges opport.	I see challenges as opportunities.
Outside school	Participate in activities outside of school to prepare for my future.
Studying matters	Studying is important to me
Educ matters	I go to school because education is important for getting a job later.
Negotiate	I believe that achieving my goals requires negotiating with others.
Leadership	I can see myself in a leadership position in the future.
Set goals	I set goals for myself in order to attain the things I want.
Creativity	I try to find creative solutions to problems

As shown, with regards to trust in their own capacity to achieve their goals in the future, there are no differences between the control group and the group who participated in the Company Program. In both groups, over 80 percent of the students are confident that they will achieve their goals. After participation in the program, however, this figure increases to 93 percent.

With regards to the idea that, faced with failure, they try to figure out the reasons to succeed the next time, 83 percent of the students in the comparison group indicated that they did so, whereas 87 percent of the students who would participate in the program did. After participation, however, most (93 percent) of the students surveyed were inclined to figure out the reasons for their failures to succeed in the future.

There is also a sizeable increase in the percentage of students who come to see challenges as opportunities. The percentage of students who agreed or agreed a lot with this view increased from 62 percent before participating in the Company Program – no different to the comparison group – to 75 percent after the program.

There is a very important difference in the percentage of students who participate in out-of-school activities to prepare for their future. Before participating in the Company Program, the percentage who agreed or agreed a lot was 54 percent, whereas it was 57 percent in the comparison group. After the program, this percentage had increased to 88 percent for those surveyed.

The students included in this study believe that studying is important. Nearly 81 percent of those participating in the program agreed or agreed a lot with this statement before participating in the Company Program, compared to 85 percent of those who did not participate. We did not ask this question after participation in the program.

Along similar lines, the percentage of students who believe that education is important to obtain a job in the future is very high and does not differ across the three groups. Before participation in the program, 82 percent of the students agreed or agreed a lot with that statement, compared to 86 percent in the comparison group. After participation in the Company Program, 84 percent of them did.

Similarly, students had very favorable views towards learning before the program with 86 percent of the students who participated in the program believing that what they are learning now will help them in the future. This figure is similar to the 81 percent for those who did not participate in the program. This question was not asked of students after program participation.

Students understand that achieving their goals requires negotiating with others. Before participation in the program, 71 percent agreed or agreed a lot with this statement, compared to 78 percent in the comparison group. This figure increased to 93 percent after the program.

When asked whether they saw themselves as leaders in the future, 73 percent of them did before participating in the program, whereas after the program 82 percent did.

Most students set goals for themselves. Before the program, 81 percent of those who participated in the program did, compared to 78 percent of those who did not participate. After the program, this figure increased to 88 percent.

Students who participated in the program also report an interest in finding creative solutions to problems (84 percent). We did not ask this question to students prior to participation in the program.

To sum up, most students who were surveyed after their participation in the program score on the high end of the various dimensions explored in this section. There are few differences in these various aspects of worldviews and views of themselves between students who did not participate in the program and those who did prior to participation. When there were differences, they were in favor of those students who did not participate. However, after participation in the program, there are sizeable increases in the percentage of students who are at the high end of the scales measuring these dimensions.

6.5.2. Perceived Self-Efficacy

Students were asked to what extent they felt capable of performing a series of tasks. Table 6.4 summarizes the percentage of those students who felt capable of doing them to a great extent – values 4 and 5 in the 5-point scale. In 12 out of the 15 the dimensions evaluated, students who were surveyed after participating in the program felt more efficacious than before. There were some small differences between program participants and students in the comparison group, generally favoring students in the comparison group.

Table 6.4. Perception of Self-Efficacy of students in Saudi Arabia before and after participating in the Company Program. (Question: On a scale of 1-5, to what extent do you feel that you are able to...? Table includes percentage who answer 4 or 5.)

| | Control | Participant | |
	Before	Before	After
Teamwork	82%	79%	96%
Adapt	69%	72%	80%
Problemsolve	73%	72%	89%
Presentpeers	56%	61%	86%
Presentadult	55%	63%	82%
Resolvediff	70%	66%	91%
Purpose	81%	72%	.
Commproblem	62%	58%	76%
Persuade	64%	61%	82%
Negconflict	73%	65%	80%
Competejob	90%	83%	93%
Startbusiness	59%	69%	83%
Rolebusiness	43%	49%	50%
Leadteam	62%	66%	91%

How Injaz Al-Arab helps youth develop an entrepreneurial mindset

Research	57%	59%	63%
Learnrealworld	47%	48%	43%

Teamwork	Work with a team to accomplish a result
Adapt	Adapt to new situations
Problemsolve	Solve problems
Presentpeers	Present a topic to a group of classmates
Presentadult	Present a topic to a group of adults
Resolvediff	Resolve differences within a group to reach a solution satisfactory to most
Commproblem	Solve community problems
Persuade	Persuade a group of people about an idea
Negconflict	Negotiate personal conflicts in a peaceful way
Competejob	Be competitive in securing a good job
Startbusiness	Start and run your own business someday
Rolebusiness	Understand the role of business owners in our economy
Leadteam	Lead the members of a group to meet a deadline in producing a result
Research	Research the potential market for a company
Learnrealworld	To what extent is there a clear connection between what you are learning in school and the real world?

When asked whether they feel capable of working with a team to accomplish a result, 79 percent of them did before participating in the program, compared to 82 percent in the comparison group. This figure increased to 96 percent for students after participating in the program.

In terms of their ability to adapt to new situations, 72 percent of those participating in the program and 69 percent of those in the comparison group reported that they were able to do this, compared to 80 percent after the program.

Before participating in the program, 72 percent reported that they were able to solve problems. This figure increased to 89 percent after participation. Similarly, before the program, 61 percent feel capable of presenting a topic to a group of classmates. After the program 86 percent of them do.

When asked about their ability to present to a group of adults, 55 percent of the students in the comparison group and 63 percent of those in the

314

company program felt capable before the program, in comparison to 82 percent after the program.

Students were asked whether they were capable of resolving differences within a group to reach a solution satisfactory to most group members. Before participation in the program, 66 percent of them felt capable to do so. After program participation, this figure increased to 91 percent.

When asked whether they were able to solve community problems, 58 percent of them said they did before program participation. After participating in the Company Program, 76 percent of them did.

We asked students about their ability to persuade a group of people about their ideas. Before participation in the program, 61 percent of them felt able to do this. This figure increased to 82 percent after program participation.

Students were asked whether they were able to negotiate conflicts in a peaceful way. Before program participation, 65 percent of them did, less than 73 percent in the comparison group. After program participation, 80 percent of the students felt capable of negotiating conflicts in a peaceful way.

When asked whether they felt competitive in securing a good job, 83 percent did so before the program, compared to 93 percent after the program.

We also asked students whether they could start and run their own business someday. Before participation in the program, 69 percent felt capable of doing this, more than 59 percent in the comparison group. This figure increased to 83 percent after program participation.

We asked whether they understood the role of business owners in the economy. Before the program, 49 percent of them did, compared to 43 percent in the control group. After program participation, 50 percent did.

Students were asked whether they felt capable of leading the members of a group to meet a deadline in producing a result. Before program participation, 66 percent did. After program participation, this figure increased to 91 percent.

We asked students whether they could research the potential market for a company. Before program participation, 59 percent of them did; a figure that rose to 63 percent for those who completed the program.

When asked to what extent there was a clear connection between what they learned in school and the real world, 48 percent of them before participation in the program said there was one. This figure declined to 43 percent after program participation. It is possible that engaging in the design of an actual entreprise may have heightened students' interests in real world problems and, as a result, they became slightly more critical of their schooled experiences.

6.5.3.   Educational Aspirations

When asked about their educational aspirations before program participation there are some differences between the three groups, with the comparison group including students with somewhat lower aspirations as 8 percent of the students in that group hope to only complete secondary, 4 percent post-secondary training or diploma, 24 percent university and 64 percent post-graduate training. Before participating in the program, less than 2 percent hoped to only finish secondary, 3 percent post-secondary training or diploma, 21 percent university and 74 percent post-graduate training. After participating in the training program 2 percent hope to finish post-secondary training, 30 percent university and 38 percent post-graduate training.

When asked about their immediate plans after leaving secondary school, most of the students in both groups before participating in the program said they planned to establish their own business; 66 percent in the control group and 72 percent in the participant group (pre-survey). After

316

program participation, only 12 percent planned to immediately establish their own business. Similarly, there is a shift in the percentage that plan to continue with their studies or in additional training programs. Among students in the control group, 20 percent plan to do this, compared to 14 percent in the participant group before the program and 56 percent of the students after the program.

6.5.4. Motivations for Choosing a Job

We asked students to what extent a range of reasons were important to them in choosing a job. The differences here are smaller than in the previous two domains. The largest differences seem to be that students who participate in the Company Program have more confidence in their ability to successfully complete a job interview and to work in the private sector than before participation (Table 6.5).

Before the program, high status of a job was important to 69 percent of the students of participated in the Company Program, relative to 79 percent of those in the comparison group. This figure increases, after program participation, to 72 percent. Ability to earn a lot of money was important to 80 percent of the students before the program and decreases to 74 percent after participation. Good promotion prospects were important to 88 percent of the students before the program, and did not change after program participation. The opportunity to use their skills and abilities was a motivation for 94 percent of the students before the program and to 91 percent of them after the program. Job security was important to 93 percent of the students before the program, and to 86 percent after the program.

The autonomy to have a role in decision making was important to 87 percent of the students before the program in the participant group but to only 65 percent of the students in the control group, and to 89 percent of the students after participating in the program. Having a lot of vacation time was mentioned by 46 percent of the students before the program, and by 54 percent of the students after the program. Easy pace of work was mentioned by 62 percent of the students before the program in the participant group, and by 54 percent of the students in the control group, and by 57 percent after program participation. Ability to work independently without supervision was mentioned by 55 percent of the students before the program, and by 70 percent of the students after the program. A job that is family friendly was mentioned by 80 percent of the students before the program and by 67 percent of the students after the program. For the group of students who had participated in the program, 73 percent mentioned the kind of people they would work with as an important factor (this question was not asked of students before the program).

When asked how confident they were that they could complete successfully a job interview, 73 percent of the students before participating in the company program felt confident, compared to 89 percent after participating in the program. We also asked students how much confidence they had that they would be hired to work in the private sector. Before participating in the program, 59 percent felt very confident, compared to 80 percent after program participation.

Table 6.5. Motivations for Choosing a Job of students in Saudi Arabia before and after participating in the company program. (Question: On a scale of 1 to 5, to what extent are the following reasons important to you in choosing a particular job? Percentage who answer 4 and 5.)

	Control	Participant	
	Before	Before	After
Status	79%	69%	72%
Money	82%	80%	74%
Career	85%	88%	89%
Uses skills	89%	94%	91%
Job security	91%	93%	86%
Role deciding	65%	87%	89%
Ample vacation	48%	46%	54%
Easy pace	54%	62%	57%
Autonomy	50%	55%	70%
Family friendly	68%	80%	67%
Jobcolleagues			73%
Confidence interview	71%	73%	89%
Confidence hired	58%	59%	80%

Status	High status of job
Money	Ability to earn a lot of money
Career	Good promotion prospects, clear career path
Uses skills	Uses my skills and abilities
Job security	Job security
Role deciding	Gives me a role in decision making
Ample vacation	Has a lot of vacation time
Easy pace	Easy pace of work
Autonomy	Ability to work independently without supervision
Family friendly	Job that is family friendly
Confidence interview	How much confidence do you have that you could successfully complete a job interview?
Confidence hired	How much confidence do you have that you could be hired to work in the private sector?

6.5.5. Interest in Starting a Business and Motivations for Business Creation

Before participation in the program we asked students if they thought there was more job security owning their own business versus working for the private sector. About 40 percent of the students in the control group replied that owning their own business, compared to 52 percent in the participant group. At the same time, 18 percent in the control group, compared to 20 percent in the participant group, replied that working for the private sector, and 42 percent in the control group and 28 percent in the participant group did not know. We did not ask this question of the group after participation in the program.

Students were asked for their views on the ease of starting a business and their interest in starting one. When asked how easy they thought it was to start a business in their country today, 59 percent in the control group and 50 percent in the participant group said it was easy or very easy before participating in the Company Program. After participating in the Company Program the figure decreased to 36 percent (Table 6.6).

In response to the question of how interested they were in starting a business someday in the country, 72 percent of them said they were interested or very interested before participating in the company program. After participation in the program, this figure increased to 82 percent.

To the group after participation in the Company Program, we asked how interested they were in someday joining somebody else's business. Half said that they were interested or very interested.

When asked if they had an idea for a business they would like to start, 34 percent of the students in the control group and 25 percent of the students in the participant group said they did; this figure increases to 43 percent after participation in the program.

Table 6.6. Interest in opening a business among students in Saudi Arabia before and after participating in the company program. (Question are on a scale of 1 to 5. Table includes percentage who answer 4 or 5 indicating high agreement.)

	Control	Participant	
	Before	*Before*	*After*
Easy start	59%	50%	36%
Interest	75%	72%	89%
Joininterest			50%
Idea	34%	25%	43%

Easy start	In general, how easy is it to start a business in your country today?
Interest	How interested are you in someday starting your own business?
Joininterested	How interested are you in someday joining somebody else's business?
Idea	Do you have an idea for a business you would like to start

A number of questions in the survey explored the motivations students had to start a business. These are summarized in Table 6.7. There are differences before and after program participation in most of the eight dimensions explored. After participation students are more likely to want to open a business as a way to work for themselves, to resolve important social problems, to earn more money, to create jobs, and to gain fame.

Table 6.7. Importance of various factors in eventual decision to open a business among students in Saudi Arabia before and after participating in the Company Program. (Question: If you were to start your own business in the future, indicate on a scale of 1-5 how important each of the following is in your decision to start a business. Percentage who answer 4 or 5.)

	Control	Participant	
	Before	*Before*	*After*
Work for self	64%	61%	78%
Use skills	83%	89%	85%
Create new ideas	81%	83%	85%
Solve problems	70%	74%	84%
Earn more	69%	77%	85%
Create jobs	68%	68%	76%
Fame	65%	58%	65%
Friends	41%	44%	56%

Work for self	Prefer to work for yourself rather than someone else
Use skills	To use your skills effectively
Create new ideas	To be able to create and develop new ideas
Solve problems	To resolve important social problems
Earn more	You can earn more money running your own business
Create jobs	To create jobs and foster economic growth
Fame	To become a famous entrepreneur
Friends	Your friends want to start a business

Before participating in the Company Program, the percentage who would open a business as a way to work for themselves rather than someone else was 61 percent in the participant group and 64 percent in the comparison group. This figure increased to 78 percent after the program. The percentage who indicated that they would want to do this to use their skills effectively was 89 percent before the program and 85 percent after the program. Those who indicated that this would allow them to create and develop new ideas were 83 percent before the program and 85 percent after the program. Those who mentioned the ability to resolve important problems were 74 percent before the program and 84 percent after the program. Those who mentioned that they could earn more money running their own business were 77 percent before the program

322

and 85 percent after the program. Those who mentioned the ability to create jobs and foster economic growth increased from 68 percent before the program, to 76 percent after the program. The figures for becoming a famous entrepreneur were 58 percent before and 65 percent after. Having friends who want to start a business was a reason for 44 percent of the surveyed group before the program and 56 percent after the program.

6.5.6.   Financial Management

Students were asked about their financial management habits in terms of whether they planned how to spend money, used a budget and saved regularly. There are no differences between the students who participate in the program at pre-test and those in the comparison group in these dimensions. Table 6.8 summarizes these results.

Table 6.8. Financial management habits among students in Saudi Arabia before and after participating in the Company Program. (0=no, 1=yes)

	Control	Participant	
	Before	*Before*	*After*
Plan finances	86%	86%	.
Budget	65%	70%	.
Save	60%	63%	.

Plan finances	When you have money, do you plan ahead for how to spend it?
Budget	Do you use a budget to manage your spending?
Save	Do you regularly save money?

Before the program, 86 percent of participants planned ahead how to spend their money, 70 percent used a budget to manage spending, and 63 percent saved regularly.

6.5.7.   Attitudes towards Entrepreneurship and Business

Students who participated in the Company Program and those who did not were similar in their attitudes towards entrepreneurship before the program. After participation, however, their attitudes differed in several dimensions.

As seen in table 6.9, the percentage of students who agreed that people in the country can get ahead by working hard increased from 56 percent before participating in the Company Program to 65 percent after the Company Program. Those who think that entrepreneurs only think about their own gain declined from 60 percent to 36 percent. Those who believe that women can play an important role in the success of a business increased from 67 percent to 74 percent after participating in the Company Program. There was no difference in the percentage of those who believed that most people should be trusted (only one in five students). Those who believe that there is potential in Saudi Arabia for an entrepreneur to become successful increased from 57 percent to 63 percent. Those who think that men are better qualified than women to be business leaders decreased from 56 percent to 33 percent. There was a significant increase in the percentage of those who think that entrepreneurs create jobs for others from 34 percent to 52 percent. The percentage who thinks that men should have more rights to a job than women when jobs are scarce was 56 percent before the program versus 52 percent after the program. Those who think that entrepreneurs contribute to the economic development of the country represent 39 percent before the program compared to 48 percent after the program.

Table 6.9. Attitudes towards Entrepreneurship in Saudi Arabia. (Question: On a scale of 1-5, to what extent do you agree or disagree with the following statements…?)

	Control	Participant	
	Before	*Before*	*After*
Hard work	53%	56%	65%
Entrepreneurs selfish	63%	60%	36%
Women lead	58%	67%	74%
Trust	21%	28%	24%
Entrepreneurs succeed	52%	57%	63%
Men lead better	57%	56%	33%
Entr. create jobs	34%	34%	52%
Men more rights	59%	56%	52%
Entrepreneurs contribute	35%	39%	48%

Hard work	People in your country can get ahead by working hard.
Entrepreneurs selfish	Entrepreneurs only think about their own gain.
Women lead	Women can play an important role in the success of a business.
Trust	Most people can be trusted.
Entrepreneurs succeed	There is potential in your country for an entrepreneur to become successful.
Men lead better	Men are better qualified than women to be business leaders.
Entr. create jobs	Entrepreneurs create jobs for others.
Men more rights	When jobs are scarce, men should have more rights to a job than women.
Entrepreneurs contribute	Entrepreneurs contribute to the economic development of the country.

In addition, students were asked whether they knew someone who was an entrepreneur. Most students know entrepreneurs who are relatives, family members or friends. There are no differences in this respect between the students who participate in the Company Program and those who do not, except that those participating are slightly more likely to have a parent who is an entrepreneur. There are differences between the pre- and post-responses, which suggest that the students who remain in the program are those who are less likely to have relatives and to know other people who are entrepreneurs.

Table 6.10. Knowledge of Entrepreneurs in Saudi Arabia. (Q: Who among the following people to you know who have started their own business?)

	Control	Participant	
	Before	Before	After
Parent	40%	48%	23%
Sibling	80%	80%	63%
Family	24%	28%	9%
Neighbor	58%	53%	45%
Friend	62%	61%	42%
Teacher	75%	78%	44%
Someone else	30%	34%	26%

Furthermore, the group of students who participated in the program and those who did not are very similar in terms of where they imagine they could access funds to create a business. Before participation in the program students were also asked to what extent they could obtain financing from various sources.

Table 6.11. Sources of funding in Saudi Arabia. (Q: If you were to start a business, to what extent would you be able to depend on the following financing sources to support your new business? On scale 1-5. Table reports percentage who answered 4 or 5.)

	Control	Participant	
	Before	Before	After
Nuclear family	56%	49%	61%
Extended family	25%	22%	33%
Friends	14%	19%	27%
Bank	41%	44%	45%
Grant	56%	49%	40%

Nuclear family	Nuclear family
Extended family	Extended family
Friends	Friend
Bank	Bank loans
Grant	Government grants

6.5.8. Knowledge about Entrepreneurship

A few questions in the survey assessed student knowledge of basic concepts of entrepreneurship and business. There are no differences between the control group and the participant group before participating in the program. After the program, a greater percentage of students demonstrated knowledge of such basic concepts, although this percentage is far from 100 percent as seen in Table 6.12.

Table 6.12. Knowledge about entrepreneurship in Saudi Arabia. (Multiple choice questions)

	Control	Participant	
	Before	*Before*	*After*
Entrepredefine	47%	44%	Not asked
Sell shares	33%	35%	46%
Vision	34%	45%	70%
Marketing	69%	70%	72%
Liquidation	17%	12%	25%
Company	51%	40%	51%

Entrepredefine   An entrepreneur is someone who

Sell shares   Selling shares of stock to get start-up money for a new company is called:

Vision   A _____ represents a company's dream of where it wants to go and what it wants to be.

Marketing   The work you completed in this scenario above is an example of which of the following…?

Liquidation   When a company liquidates, it does which of the following:

Company   By definition, a company must have which of the following

Before participation in the Company Program, students were asked to define an entrepreneur. Only 44 percent correctly identified 'creates a business' as the correct answer. This question was not asked in the follow up.

When asked to identify the term for selling shares of stock to get start-up money for a new company, only a third identified the correct option capitalization before the program, and 46 percent did so after the program.

When asked to fill in the term for the definition of a vision statement, only 45 percent of the students did so correctly before participating in the program, compared to 70 percent after participating in the program. It is noteworthy that most students, before and after the program, selected 'a business plan' as the correct definition of 'a company's dream of where it wants to go and what it wants to be'.

When asked to recognize a scenario representing a marketing strategy, 70 percent of the students did so correctly before participating in the Company Program, compared to 72 percent after program participation.

When asked to recognize the definition of liquidation, 12 percent did so correctly before participating in the Company Program versus 25 percent after program participation.

Lastly, when asked to identify that a company must have stockholders, 40 percent of the students did so before participating in the program, compared to 51 percent of those who had participated in the program.

6.6. How Do Participants in the Company Program Describe the Effects of the Program?

When asked to rate their abilities in a series of questions about possible effects of the program, most participants who were surveyed after the program are very favorable about the changes they observe in themselves.

After participating in the Company Program and attending the national competition, nine in ten students feel more empowered to take a leadership role in the workforce in the future (Table 6.13). Nearly 89 percent of the students say they understand the importance of managing their finances, 93 percent say that they have further developed their educational goals, 84 percent of participants say they have developed their career goals, 96 percent say that they now feel more confident about their ability to successfully compete in the workforce in the future. About 84 percent say they now know more about entrepreneurship, and 91 percent say they are now more interested in starting their own business.

Table 6.13. Retrospective experience in Saudi Arabia (Compare yourself now to where you were at the beginning of the school year. On a scale of 1-5, to what extent do you agree with the following statements about yourself...?)

	Control	Participant	
	Before	Before	After
Leadership	.	.	91%
Finances	.	.	89%
Education goals	.	.	93%
Career goals	.	.	84%
Competitive	.	.	96%
Know entrepreneurship	.	.	84%
Start business	.	.	91%

Leadership	I feel more empowered to take a leadership role in the workforce in the future.
Finances	I realize more that knowing how to effectively manage my finances is important.
Education goals	I have developed (or further developed) my educational goals.
Career goals	I have developed (or further developed) my career goals.
Competitive	I am more confident in my ability to successfully compete in the workforce in the future.
Know entrepreneurship	I know more about entrepreneurship.
Start business	I am more interested in starting my own business.

When asked specifically about the Injaz Company Program, 95 percent of participants found it valuable or very valuable (Table 6.14). More than 90 percent of participants felt that the Injaz Company Program helped them develop the ability to work with others as a team, helped them develop the capacity to innovate and to think more creatively, taught them how to manage a budget, and helped them learn to communicate with others and negotiate differences. More than 80 percent reported that the Company Program had taught them critical thinking skills, helped them develop initiative and self-motivation, aided them in developing leadership capabilities, helped them learn to speak in public more easily, and helped them learn to solve problems.

Table 6.14. Contribution of the Company Program in Saudi Arabia. (In your opinion, on a scale of 1-5, to what extent did your participation in the Injaz Company Program help you with the following...?)

	Control	Participant	
	Before	Before	After
Valuable	.	.	95%
Team work	.	.	91%
Innovation	.	.	93%
Critical thinking	.	.	84%
Initiative	.	.	87%
Leadership	.	.	84%
Budgeting	.	.	95%
Problem solve	.	.	80%
Communicate	.	.	91%
Negotiate	.	.	93%
Sell	.	.	89%
Speak	.	.	84%
Creativity	.	.	91%

Team work	It helped me develop the ability to work with others as a team.
Innovation	It helped me develop the capacity to innovate.
Critical thinking	It taught me critical thinking skills.
Initiative	It helped me development initiative and self-motivation.
Leadership	It helped me develop my abilities as a leader.
Budgeting	It taught me how to manage a budget.
Problem solve	It helped me learn to solve problems.
Communicate	It helped me learn to communicate with others.
Negotiate	It helped me learn to negotiate differences with people.
Sell	It helped me learn to sell ideas or products.
Speak	It helped me learn to speak in public more easily.
Creativity	It inspired me to think more creatively about problems.

Students were also asked to evaluate some of the components of the program (Table 6.15). Three in four of them say the lectures aroused their interest in the topics, and that the volunteer delivered the lectures in an interactive manner. About 67 percent say the volunteer presented the content clearly and about 80 percent say that the volunteer was helpful and responsive to questions. Finally, 67 percent of them found the Student Guide useful or very useful.

Table 6.15. Evaluation of the Components of the Program in Saudi Arabia. (On a scale of 1-5, to what extent do you agree with the following comments about the Injaz Company Program…?)

	Control	Participant	
	Before	*Before*	*After*
Lecture	.	.	73%
Volunclear	.	.	67%
Volunrespond	.	.	80%
Studyguide	.	.	67%
Volunlecture	.	.	76%
Lecture		Company Program lectures aroused my interest for the topics being discussed.	
Volunclear		The volunteer presented the program's content in a clear way.	
Volunrespond		The volunteer was helpful and responsive to our questions.	
Studyguide		The Student Guide was useful.	
Volunlecture		The volunteer held lectures in an interactive way.	

6.7. A Qualitative Analysis of Student Descriptions of Program Effects

Within the follow-up survey, students were provided the opportunity to answer an open-ended question regarding their experience with the Company Program: "Use the following space to provide any comments – positive or negative – about your experience in the Injaz Company Program." Of the 107 participants for whom we secured follow-up surveys, including both those students in the schools surveyed as part of the pre-survey and other students participating in the program who were not surveyed in the pre-test, 50 used this opportunity to express views – either positive or negative – about the program. Most responses were favorable. In fact, 62 percent of responses were entirely positive, while 28 percent provided critiques in the context of otherwise positive feedback. Overall, while student responses were not generally detailed, the feedback provides information that provides further understanding to our quantitative analysis of the program while providing criticism that can help Injaz improve the implementation of its program in the future.

On the positive side, many respondents emphasized that the program had prepared them to understand business and how to start and run their own business (24 percent). About 22 percent of respondents felt that the program had improved their self-confidence and sense of self-reliance. A large share of participants also noted how the program had enhanced their ability to communicate effectively with people (20%) or to work cooperatively within teams (16 percent). Improved leadership capacity and time management ability were each addressed by 8 percent of respondents. Other views expressed by individual participants focused on the benefit of the program in regard to helping them gain respect for others' opinions, improved critical thinking, better ability to manage responsibilities and finances, adaptability to changing environments, understanding and working with customers, and greater capacity to interview and compete for jobs.

Most negative program critiques focused on time constraints in the context of tight schedules and other academic responsibilities (10 percent of respondents). Several students built on this, noting specifically that their schools had not cooperated with them in giving them enough time to develop their student companies (4 percent of respondents) or that the program's delivery was not efficiently carried out (4 percent). Others felt that they did not have the capacity or access to the market needed to develop their company ideas or that they did not have the resources to compete with student companies that had more financial resources (6 percent). Two students complained that their volunteer had not met with them on a timely basis or was not qualified. Another two students felt that the competition rules were unclear and that they did not have enough information to prepare their companies to compete effectively in the competition.

6.8. Discussion

The results of this study suggest that after participating in the Company Program, students have higher aspirations, more ambitious views towards the future and feelings of empowerment than before participating, although their perspectives on these issues are generally positive even before program participation. Students report also higher self-efficacy in a range of soft skills such as ability to work with others, adapt to new situations, solve problems or make presentations to peers and adults, resolve differences and others after program participation. Students' educational aspirations are also higher after program participation.

There are no obvious differences in the motivations students have for choosing a job after participating in the program. However, the percentage of students interested in starting a business and having an idea to start a business is higher after program participation than before. The motivations to start a business also change after program participation, with students more likely to prefer to work for themselves, to resolve important social problems, to earn more money, to create jobs or become famous entrepreneurs. Attitudes towards entrepreneurship in general become more favorable after participating in the program. Participation in the program does not seem to affect the financial management skills of students, but participating students demonstrate higher knowledge of basic concepts about entrepreneurship and business.

Overall students who participate in the program attribute to the program an increase in their leadership skills, understanding the importance of effective financial management, more developed educational and career goals, greater confidence in their ability to compete, more knowledge about entrepreneurship and more interest in starting their own business. They also think the program increased their competency in a range of soft-skills from valuing the views of others to the ability to work in a team to thinking creatively.

In considering these favorable results, however, we should keep in mind that the design of this study does not allow us to establish that the program caused these observed differences. The fact that the group who participated in Injaz is in general very similar, in the outcomes we measured, to the comparison group, and the fact that there are differences in numerous outcomes between the pre- and post-surveys suggests that the program *may have* produced those changes. However, these changes could also be the result of differences between the students who took the post-survey and those who took only the pre-survey – we do now know how the students who did not finish the program differ from those who did—or they could be due to the influence of other factors, independent of the program, that took place concurrently with program participation.

The consistently positive differences, however, as well as the attributions made by the students, suggest that it is plausible that Injaz provides unique opportunities to develop skills and dispositions which are not typically provided by schools in Saudi Arabia.

6.9. Policy and Program Implications

Although our results must be viewed with caution given potential bias, the data – and participant feedback on the experience provided by the program – strongly suggest that it has significant benefits in exposing youth to entrepreneurship and, perhaps more importantly for many youth, in regard to soft skills development, job-relevant skills and self-efficacy. The experiential learning opportunity provided by the Company Program is a unique learning experience for many youth, one that provides tangible skill development and makes students aware of skills they already possess but are not aware that they have. As such, it is reasonable to expect that Saudi youth would benefit from expansion of this program.

Such an expansion will also require addressing key challenges that have faced Injaz staff over the past year. Discussions with staff indicate that there are several concerns on the programmatic side that must be addressed. First, securing the commitment of volunteers to the program, even though it is only run over 12 weeks in Saudi Arabia, has proven difficult. Moreover, the staff have struggled to secure volunteers of the caliber sought, volunteers that are able to truly mentor and assist students creatively in selecting products and building their businesses. These challenges will only become more acute as the program expands in scope.

Another logistical concern is related to the ability to provide female participants with the full scope of the program's potential in an environment wherein they have restricted access to the public sphere, given the conservative nature of Saudi society. Generally, female students do not have the ability to go out into the marketplace, particularly industrial areas, to work with potential product manufacturers or service providers. Ensuring that young women get the most out of the program's experience in the future will require significant efforts to engage parents and educate them on the positive outcomes of the Company Program so that they provide the support needed for their students to fully participate.

A third issue raised by Injaz staff is a realization that the curriculum documents, student materials and the descriptions of roles for various departments of the student companies (finance, HR, marketing, etc.) need to be revised. The curriculum documents must be made clearer, simpler and more streamlined to allow students and volunteers to quickly digest them and move on to the experiential aspects of the program. Injaz is aware of concerns raised both by volunteers and students in this regard and are taking steps to alleviate the problem.

Finally, expansion of the program comes at a financial cost at a time when the local Saudi office feels that they are already lacking in the financial capital needed to run the program to its maximum output. As such, Injaz

Saudi Arabia must reach out to members of the Saudi business community to ensure that they understand better the benefits of investing in what truly seems to be a substantive and significant program for young Saudis, both in terms of preparing them for employment in the Saudi private sector and as future business owners.

How Injaz Al-Arab helps youth develop an entrepreneurial mindset

Chapter 7. An exploratory study of the Injaz Company Program in the United Arab Emirates

7.1. Introduction

With a per capita GDP of nearly $39,600, the United Arab Emirates (UAE) is one of the wealthiest countries in the Arab world. The country's wealth is driven by its substantial oil reserves, but the development of Dubai into a regional hub for investment and transportation has helped to diversify the country's economy. As such, despite a serious contraction during the global economic downturn, the country's private sector has boomed, and Dubai attracts businesses and entrepreneurs from across the region and the world.

In turn, the UAE has been extremely successful in creating jobs, attracting workers from all over the world. For Emirati youth, however, there are notable challenges in regard to employment. In fact, the unemployment rate among Emirati youth (ages 15-24) in 2009 was nearly 28 percent, compared with a total unemployment rate of only 4 percent and an unemployment rate for Emirati nationals of 14 percent. The high rate of unemployment among young nationals is driven by several structural challenges related to the nature of the UAE economy and the role of Emiratis therein.

First, there is a legacy of labor market segmentation in the country, with nationals favoring public sector employment and private sector employment being dominated by expatriate workers. In fact, over 90 percent of employed Emirati workers are found in the public sector or quasi-public enterprises. This segmentation of the labor market is driven by several factors, including the high wages, benefits and job security provided in the public sector, which causes young Emiratis to queue for such jobs rather than seeking private sector employment or starting their own businesses.[16] On the other hand, private sector firms are more eager to hire expatriates given the lower wage expectations among these workers and the greater flexibility they have in hiring and firing these workers compared with Emiratis.

The lure of public sector employment also shapes the investments that young Emiratis are making in education. By and large, youth seek university degrees that enable them to access public sector jobs rather than degrees that make them competitive in the private sector. Moreover, especially for young men, opportunities in the military and police often discourage them from pursuing university education. On top of these labor market drivers, the public education system is troubled by issues of quality. Despite increased efforts to reform the education system, curricula are still dominated by rote memorization and teacher-centered instruction. Students have few opportunities to apply practical skills or to develop broader soft skills (teamwork, communication, problem solving, etc.) that would benefit them in their future career development.

Despite the country's wealth, Emirati youth facing the school-to-work transition are placed in a difficult situation. Rationally, they pursue public sector employment that is increasingly difficult to attain, while their efforts in doing so ensure that they are less competitive for private sector jobs. Policy makers have tried to push the private sector to employ more Emiratis through the provision of quotas, as well as increasing the attractiveness of private sector employment for Emiratis by passing legislation that makes it illegal to dismiss Emirati workers unless they commit legal infractions. While this has increased hiring to some degree, such regulations have had a perverse effect in making it less desirable for firms to hire Emiratis and encouraging many firms to find ways around the rules. More recently, policy makers have considered wage subsidies

---

[16] Many Emiratis are entrepreneurs, but they generally start their own businesses after securing a public sector job that allows them the financial security on which to build their new enterprises.

as a replacement for quotas; this strategy is yet untested and would prove to be extremely costly to sustain with public finance.

In this context, new approaches to employment for young Emiratis are necessary. The promotion of youth entrepreneurship is an increasingly attractive alternative to bolstering employment in the public sector and increased regulation or subsidization of the private sector. There are a growing number of organizations – both public and private – with the focus of preparing young Emiratis to take on the challenges of business ownership and to support them with seed funding and incubation as they do so.

7.2. Injaz UAE and the Company Program

Towards this end, Injaz has been working with local schools, both private and public, in the United Arab Emirates to deliver a broad base of entrepreneurship training opportunities to Emirati and expatriate youth through schools. By working with local volunteers from the business community, Injaz seeks to provide youth in the UAE with opportunities to develop the basic business skills and the financial literacy they need to start and run their own businesses, while developing the softer job-ready skills that are in increasing demand by the private sector through an experiential learning environment.

As such, Injaz UAE offers intermediate and secondary students with a number of programs in which they are able to participate as part of their school curriculum (see Table 7.1). For each of these programs, Injaz provides instructional materials, secures and trains volunteers to run the programs, and works with local school administrators to arrange for program delivery within schools. Particular programs range from day-long interventions like Innovation Camp to programs carried out over the course of the academic year, like the Company Program. The *Company Program* is the most important program among Injaz's offerings in the UAE.

Table 7.1: Injaz Programs Offered in the United Arab Emirates

Program name	Duration	Age group	Purpose
Banks in Action	8 sessions	Secondary/ university	Promotes understanding of banking fundamentals and operations of competitive banks.
Be Entrepreneurial	Variable	Secondary	Interactive classroom activities aimed to encourage youth to start their own businesses before leaving school.
Business Ethics	7-12 sessions	Secondary	Fosters student's ethical decision-making as they prepare to enter the workforce
Success Skills	7 sessions	Secondary	Works with students to prepare them for job search and interview skills.
Job Shadow	4 sessions	Secondary/ university	Prepares students for careers with 3 classroom sessions and an on-site orientation in the workplace.
Economics for Success	6 sessions	Secondary	Introduces students to personal finance and educational and career options.
More than Money	6 sessions	Grades 3-5	Teaches students about earning, saving and spending money responsibly.
Entrepreneurship Master Class	1 day	Grades 10-12	Provides an introduction to entrepreneurship and self-employment
Community Citizenship	Variable	Secondary/ university	Provides an opportunity to participate in a community service project
Innovation Camp	1 day	Secondary/ university	Provides an opportunity to discuss a particular business challenge and develop potential solutions.
Company Program	4-6 months	Secondary/ university	Provides an opportunity for participants to develop a business plan, launch a business, market and sell their product and then liquidate the business for first-hand experience in entrepreneurship.

Logistical impediments caused modifications to the original study design described in chapter one. In the UAE, the team was not able to identify any viable control groups, because the Company Program was provided to all comparable students within the relatively small schools in which the program was run and because the survey team could not identify any other schools willing to provide access to students. As such, our results reflect only a pre- and post-assessment of participants with *no counterfactual* allowing for net impact assessment.

At baseline, we surveyed 79 students who participated in the Company Program. These students were from two public schools (one boys' school and one girls' school) in Dubai.[17] In all, they represented 6 student companies (3 from each school). After the completion of the program, 61 of those who participated in the program completed surveys, as well as 13 who did not complete the program. Based on student names and contact information, we were able to match pre- and post-results for 58 students who completed the program, of which 32 are girls. The quantitative analysis in this report is based on these 58 students that we could match.

---

[17] A total of four schools participated in the Company Program during 2010-2011. These included the two public schools under study, as well as another girls' public school and a Dubai private school for which we were not able to secure access to survey students.

7.3. Who Participates in the Company Program?

In this section of the report, we characterize these 58 students when they completed the questionnaire before participating in the Company Program. This allows us to detail the demographics of Injaz participants in UAE.

As mentioned, 55 percent of the participants in the program are women. In terms of age, 7 percent of the students are 15 years old, 83 percent are 16, and 10 percent are 17 years old.

The level of parental education ranges among students and is higher, on average, for fathers than for mothers. The education of fathers ranges from one student whose father had no formal education to 5 percent of the students whose fathers had post-graduate education. About 57 percent have secondary education or less, and a third have intermediate education or less. Thirty-one percent have university or graduate studies. For mothers, 35 percent have intermediate studies or less and 69 percent have secondary studies or less, and 23 percent have university studies or graduate studies.

Fathers of the students have a range of occupations, but 55 percent of them work in government administration, policy, the armed forces, or in a public sector company. About 11 percent are farmers and 18 percent are retired or outside the labor force. Only 2 percent work in a large private sector company. A large percentage of mothers (37 percent) are involved in housework, while 18 percent are unemployed and 8 percent are students. About 13 percent work in government administration, policy, the armed forces, or in a public sector company, and none of them work in a private company.

Regarding how literacy is valued, 37 percent of the students come from homes where there are less than 25 books. An additional 30 percent of them live in homes where there are between 26 and 100 books. A third of the students live in homes with more than 100 books.

Finally, we asked the students how satisfied they were with their standard of living, and most are satisfied: 52 percent are very satisfied, and an additional 28 percent are satisfied. Only 5 percent of the students are not satisfied or somewhat satisfied.

7.4. How Do Participating Students Spend Their Time?

Students were asked, in the pre-questionnaire, how much time they spent in several activities.

Most students (74 percent) report that they study, followed by watching TV, chatting with friends, entertainment and with their parents. Only about a quarter of the students devote time to study career options, research business opportunities or follow the news. These figures are summarized in Table 7.2.

Table 7.2. How much time do students in the United Arab Emirates spend on the following activities in a typical week? Responses before participating in the company program (Question: On a scale of 1-5, how much time to you spend on the following activities. Table includes percentage who answer that they spent *much time* (4) or a *lot of time (5)*.)

	Participant	
	Before	*After*
Careers	27%	
Research	30%	
News	27%	
Talk parents	53%	
Studying	74%	
Entertainment	60%	
Chatting		
Friends	63%	
TV and Radio	67%	

Careers	Investigating career possibilities
Research	Research potential ideas for a new business
News	Following the news
Talk parents	Talking to your parents about career possibilities
Studying	Studying or working on school-related activities
Entertainment	Keeping up-to-date on entertainment, fashion or sports
Chatting friends	Chatting with friends
TV and Radio	Watching TV or listening to music

7.5. How Do Participants Differ before and after Participation?

In this section, we compare the 58 students before and after participation in the program. We also performed a statistical test of the significance of these differences. Since we do not have a similar comparison for a control group, we do not know whether the differences observed are due to participation in the program, or the result of other influences in the lives of the students during the period when they participated in the Company Program, or simply maturation.

7.5.1. Aspirations, Views of Self and Worldviews

Overall, students have high aspirations and broad worldviews before as well as after the program. These aspirations, however, are higher after participation in the program than before in most of the dimensions measured. For example, 78 percent of the students believed that they could achieve their goals in the future before program participation; after participating in the program, this percentage had increased to 83 percent. Similar increases are observed in all dimensions except for believing that education is important to getting a job and believing that negotiation is necessary to resolve differences. The largest difference observed is in participation in activities outside school to prepare for the future, which is 63 percent after participation in the program but only 33 percent before program participation.

Each of these aspirations and worldviews was measured with a five-point scale in which students were asked to rate themselves from completely disagree (1) with completely agree (5). In table 7.3, we have calculated the percentages for each item represented by the students who selected agree or completely agree (points 4 and 5 in the scale).

Table 7.3. Aspirations and worldviews towards future and self of students in the United Arab Emirates before and after participating in the Company Program. (Question: On a scale of 1-5, to what extent do you agree or disagree with the following statements about yourself. Table 7.3. includes percentage who answered 4 or 5.)

	Participant	
	Before	*After*
Achieve goals	78%	83%
Learn from failure	86%	91%
Challenges opport.	66%	86%
Outside school	33%	63%
Studying matters	88%	..
Educ matters	93%	90%
Learnfuture	84%	90%
Negotiate	81%	74%
Leadership	74%	78%
Set goals	76%	81%

Achieve goals	I trust that in the future, I will achieve my goals.
Learn from failure	If I fail at something, I try to figure out why so that I can succeed the next time.
Challenges opport.	I see challenges as opportunities.
Outside school	Participate in activities outside of school to prepare for my future.
Studying matters	Studying is important to me
Educ matters	I go to school because education is important for getting a job later.
Learnfuture	The things that I am learning now will help me in the future.
Negotiate	I believe that achieving my goals requires negotiating with others.
Leadership	I can see myself in a leadership position in the future.
Set goals	I set goals for myself in order to attain the things I want.
Creativity	I try to find creative solutions to problems.

Formal tests of the statistical significance of the differences between before and after the program showed that in the post-survey students are more likely to see challenges as opportunities and are more likely to participate in extra-curricular activities to prepare for their future. The differences in these dimensions are statistically significant at the 5 percent level (Table 7.4).

Table 7.4. Differences in Aspirations and worldviews towards future and self of students in the United Arab Emirates before and after participating in the Company Program. (Question: On a scale of 1-5, to what extent do you agree or disagree with the following statements about yourself)

	Participant			
	Before	After	*PA - PB*	
Achieve goals	4.31	4.34	0.03	
	(0.80)	(0.98)	*0.21*	
Learn from failure	4.45	4.59	0.14	
	(0.84)	(0.77)	*0.92*	
Challenges opport.	3.96	4.44	0.47	**
	(1.10)	(0.82)	*2.60*	
Outside school	3.07	3.65	0.58	**
	(1.24)	(1.38)	*2.36*	
Educ matters	4.70	4.59	-0.12	
	(0.71)	(0.90)	*-0.77*	
Negotiate	4.19	4.12	-0.07	
	(0.97)	(1.06)	*-0.38*	
Leadership	4.12	4.33	0.20	
	(1.04)	(0.87)	*1.15*	
Set goals	4.17	4.25	0.07	
	(0.98)	(0.89)	*0.42*	

*** significant at 1% level, ** at 5% level, * at 10% level.
Standard deviations in parentheses, t-statistics in *italics*.

7.5.2. Perceived Self-Efficacy

Students were asked to what extent they felt capable of performing a series of tasks. Table 7.6 summarizes the percentage of those students who felt capable of doing them to a great extent (values 4 and 5 in the 5-point scale). While most students tend to report high levels of self-efficacy on those dimensions, there are important gains after participation in the Company Program in most dimensions. There are gains in perceived self-efficacy to work with a team to accomplish results, to adapt to new situations, to solve problems, to present to a group of peers or to adults, to resolve differences within a group to reach a solution satisfactory to most, to persuade a group of people about an idea, to be competitive in securing a job, to start and run a business someday, and to lead a team. There are no differences in ability to solve community problems, to negotiate personal conflicts in a peaceful way, understanding the role of business owners in the economy, researching the potential market for a company and seeing a relationship between what is learned in school and the real world. The results are presented in Table 7.5.

Table 7.5. Perception of Self-Efficacy of students in the United Arab Emirates before and after participating in the Company Program. (Question: On a scale of 1-5, to what extent do you feel that you are able to. Table includes percentage who answer 4 or 5)

	Participant	
	Before	*After*
Teamwork	76%	81%
Adapt	64%	79%
Problemsolve	67%	76%
Presentpeers	49%	67%
Presentadult	47%	55%
Resolvediff	64%	71%
Purpose	85%	..
Commproblem	64%	66%
Persuade	64%	71%
Negconflict	72%	68%
Competejob	85%	93%
Startbusiness	54%	69%
Rolebusiness	41%	41%
Leadteam	59%	71%
Research	52%	48%
Learnrealworld	54%	59%
Teamwork	Work with a team to accomplish a result	

Adapt	Adapt to new situations
Problemsolve	Solve problems
Presentpeers	Present a topic to a group of classmates
Presentadult	Present a topic to a group of adults
Resolvediff	Resolve differences within a group to reach a solution satisfactory to most
Purpose	Understand your purpose in life
Commproblem	Solve community problems
Persuade	Persuade a group of people about an idea
Negconflict	Negotiate personal conflicts in a peaceful way
Competejob	Be competitive in securing a good job
Startbusiness	Start and run your own business someday
Rolebusiness	Understand the role of business owners in our economy
Leadteam	Lead the members of a group to meet a deadline in producing a result
Research	Research the potential market for a company
Learnrealworld	To what extent is there a clear connection between what you are learning in school and the real world?

The results of the statistical analysis of these differences show that (at the 5% significance level) students after the program are more likely to feel that they are able to adapt to new situations and present a topic to a group of classmates. Also, they are (at the 10% significance level) more likely to feel that they are able to work in teams to accomplish a result, to start and run their own business someday, understand the role of business owners in the economy, and lead a team to produce a result. Most of the differences in the other dimensions are not statistically significant although the direction of these differences tends to be positive after program participation.

Table 7.6. Differences in Perception of Self-Efficacy of students in the United Arab Emirates before and after participating in the company program. (Question: On a scale of 1-5, to what extent do you feel that you are able to…?)

| | Participant | | |
	Before	After	PA - PB
Teamwork	4.00	4.28	0.28 *
	(0.96)	(0.81)	1.68
Adapt	3.79	4.19	0.40 **
	(1.04)	(0.85)	2.25
Problemsolve	3.95	4.17	0.23
	(0.95)	(0.88)	1.31
Presentpeers	3.36	3.86	0.50 **
	(1.35)	(1.02)	2.25
Presentadult	3.43	3.66	0.23
	(1.24)	(1.12)	1.04
Resolvediff	3.81	4.03	0.22
	(1.12)	(1.03)	1.13
Commproblem	3.77	3.88	0.11
	(0.96)	(1.04)	0.57
Persuade	3.82	3.90	0.08
	(1.04)	(0.99)	0.41
Negconflict	3.98	3.95	-0.04
	(1.01)	(1.03)	-0.18
Competejob	4.47	4.60	0.14
	(0.98)	(0.72)	0.86
Startbusiness	3.59	4.03	0.45 *
	(1.26)	(1.18)	1.98
Rolebusiness	3.02	3.38	0.36 *
	(1.25)	(1.04)	1.70
Leadteam	3.60	4.00	0.40 *
	(1.20)	(1.09)	1.86
Research	3.54	3.43	-0.11
	(1.18)	(1.03)	-0.55
Learnrealworld	3.60	3.79	0.19
	(0.85)	(0.89)	1.12

*** significant at 1% level, ** at 5% level, * at 10% level.
Standard deviations in parentheses, t-statistics in *italics*.

7.5.3. Educational Aspirations

There is a small increase in the educational aspirations of students after participating in the program. Before the program, 7 percent of the students aspired to complete a post-secondary diploma, 25 percent a bachelor's degree, and 64 percent post-graduate studies (with 4 percent having other educational aspirations). After participation in the program, only 2 percent aspire to post-secondary diploma, while 30 percent aspire to complete a bachelor's degree, and 68 percent aspire to complete a post-graduate degree. A slightly higher percentage of students plan to continue with their studies immediately after finishing secondary school when asked after participation in the Company Program. This percentage is 89 percent before participation and 93 percent afterwards.

7.5.4. Motivations for Choosing a Job

We asked students to what extent a range of reasons were important to them in choosing a particular job. There are modest differences in these motivations (Table 7.9). After program participation students are less likely to be interested in the high status of a job, more interest in a clear career path, somewhat more interested in a job that gives them a role in decision making, more interested in the ability to work independently (without supervision), and more open to a job that is not family-friendly (in regard to work hours or flexibility). They were also more interested in having more vacation time and an easy pace of work. They were equally interested in earning a lot of money, in a job that uses their skills and abilities, and in job security. Overall, students were more confident that they could complete a job interview and that they could be hired to work in the private sector. The only statistically significant difference, however, is observed in the confidence to complete a job interview.

Table 7.7. Motivations for Choosing a Job of students in the United Arab Emirates before and after participating in the company program. (Question: On a scale of 1 to 5, to what extent are the following reasons important to you in choosing a particular job? Percentage who answer 4 and 5)

| | Participant | |
	Before	After
Status	88%	79%
Money	87%	88%
Career	88%	93%
Uses skills	92%	93%
Job security	88%	86%
Role deciding	81%	84%
Ample vacation	45%	54%
Easy pace	66%	72%
Autonomy	55%	65%
Family friendly	76%	66%
Jobcolleagues	.	84%
Confidence interview	73%	93%
Confidence hired	66%	71%

Status	High status of job
Money	Ability to earn a lot of money
Career	Good promotion prospects, clear career path
Uses skills	Uses my skills and abilities
Job security	Job security
Role deciding	Gives me a role in decision making
Ample vacation	Has a lot of vacation time
Easy pace	Easy pace of work
Autonomy	Ability to work independently without supervision
Family friendly	Job that is family friendly
Confidence interview	How much confidence do you have that you could successfully complete a job interview?
Confidence hired	How much confidence do you have that you could be hired to work in the private sector?

7.5.5. Interest in Starting a Business and Motivations for Business Creation

Students were asked for their views on how easy it is to open a business and their interest in starting one. There are no clear differences before and after program participation. About a third of the students think that starting a business is easy. About half are interested in doing so, and about a third would be interested in joining someone else's business. One in five has an idea for a business they would like to start one day. There are no statistically significant differences when comparing the average values for these dimensions before and after the program.

Table 7.8. Interest in opening a business among students in the United Arab Emirates before and after participating in the Company Program. (Question: On a scale of 1 to 5. Table includes percentage who answer 4 or 5)

	Participant	
	Before	*After*
Easy start	37%	28%
Interest	47%	52%
Joininterest	..	38%
Idea	19%	22%
Easy start	In general, how easy is it to start a business in your country today?	
Interest	How interested are you in someday starting your own business?	
Joininterest	How interested are you in someday joining somebody else's business?	
Idea	Do you have an idea for a business you would like to start?	

A number of questions in the survey explored the motivations students had to start a business. These are summarized in Table 7.9. In all questions, more students had increased their motivation to start a business. After program participation, they were more likely to seek self-employment to work for themselves rather than someone else, to use their skills effectively, to be able to create and develop new ideas, to resolve important social problems, to earn money running their own business, to create jobs, to become a famous entrepreneur, and because their friends want to start a business.

Table 7.9. Importance of various factors in eventual decision to open a business among students in the United Arab Emirates before and after participating in the Company Program. (Question: If you were to start your own business in the future, indicate on a scale of 1-5 how important each of the following is in your decision to start a business. Percentage who answer 4 or 5)

	Participant	
	Before	*After*
Work for self	56%	63%
Use skills	86%	93%
Create new ideas	81%	86%
Solve problems	64%	70%
Earn more	59%	75%
Create jobs	47%	73%
Fame	61%	70%
Friends	32%	55%

Work for self	Prefer to work for yourself rather than someone else
Use skills	To use your skills effectively
Create new ideas	To be able to create and develop new ideas
Solve problems	To resolve important social problems
Earn more	You can earn more money running your own business
Create jobs	To create jobs and foster economic growth
Fame	To become a famous entrepreneur
Friends	Your friends want to start a business

When asked to rate the importance of various factors in their eventual decision to start a business, students were more likely after participating in the Company Program to say that their motivation would be to create jobs and foster economic growth and because they had friends who also wanted to start a business. There were no differences after participation in the Company Program and before with regards the other dimensions. Table 7.10 summarizes these differences.

Table 7.10. Differences in the importance of various factors in eventual decision to open a business among students in the United Arab Emirates before and after participating in the Company Program. (Question: If you were to start your own business in the future, indicate on a scale of 1-5 how important each of the following is in your decision to start a business.)

| | Participant | | |
	Before	After	PA - PB
Work for self	3.66	3.75	0.09
	(1.33)	(1.08)	0.42
Use skills	4.45	4.55	0.11
	(0.82)	(0.76)	0.71
Create new ideas	4.33	4.54	0.21
	(0.89)	(0.79)	1.33
Solve problems	3.91	4.09	0.18
	(0.94)	(0.96)	0.99
Earn more	3.53	4.11	0.58
	(1.02)	(1.04)	3.00
Create jobs	3.36	4.04	0.67 ***
	(1.29)	(1.04)	3.06
Fame	3.57	3.84	0.27
	(1.51)	(1.30)	1.02
Friends	2.76	3.54	0.78 ***
	(1.23)	(1.13)	3.51

*** significant at 1% level, ** at 5% level, * at 10% level.
Standard deviations in parentheses, t-statistics in *italics*.

7.5.6. Financial Management

Students were asked about their financial management habits in terms of whether they planned how to spend money, used a budget and saved regularly. Table 7.11 summarizes these results. Most of the students participating in the program planned how to spend their money, used a budget to manage their spending and save regularly. They become even more likely to do this after program participation. However, we do not find statistically significant differences when comparing the average values of these dimensions before and after the program.

Table 7.11. Financial management habits among students in the United Arab Emirates before and after participating in the Company Program. (0=no, 1=yes)

	Participant	
	Before	*After*
Plan finances	85%	91%
Budget	73%	79%
Save	63%	76%
Plan finances	When you have money, do you plan ahead for how to spend it?	
Budget	Do you use a budget to manage your spending?	
Save	Do you regularly save money?	

7.5.7. Attitudes towards Entrepreneurs and Business

The students participating in the program had favorable views toward entrepreneurship and business before participation, but these views became more favorable after participating in the program in all dimensions. After participation in the program, a greater percentage of students thought that people in the UAE could get ahead by working hard, fewer of them thought that entrepreneurs only think about their own gain, more thought that women can play an important role in the success of a business, more believe that most people can be trusted (though only a third of the students believe this), more believe that entrepreneurs create jobs for others, and that entrepreneurs contribute to the economic development of the country. Paradoxically, after program participation, students were more likely to believe that men were better business leaders than women and to believe that men should have priority in access to jobs over women if jobs were scarce.

Table 7.12. Attitudes towards Entrepreneurship in the United Arab Emirates. (Question: On a scale of 1-5, to what extent do you agree or disagree with the following statements. Percentage who answer 4 or 5)

	Participant	
	Before	*After*
Hard work	73%	86%
Entrepreneurs selfish	40%	35%
Women lead	86%	88%
Trust	18%	32%
Entrepreneurs succeed	72%	86%
Men lead better	35%	46%
Entr. create Jobs	39%	70%
Men more rights	42%	54%
Entrepreneurs contribute	56%	74%

Hard work	People in your country can get ahead by working hard.
Entrepreneurs selfish	Entrepreneurs only think about their own gain.
Women lead	Women can play an important role in the success of a business.
Trust	Most people can be trusted.
Entrepreneurs succeed	There is potential in your country for an entrepreneur to become successful.
Men lead better	Men are better qualified than women to be business leaders.
Entr. create jobs	Entrepreneurs create jobs for others.
Men more rights	When jobs are scarce, men should have more rights to a job than women.
Entrepreneurs contribute	Entrepreneurs contribute to the economic development of the country.

The statistical analysis of the differences in attitudes towards entrepreneurship is summarized in Table 7.13. Although most of the differences tend to be positive, the only statistically significant differences are found in the beliefs that entrepreneurs create jobs for others and that entrepreneurs contribute to the economic development of the country.

Table 7.13. Differences in Attitudes towards Entrepreneurship in the United Arab Emirates. (Question: On a scale of 1-5, to what extent do you agree or disagree with the following statements.)

| | Participant | | |
	Before	After	PA – PB
Hard work	3.97	4.26	0.30 *
	(0.95)	(0.92)	1.71
Entrepreneurs selfish	3.31	3.05	-0.26
	(1.20)	(1.20)	-1.15
Women lead	4.47	4.54	0.07
	(0.91)	(0.89)	0.42
Trust	2.76	2.96	0.21
	(1.00)	(1.22)	0.99
Entrepreneurs succeed	3.97	4.33	0.37
	(0.94)	(0.81)	2.26
Men lead better	3.09	3.29	0.20
	(1.20)	(1.38)	0.82
Entr. create jobs	3.23	3.79	0.56 ***
	(1.04)	(1.11)	2.79
Men more rights	3.23	3.35	0.12
	(1.40)	(1.53)	0.45
Entrepreneurs contribute	3.67	4.05	0.39 **
	(1.01)	(1.03)	2.03

*** significant at 1% level, ** at 5% level, * at 10% level.
Standard deviations in parentheses, t-statistics in *italics*.

In addition to these questions about their views on entrepreneurs, business and related social issues, students were asked whether they knew someone who was an entrepreneur. Most students know entrepreneurs who are parents, siblings, teachers or friends.

Learning to Improve the World: Entrepreneurship Education in the Middle East

Table 7.14. Knowledge of Entrepreneurs in the United Arab Emirates. (Q: Who among the following people do you know who have started their own business?)

	Participant	
	Before	After
Parent	74%	
Sibling	88%	
Family	27%	
Neighbor	79%	
Friend	67%	
Teacher	91%	
Someone else	52%	

When asked where they could find access to financing for a business venture, about half mentioned that they were confident or very confident that they could do so from their nuclear family, bank or government grant.

Table 7.15. Sources of funding in the United Arab Emirates. (Q: If you were to start a business, to what extent would you be able to depend on the following financing sources to support your new business? On scale 1-5. Table reports percentage who answered 4 or 5)

	Participant	
	Before	After
Nuclear family	40%	.
Extended family	14%	.
Friends	9%	.
Bank	42%	.
Grant	51%	.

Nuclear family	Nuclear family
Extended family	Extended family
Friends	Friend
Bank	Bank loans
Grant	Government grants

7.5.8. Knowledge about Entrepreneurship

A few questions in the survey assessed student knowledge of basic concepts of entrepreneurship and business. Those levels are moderate before participation in the program and somewhat higher afterwards, but there are large gaps in knowledge even after participating in the program. For example, about half of the students can define an entrepreneur. Only about a fourth of the students can define capitalization, and this percentage diminishes after program participation. Most students can define a vision for a company and marketing. About a tenth of the students could define liquidation before participating in the program, and this figure increases to a third after program participation. A quarter of the students could define a company before participating in the program and this percentage increase to about half after participation. The differences in these two last dimensions were statistically significant at the 5% level. Percentages of students who answered correctly these various knowledge questions are reported in Table 7.16.

Table 7.16. Knowledge about entrepreneurship in the United Arab Emirates. (Multiple choice questions. Percentage who answered correctly.)

	Participant	
	Before	After
Entrepredefine	55%	.
Sell shares	25%	14%
Vision	68%	79%
Marketing	78%	79%
Liquidation	8%	31%
Company	28%	47%
Entrepredefine	An entrepreneur is someone who	
Sell shares	Selling shares of stock to get start-up money for a new company is called:	
Vision	A _____ represents a company's dream of where it wants to go and what it wants to be.	

Marketing	The work you completed in this scenario above is an example of which of the following:
Liquidation	When a company liquidates, it does which of the following:
Company	By definition, a company must have which of the following:

7.6. How Do Company Program Participants Describe the Effects of the Program?

When asked to rate themselves in a series of questions about possible effects of the program, most participants who were surveyed after the program rate highly the changes they observe in themselves. To further examine the effects that students who participated in the Company Program attribute to their participation, students were asked a series of additional questions following the national competition. This section focuses on these retrospective questions. These questions asked the students to compare themselves at the end of the school year to where they were at the beginning of the school year and to assess their capabilities in a variety of areas. Table 7.19 reports the answers from matched participants (those for whom we have specific results both from pre- and post-surveys).

On balance, the majority of the students feels that the program has increased their competencies in a range of leadership domains. Most students feel more empowered to take a leadership role in the workforce in the future, realize the importance of managing their finances effectively, have further developed their educational and career goals, feel more confident in their ability to compete in the future and know more about entrepreneurship. The area in which there is a lower percentage of students who feel they have gained from the program is in being more interested in starting their own business, which refers to 60 percent of the students.

Table 7.17. Retrospective experience in the United Arab Emirates (Compare yourself now to where you were at the beginning of the school year. On a scale of 1-5, to what extent do you agree with the following statements about yourself. Table reports percentage who answered 4 or 5.)

	Participant	
	Before	*After*
Leadership		86%
Finances		84%
Education goals		79%
Career goals		74%
Competitive		79%
Know entrepreneurship		67%
Start business		57%

Leadership	I feel more empowered to take a leadership role in the workforce in the future.
Finances	I realize more that knowing how to effectively manage my finances is important.
Education goals	I have developed (or further developed) my educational goals.
Career goals	I have developed (or further developed) my career goals.
Competitive	I am more confident in my ability to successfully compete in the workforce in the future.
Know entrepreneurship	I know more about entrepreneurship.
Start business	I am more interested in starting my own business.

A large percentage of students also attribute to the program gains in their capacity for empathy, working with others, developing citizenship skills, being innovative, thinking critically, having business skills, developing initiative and self-motivation, leading others, managing a budget, solving problems, making better decisions, communicating with others, negotiating differences, selling ideas or products, speaking in public and thinking creatively. These figures are presented in Table 7.18.

Table 7.18. Contribution of the Company Program in the United Arab Emirates. (In your opinion, on a scale of 1-5, to what extent did your participation in the Injaz Company Program help you with the following. Table reports percentage who answered 4 or 5.)

	Participant	
	Before	After
Valuable		70%
Empathy		67%
Team work		74%
Citizenship		69%
Innovation		71%
Critical thinking		61%
Business		73%
Initiative		72%
Leadership		66%
Budgeting		66%
Problem solve		68%
Decide		74%
Communicate		73%
Negotiate		65%
Sell		70%
Speak		67%
Creativity		61%

Empathy	It helped me develop understanding of other people's views.
Team work	It helped me develop the ability to work with others as a team.
Citizenship	It helped me develop citizenship skills.
Innovation	It helped me develop the capacity to innovate.
Critical thinking	It taught me critical thinking skills.
Business	It taught me useful business skills.
Initiative	It helped me development initiative and self-motivation.
Leadership	It helped me develop my abilities as a leader.
Budgeting	It taught me how to manage a budget.
Problem solve	It helped me learn to solve problems.
Decide	It helped me to become a better decision maker.

Communicate	It helped me learn to communicate with others.
Negotiate	It helped me learn to negotiate differences with people.
Sell	It helped me learn to sell ideas or products.
Speak	It helped me learn to speak in public more easily.
Creativity	It inspired me to think more creatively about problems.

Finally, students were also asked to evaluate some of the components of the program (Table 7.19). Most of them said lectures increased their interest in the topics, and that the volunteer presented the content clearly, held lectures in an interactive way, and was helpful and responsive to questions. Many found the "Student Guide" useful or very useful. Finally, the majority of the participants would recommend the Company Program to friends or family.

Table 7.19. Evaluation of the Components of the Program in the United Arab Emirates. (On a scale of 1-5, to what extent do you agree with the following comments about the Injaz Company Program. Table reports percentage who answered 4 or 5.)

	Participant	
	Before	*After*
Lecture		64%
Volunclear		80%
Volunrespond		73%
Studyguide		56%
Volunlecture		75%
Recommend		69%

Lecture	Company Program lectures aroused my interest for the topics being discussed.
Volunclear	The volunteer presented the program's content in a clear way.
Volunrespond	The volunteer was helpful and responsive to our questions.
Studyguide	The Student Guide was useful.
Volunlecture	The volunteer held lectures in an interactive way.
Recommend	Would you recommend participating in the Injaz Company Program to friends or family members? (1=YES, 0=NO)

7.7. A Qualitative Analysis of Student Descriptions of Program Effects

Within the post-survey, students were provided the opportunity to answer an open-ended question regarding their experience with the Company Program: "Use the following space to provide any comments – positive or negative – about your experience in the Injaz Company Program." Of the 74 participants who started the program and for whom we received post-surveys, 40 used this opportunity to express views – either positive or negative – about the program. Most responses were not detailed. However, a review of these responses provides an opportunity to round out our understanding of the outcomes most important to the program's participants while providing some critiques for Injaz to use in revising operational approaches in coming years. To complement these, the evaluation team conducted focus groups with participants and volunteers, outcomes of which are described below.

7.7.1. Survey Comments

By and large, the responses from students in the post-survey were positive. In fact, 16 respondents (40 percent) used this question only to provide positive reactions to their participation, and 10 (25 percent) provided generally positive answers while critiquing aspects of the program. The remaining 14 respondents (35 percent) used the space to criticize aspects of the program, although it should be noted that most of these individuals belonged to the one student company that failed to complete the course due to problems with the volunteer instructor's ability to finish the program (see below).

On the positive side, few respondents were specific about aspects of the program they thought were of benefit. Instead, they were broadly, and enthusiastically, supportive. For example, one student replied: "Injaz is a success, and I encourage those who do not have any experience in trade to participate because it tells us a lot in our lives." Others highlighted their increased knowledge about business and how to start a business (10 respondents, with one emphasizing that because of the Company Program he is now thinking of starting his own business). Specific gains in self-efficacy noted by some students include an improved ability to cooperate with others and to work with a team (4 respondents), an increase in self-confidence (3), a greater appreciation for hard work and perseverance (2), and ability to better solve problems (1). Several students highlighted the positive engagement they had with their volunteer and the competition judges as a highlight of the program.

Critiques from student responses focused on several issues. Two students noted that the experience was generally unhelpful, although it should be noted that these students were among those that stopped meeting because of the volunteer's departure from the program. Five students felt that they lacked time needed to dedicate to the program in the context of busy academic schedules. Several others felt that expectations from the program (and from the judging of the national competition) were not clear from the beginning and that they wasted time because of this. A relatively large number (7) felt that the judging of the national competition itself was not fair, although few were clear about how the assessment was unfair. One noted that awards were only given to those students who represented each student company in the national competition (managers of the student companies) and felt that this was unfair. Finally, several noted that their volunteer was unhelpful (again, these were students who belonged to the company where the volunteer dropped out).

7.7.2. Focus Groups with Participants

Our findings from the open-ended question are largely in line with student comments documented during two focus groups held prior to the national competition. Each of these focus groups was held at a different participating school (one boys' school and one girls' school), consisting of 2 or 3 representatives from each student company at that school. These students participated in the management team of each student company and were thus leaders of their student companies.

In discussions about what they had learned from participation in the program, focus group participants emphasized a greater understanding of how to start and run a business, including how to deal with suppliers (developing a final product design and manufacturing it, negotiating over price) and how to market their products to new customers. All generally agreed that starting one's own business was an extremely risky venture, but one that could be successful with careful planning.

That said, most of the interviewed students noted that they did not have any immediate plans to start businesses of their own. Most planned to go on to university and then planned to find a job, with a decided favoritism shown towards securing a stable and secure public sector job. While most agreed that the private sector provided more creative, interesting work, they emphasized that it does not offer the stability found in the public sector. Moreover, work timings were important, particularly for the girls interviewed: government jobs allow them to work and yet be at home by 4 PM to be with their families. In the UAE, one noted, the time to become an entrepreneur is after one has worked in the public sector and then retired early, a comment that provides a simple but profound understanding of the challenges faced by programs like Injaz when labor market signals favoring public sector employment are so strong.

Interviewed students were more enthusiastic about the soft skills that they felt they had developed through the program. Students stressed that they now had a greater appreciation for the perspectives of others, were more willing to hear out the arguments of others, and were more inclined to negotiate with others to reach a mutually agreeable solution. As one student stated, "I have learned how to argue effectively and peacefully. When I argue with someone now, I don't want to just get my point across. Now I discuss our differences. Maybe I am more open now to their perspectives, and because of this I experience more and learn more."

Students also praised the opportunity to take on responsibility. They noted that upon graduation, they would carry responsibilities in their jobs and with their families, but they really had no experience with shouldering responsibility. The Injaz Company Program gave them an opportunity wherein they were responsible for the success of their own student company, an experience that they felt helped prepare them for the real world. As one student noted, "This was the biggest responsibility ever in my life. I don't have much responsibility at home, so this was a great experience."

Overall, the students described completing the Company Program as challenging but were extremely satisfied when they were able to overcome these challenges and to see their projects come to fruition. Students described various challenges related to raising money and selling shares in their company, finding capable and willing suppliers, and in marketing their products. However, each of these challenges was presented in the context of the students having overcome it. Looking back on these challenges, they were proud at what they had accomplished and enjoyed the process. As one noted, "We were very happy to see something we had accomplished." Another stated, "This was so different than other subjects. With Injaz, we got to experience something. We were trying something we have never done before and we are doing it on our own. With other subjects, it is not this way."

At the same time, when asked whether they felt that the Injaz program should be provided to all 11th graders, many said no. Asked why, students described how difficult it had been to motivate some of the students to play any kind of constructive role in developing the company. One frustrated company leader said, "People want to get a diploma and get out and not work. Some students in the UAE study to finish school and then go play... If it is provided to everyone, it will fail because there are a lot of students who are not serious." Others took a more holistic perspective: "We really had a problem with students not participating, students that were not engaged... But the course was also a lesson in how to motivate these people or at least understand their limitations."

One of the challenges that interviewees focused on was that of time. No one felt that they had enough time to develop their student companies and meet as a group. Several put the blame more on their schools, saying that administrators did not give them any flexibility in timing. Most, however, focused on the other academic demands that they had and the difficulty of balancing their school work and participation in the program. Many stated that the program should be taught over the summer. Wisely, one student noted, "I told my mom that we did not have time to do this, but she said, 'When you get to college or graduate and begin to work, you won't have time either.'" As such, the Injaz program was an exercise in time management.

Overall, students described their volunteers in favorable terms as engaged, interesting and helpful in guiding their projects forward. Several volunteers went out of their way to provide transportation to participants as they visited potential suppliers and service providers. Importantly, the volunteers brought personal experience and perspectives with them, which rounded out student understanding of how to develop their projects. However, as described above, one volunteer was regularly absent and eventually was no longer able to work with the students. While Injaz was able to provide some basic direction, one student in this company said simply, "We had no one. We had to do it on our own." Eventually, this student company did not complete the program nor compete in the national competition.

7.7.3. Volunteer Interviews

To supplement our surveys and interviews with students, we interviewed several of the volunteers who worked with the students during the Company Program. Most volunteers felt that they were well prepared to lead the program through the initial training session delivered by Injaz. However, one had not been able to attend that training and there were no additional training sessions held. Another felt that the material was pressed into one long session and would have been absorbed more readily had the initial training taken place over 2 or 3 shorter sessions. Nearly all of the volunteers felt that they would have benefitted from the ability to engage former volunteers about lessons learned from past experience and to share best practices.

Throughout the program, volunteers felt that the Injaz staff provided them with exceptional support. However, they did note that it would be beneficial if volunteers were more involved in developing the overall structure for program delivery. One noted that instead of providing volunteers with highly detailed agendas, Injaz should merely provide basic deadlines and deliverables and allow volunteers flexibility in how to deliver the program. At the same time, volunteers felt that they did not have enough information about school schedules and examinations, which posed problems during the delivery of the program. Finally, one volunteer wished that Injaz had provided some advice on dealing with cultural and language barriers. This comment is particularly relevant to the UAE context, where young Emiratis do not necessarily have strong English skills, but where many of the private sector volunteers are English-speaking expatriates and the Injaz program is delivered in English.

Most volunteers voiced strong concerns about the Student Guide, noting that it needs to be provided in Arabic (or in English and Arabic in parallel) and needs to be revised to reflect local context; i.e., examples should be localized, rather than reflecting examples within the United States. At the same time, volunteers suggested moving away from the comprehensive guide and instead providing more streamlined guidelines and expected results for each step of the Company Program. Overall, the guide is seen as thorough, but too complex for the needs of students with limited time.

Time was a concern for most volunteers. Most volunteers felt that the Company Program tried to cover too much ground in too short of a time. "Expectations of program delivery did not take into consideration the time allocated for program completion." The Company Program schedule did not consider the school schedules, particularly examination schedules, which put strains on student participants. Overall, volunteers felt that the program should be extended beyond the 15 weeks in which it was run. Moreover, the class sessions themselves were, according to one volunteer, too short to get everything done.

While volunteers provided considerable criticism of the program, they were enthusiastic about the program as a learning experience for the students (and for themselves):

"I will always cherish this experience – the excitement and creativity of the girls and their natural ability to think business-like was amazing."

"Dealing with teenagers is a big challenge. Keeping them involved, interested and motivated was the hardest part, but it has taught me the most."

"I took them to my office to meet different departments and they asked a lot of questions, which I did not expect. During the management elections, they were very motivated. One day, only half the team was there… the ones who would never talk to me. They were very open and talked a lot, as well as asking lots of questions."

"When an idea came together, the girls saw results and benefited from seeing success at what they wanted to do."

"The excitement and proactivity of students is amazing. The program helps bring the best out of them. There is a need for many similar platforms."

Finally, several volunteers felt that the most important factor for improving the Company Program was to communicate with schools and parents to ensure that both family and school support their students' participation in the program. Volunteers noted that there was little or no parental support for the program, and parents were often upset that it conflicted with their children's studies. In turn, they would not provide transport for after-school activities or trips to visit potential suppliers. This lack of parental support was particularly an issue for female participants.

7.8. Discussion

As discussed above, the results of our study must be viewed with caution about the plausible effects of Injaz's Company Program, given that there is no counterfactual with which to compare results. Because we cannot compare participant outcomes with outcomes for comparable students who did not participate in the program, it is impossible to assess what the net effects of the program are and whether the identified changes in outcomes for participants were the result of program participation or other factors. Moreover, given the small number of surveys that we were able to collect and the limited range of variability within the results, few of our results have proven to be statistically significant, even when the observed differences between pre- and post-surveys appear to suggest positive program effects.

With these caveats in mind, however, the generally positive results, mixed with student views of how the program affected them (both quantitative and qualitative), suggest that the Company Program offers a learning environment that provides youth in the UAE with valuable experiences and skills, which they would not otherwise experience within the traditional school curriculum. The student participants we assessed, it seems, benefit from improvements related to valuable soft skills, knowledge about business and entrepreneurship, and more inclusive worldviews, if not demonstrating a decidedly bolstered interest in starting their own businesses in the future. After participating in the program Emirati students have higher aspirations and self-efficacy. They also have higher educational aspirations. There are no systematic differences in their motivations for choosing a job.

In regard to Injaz's primary goal of encouraging more youth to become entrepreneurs, results are mixed. Injaz Company Program participants were not significantly more inclined after the program to want to start a business of their own, even though 52 percent of them express an interest in doing so at some point. Less than one in four students have an idea for a business they would like to start in the future at the end of the program. After program participation, students are more likely to indicate that if they were to open a business it would be to create jobs, to seek self-employment, to create and develop new ideas, to resolve important social problems, and to earn more money.

There are no differences in the financial management skills of students after participating in the program. Students' knowledge of entrepreneurship does increase after program participation, but there are important gaps in knowledge of basic concepts related to business and entrepreneurship even after participating. Overall, however, views towards entrepreneurs and their role in the economy become more positive after program participation.

Our analysis suggests that the Company Program experience does have a direct, tangible bearing on student development in regard to soft skills development and self-efficacy. In both the quantitative and qualitative analysis, participant responses point to considerable gains regarding their self-perceived abilities to work with teams, to resolve differences peacefully and to negotiate conflict, to adapt to new situations, to solve problems and to lead a team. They felt more that they were better able to run a business successfully and to research potential markets effectively. Moreover, a large share of participants felt that they were better able to compete for jobs. Importantly, the majority of surveyed students either agreed or strongly agreed that their participation had had a direct bearing on their improvement in these areas.

Finally, while the qualitative responses from students to the open-ended question and volunteer feedback are not quantifiable, they provide overall a strong argument in favor of the Injaz Company Program. While feedback on specific impacts are limited, both student responses and volunteer responses paint a picture of the Injaz Company Program as a unique and transformative learning experience, a picture that is reinforced by extremely positive quantitative responses to questions about the direct impact that program participation has had on them. Importantly, the student-centered, experiential nature of the program ensures that students are not only receiving knowledge, but are engaged in practicing the skills they are intended to learn. Learning by doing is the only effective way to develop many of these skills, particularly those known collectively as soft skills, and for many of these students, Injaz stands alone as an opportunity to engage in this type of learning.

7.9. Policy and Program Implications

Although our results must be viewed with caution given potential bias, the data – and participant feedback on the experience provided by the program – strongly suggest that it has significant benefits in exposing youth to entrepreneurship and, perhaps more importantly for many youth, in regard to soft skills development, job-relevant skills and self-efficacy. The experiential learning opportunity provided by the Company Program is a unique experience for many youth, one that provides tangible skill development and makes students aware of skills they already possess but are not aware that they have. As such, there should be significant gains for Emirati youth were the program to be expanded.

Notably, the Company Program – at least during the 2010-2011 school year– was only offered in four schools in Dubai. As such, there is ample room for expanding the program both within the Emirate of Dubai and within the country. Importantly, Injaz should consider providing the program to youth in more disadvantaged or rural areas, where youth do not have the educational opportunities or access to formal sector public and private jobs that youth in Dubai might have and where self-employment can provide immediate benefit.

Expanding the delivery of the program would elevate costs for Injaz, but more importantly will impose logistical challenges. First among these is identifying and engaging a larger number of (quality) volunteers to deliver the program to a growing number of young participants and maintaining program quality. To date, Injaz UAE has been able to work with a small but highly engaged number of volunteers from the private sector. In expanding the program, Injaz UAE may face growing difficulty in securing volunteers who have the significant private sector experience and personal dynamism that make them effective instructors for this program. This is a challenge outside of Dubai (the commercial center of UAE). As such, expansion of the program – as with all programs – must be done carefully to avoid diminishing returns to scale. Challenges would stem from the potential language gap, since many of the volunteers would be from the English-speaking expatriate population and many of the youth outside of Dubai do not necessarily have a firm grasp on English.

Expanding the services provided through Injaz would require support from the Ministry of Education and local school administrators, all of whom are already facing challenges related to the administration of school calendars and curriculum demands. Injaz should begin to strategically engage representatives of the Ministry of Education and, particularly important, local school administrators to begin developing plans for expansion in the future. Working on an expanded timeline will help ensure that education planners understand the merits of the Company Program and are providing space in the school calendar for the Company Program.

At the same time, our analysis raises some program process issues that Injaz UAE should address as it works to expand its offerings within UAE. First, in the future, Injaz must work more closely with the Ministry of Education to ensure that it has early access to school at the beginning of the school year and is able to implement the Company Program in a way that imposes less stress on student participants. According to feedback from students, this means extending the course over a longer time period and holding the national competition at a time when it does not conflict with examinations.

Injaz might also consider offering the program as an extra-curricular activity for those seeking to participate, rather than integrating into the curriculum. While this means that fewer students might participate, evidence from other countries in this study suggests that the extra-curricular approach ensures that those who do participate get more out of the program because their peers are similarly engaged. At the same time, however, Injaz needs to find a way to attract more students to participate and who are willing to stick with the program over time. Offering other Injaz programs, such as the Innovation Camp program, to all students as an introduction to entrepreneurship helps to expose a broader number of youth to the basics of entrepreneurship. Such programs can also be used as screening mechanisms to identify youth who would most benefit from the more rigorous program of learning offered by the Company Program.

In this area, our findings suggest that securing parental support for student participation is important as well in making sure that youth are fully engaged in the program. As such, Injaz must find a way to engage parents, informing them of the merits of program participation for their children and ensuring that they understand what activities students will be involved in during the program. In garnering parental support, Injaz will not only secure more students, but participating students will have more leeway in going out into the community to work with service and material providers needed to manufacture products and with potential consumers.

This language gap is a specific challenge related to the unique structure of the Emirati economy. Given the need for English language skills within the economy, it is perhaps right that the program in the UAE is run in English. Moreover, given that so many of the potential Injaz volunteers speak only English, it is a logistical necessity. Still, efforts must be taken to help bridge the potential communications gap between students and volunteers. Starting with a complete revision and translation of the Student Guide would help. Providing translators is perhaps going too far, especially given that there are generally at least one or two students in each class who can translate when needed.

The issues of volunteer identification should also be addressed. One of the great benefits of the Injaz program is that it is taught by volunteers from the private sector, who are able to bring real-world perspectives to the topics and exercises addressed during the program. However, the dependence on volunteers also makes Injaz vulnerable to the other demands on these volunteers' time. The risks related to this are quite evident in the one case in the UAE wherein a volunteer started working with one student company but then failed to complete the course. Students were disappointed and left to see their initial work falter when they could not get the volunteer support to help them complete the program, but also school administrators at the school in question were upset. Such an experience could make it more difficult for Injaz to run the program in the future at that school. As such, Injaz must strike a careful balance in engaging volunteers while putting in place controls to ensure that children are not left in the lurch should a volunteer's time be restricted. Injaz should consider teaming two volunteers for each student company or other measures that provide flexibility while ensuring that student companies have access to capable expertise.

Finally, while our results strongly point to a significant impact of the program on student self-efficacy, soft skills development and interest in business (both self-employment and private sector employment), it should be noted that the results herein should not be taken to represent the causal evidence of impact that would be provided in the context of a more rigorous impact evaluation. The team suggests that Injaz engage in an experimental evaluation that is able both to determine the exact causal relationship between participation in the program and outcomes in regard to entrepreneurial activity, job-relevant skills development, and employment. Moreover, such an evaluation should take place over a longer time span, allowing for an assessment of actual outcomes within the labor market after youth leave school.

How Injaz Al-Arab helps youth develop an entrepreneurial mindset

Conclusion: Seven lessons learned from the company program.

Fernando M. Reimers

Concluding a study which generated scuh rich insights as this one is a real challenge. I will not attempt here to summarize or discuss the findings of this book. An overall summary is provided in chapter one, and each chapter offers a summary and discussion of findings for each of the countries included in the study. Instead, I will attempt to sketch seven high-level lessons learned from the study.

Lesson 1: Short education programs which empower students can have large effects

The motivation for this study was to understand how an education program designed to teach secondary school students to create a company empowered them. I designed a study that measured student knowledge and self-reported skills and mindsets across a very broad range of outcomes which reflected explicit goals of the program, and others not directly emphasized by the program. This was done because the study originated in a conversation I had with Soraya Salti about whether entrepreneurship education empowered youth. Many of the same instruments I had developed to evaluate the impact of a civic education program in Mexico were used in this study. I was skeptical that learning to create a business could impact youth in ways that would generalize beyond the specifics of business creation. I was wrong. To my surprise students' mindsets changed in multifaceted ways, summarized in chapter one, and discussed in detail in the remaining chapters of this book. What most surprised me is that a relatively short intervention, which engaged students over a short four-month period, would have such powerful effects.

Lesson 2: Much school-based education is not empowering

I have come to understand that much of the power of the company program rests on the contrast it represents over the rest of students' academic trajectories. This program, which brings a business leader who works as a coach to students as they decide what product they want to create and as they build a company to bring this program to market, gives students voice and agency over their education which is rare in schools in the Middle East, and indeed in the rest of the world. In Injaz Al-Arab students have choice over what they want to do, and they do it collaboratively with fellow students, supported by an adult, in a collegial relationship that is not typical of most teacher-student relationships. Perhaps this is the biggest lesson the Company Program teaches us: we should provide students more opportunities to decide what they want to learn, to work with peers in actively building a product that causes them to learn, guided by others with more experience and knowledge in ways that cultivate their sense of agency. That so much can be achieved by a four-month program should cause us to think how *much* more could be achieved if these experiences were the norm for students, from kindergarten to high school.

Lesson 3: Programs such as Injaz Al-Arab can help personalize education

I don't think that these findings necessarily suggest that all students should learn to create a business. The findings of this study show that Injaz Al-Arab works best when students opt to join the program, as opposed to been forced into it. The implication of this is that choice over how to learn is helpful to students. Some will be excited by programs that teach them to create a business, others will be excited by programs that help them solve problems in their communities, others by science and engineering programs, others by the humanities. The take-away from this study is that schools could do much better than they do in personalizing education, by providing students choice over what they want to study, and over how to do it.

Lesson 4: Simple ideas scale well

Ultimately, Injaz Al-Arab is a story about the beauty of simplicity. What could be simpler than a program in which a volunteer comes to school to work with a group of students over a four-month period to help them create a business? Simple ideas scale well. This is a powerful principle which could inspire those interested in the puzzle of why so very few educational innovations have been able to scale successfully.

Lesson 5: Program evaluation helps educators walk the talk of enlightenment values

The study shows also the power of program evaluation to help us advance the conversation about what kind of education prepares students for the twenty first century. Framing this evaluation provided very helpful goal clarification to the senior staff of Injaz Al-Arab: it reminded them of what they were trying to achieve, and stimulated valuable discussions of which outcomes were core to the program, and which of them were interesting but not core intended outcomes. In a way, an evaluation such as this one is helpful to a program even before any data are collected, because it forces a necessary clarification of the theory of action of the program which may elude most organizations given the many demands of day-to-day management of large programs. Collecting evidence is also helpful because nothing is more stimulating to those who are trying to improve the world that the stubbornness of facts. Those facts sometimes confirm our beliefs and intuitions, and at times challenge them, ultimately helping us learn and get better at what we do.

All education organizations would benefit from the commitment to learning from evidence which Soraya and her colleagues exemplified. Schools, as institutions that would serve all children, are a product of the Enlightenment, a global movement built on the audacious idea that ordinary people can improve their lives and work with others improving their communities, and the world. The philosophers of the enlightenment posited that human reason was a powerful tool to assist this project of self and world improvement, and that science was a pre-eminent instrument to support reason. John Dewey, the progressive American philosopher, used to say that "how we teach is what we teach". This is true also for those who lead education programs and organizations. If schools are to help students develop the power of reason, respect for evidence, and the value of science to help us not only understand the world, but to transform it, it is necessary that those who lead schools and education programs demonstrate the same commitment to reasoned inquiry and to evidence, in informing their work. That the evidence on the effects of entrepreneurship education programs is so scant should remind us that those leading those programs are not "walking the talk," asking their students to develop habits of reasoned inquiry in informing the creation of business, which they themselves, leading those programs, do not practice.

The real world of schools is not a laboratory, and undertaking evaluations in naturalistic settings implies plenty of risks, for example that a revolution may interfere with the design of a study, or that data may be collected in ways which do not reflect the methods planned. The real world is messy and it follows its own logic, not the designs of the evaluator. But such a messy world is also exciting, rich with opportunities to learn, including learning from what goes awry with the plans of the researcher. There are clear limits to the kind of insights that can be drawn from collecting data in settings of this sort, with challenges such as those I describe. But there are always limits to what science can teach us. All scientific knowledge is provisional, until we know better. If we are aware of such limits, we can profit from what an evaluation in a naturalistic setting can teach us. Given the paucity of evaluations of entrepreneurship education programs, much can be gained even from the descriptive information of who participates in this program, from their reports of how they benefit, and from the ways in which their knowledge and mindsets change while they participate in the program, even if our counterfactuals are imperfect.

Lesson 6: Ordinary people can change the world of education, and public-private partnerships can help

Another lesson Injaz Al-Arab teaches us is about the role of social entrepreneurs in helping advance educational innovation. As an ordinary citizen, not a government functionary, Soraya understood that the future of the Middle East would be brighter if youth had opportunities to gain voice and agency. She was excited by what she saw in Junior Achievement when she led the program in Jordan, and committed to a seemingly impossible goal: to bring the same opportunity to every country in the Middle East. That she was able to do this should serve as a reminder of the power of ordinary people to change the world. She provided educators in every country in this region an example of what was possible in helping all students develop the skills she possessed in abundance: Imagination, creativity, the capacity to work with others and to lead them, optimism about the future, the ability to work hard, the capacity to reflect and to learn from one's mistakes, and perseverance, the capacity to stay the course in the face of adversity. These are the skills and habits of mind all people will need to make the most of the fourth industrial revolution, to face the present and future challenges, in order to create a world of abundance that includes all, and where we relate to one another, and to the planet, in a sustainable way. That one person could do so much is an invitation to every teacher, school principal, administrator, education leader and policy maker of how much we could all achieve for children and youth everywhere with a similar vision and determination.

An obvious lesson of Injaz Al-Arab concerns the power of public-private partnerships. Soraya sought and cultivated relationships with governments to bring this program to scale, and governments provided the regulatory framework and the support that made this program possible. The creation of meaningful educational opportunities requires the best efforts not just of education leaders, but of all members of society. Much more can be achieved when productive public-private partnerships such as Injaz Al-Arab support innovation, and help bring it to scale.

Lesson 7: Take action!

The last (and perhaps the most enduring) lesson the Company Program teaches all of us, is that the opportunity to learn to create a business provides students the opportunity to understand that the best way to learn to improve the world is to take action, to do something. There are limits to how far an education based primarily in contemplation can take students. Engaging students in taking action involves risks, the risk that their initial ideas may be wrong, but it is the reflection and learning from those consequences of taking action that produce knowledge of value to continue to change the world. This is not just the opportunity that Injaz Al-Arab provides students, it is also the way in which it models for them what it means to improve education: take action, take risks, learn from them, and keep trying to get better. If more students indeed learn these lessons in school, they would truly be empowered to become architects of their own lives, and shapers of the future of their communities and of a better world.

We are all better because Soraya Salti took action, and invited others to join her, in the journey to build exciting education programs that bring forward the best of our humanity.

About the Authors

Fernando M. Reimers is the Ford Foundation Professor of the Practice of International Education and Director of the Global Education Innovation Initiative and of the International Education Policy Masters Program at Harvard University. An an expert in the field of Global Education, his research and teaching focus on understanding how to educate children and youth so they can thrive in the 21st century.

Recent books include *Teaching and Learning for the 21st Century, Preparing Teachers to Educate Whole Students: An International Comparative Study, Empowering Global Citizens, Empowering Students to Improve the World in Sixty Lessons. Version 1.0, Learning to Collaborate for the Global Common Good, Fifteen Letters on Education in Singapore, (Empowering All Students at Scale)*, and *One Student at a Time. Leading the Global Education Movement*

Website https://fernando-reimers.gse.harvard.edu/

Maria Elena Ortega-Hesles is co-founder and director at PraxEd, a research organization dedicated to improving education in Latin America. She works as a consultant for non-profit organizations, governments and international organizations. She specializes on the design, monitoring and evaluation of education and labor programs. Recently, she was a grantee of the Round 2 of *All Children Reading: A Grand Challenge for Development* (funded by USAID, World Vision and Australian Aid) under which the "Mundo de Libros" reading program for early grade readers was developed (www.mundodelibros.mx). María Elena is an Economist with a Master's and a Doctorate in Education from the Harvard Graduate School of Education. Her research work has received several national awards in Mexico and has been published on books and peer-reviewed journals.

Paul Dyer is an economist and senior associate at Maxwell Stamp, Inc., where his work focuses on youth, employment, and entrepreneurship in the Middle East and North Africa. He specializes in employment intervention design and the use of impact evaluation to build evidence in support of effective program development for youth. Prior to joining

Maxwell Stamp, Paul served as Knowledge Program Manager for the Research and Policy Department at Silatech. He was also a fellow at the Dubai School of Government and worked with the World Bank as a consultant in the Office of the Chief Economist, Middle East and North Africa Region. Paul holds a Master of Arts in Arab Studies with a concentration in Economics and Development from Georgetown University, where he was the Sheikh Sultan bin Mohamed Al Qassemi Scholar.

Made in the USA
Las Vegas, NV
19 November 2020